PARLIAMENTARY QUESTIONS

PARLIAMENTARY QUESTIONS

Edited by
MARK FRANKLIN
and
PHILIP NORTON

for the Study of Parliament Group

CLARENDON PRESS · OXFORD

1993

Oxford University Press, Walton Street, Oxford OX2 6DP
Oxford New York Toronto
Delhi Bombay Calcutta Madras Karachi
Kuala Lumpur Singapore Hong Kong Tokyo
Nairobi Dar es Salaam Cape Town
Melbourne Auckland Madrid
and associated companies in
Berlin Ibadan

Oxford is a trade mark of Oxford University Press

Published in the United States
by Oxford University Press Inc., New York

British Library Cataloguing in Publication Data
Data available

Library of Congress Cataloging in Publication Data
Parliamentary questions / edited by Mark Franklin and Philip Norton;
for the Study of Parliament Group.
p. cm.
Includes bibliographical references and index.
1. Interpellation—Great Britain. 2. Great Britain. Parliament—
Rules and practice. 3. Great Britain—Politics and
government—1945– I. Franklin, Mark N. II. Norton, Philip.
III. Study of Parliament Group.
JN611.P37 1993 328.41'07456—dc20 92-32478
ISBN 0-19-827317-7

Typeset by Cambrian Typesetters, Frimley, Surrey
Printed in Great Britain
on acid free paper by
Biddles Ltd., Guildford and King's Lynn

PREFACE

This volume is the result of research undertaken by the study group on parliamentary questions of the Study of Parliament Group.

The Study of Parliament Group is a private organization, formed in 1964, and is composed of academics and officers and former officers of both Houses of Parliament. Much of the Group's work is conducted through small study groups, the work of each group often resulting in a published report or edited volume. Most of these volumes have been published by the Clarendon Press. The Press was the publisher of the most substantial work to emerge so far from the Study of Parliament Group, *The House of Commons in the Twentieth Century* (1979), edited by Stuart Walkland, and more recently has published *The New Select Committees* (2nd edition, 1989), edited by Gavin Drewry, and *Parliament and Pressure Politics* (1990), edited by Michael Rush. It will also be publishing, almost simultaneously with this volume, *The House of Lords at Work*, edited by David Beamish and Donald Shell. The editors are grateful to the Press and to Tim Barton in particular for the encouragement and assistance given in the preparation of this work. The aim has been to maintain the standard set by the earlier books.

This volume is the product of five years' work by the study group. The group was set up to investigate an important but much neglected aspect of parliamentary work in the United Kingdom—Parliamentary questions. The product of this research constitutes the first book-length study of the subject since Norman Chester and Nona Bowring's *Questions in Parliament* was published by the Clarendon Press in 1962. The need for a contemporary study will be apparent from the following pages.

Mark Franklin was responsible for establishing the study group that planned the book and for the survey of MPs that forms the basis especially of Chapter 4. Philip Norton edited the book for publication. They are grateful for the assistance of all the contributors and especially Helen Irwin and her fellow clerks for reading and commenting on draft chapters. Their help has been

invaluable. Particular thanks are owing also to Jacqy Sharpe for
her meticulous reading of the manuscript.

The study group wishes to record its thanks to the Nuffield
Foundation. Without the assistance of the Foundation, this study
could not have been undertaken. A grant from the Foundation
funded meetings of the group and also the survey of MPs.

In common with all Study of Parliament Group publications,
nothing in this work represents the collective view of the Group.
The views expressed are those of the individual contributors, who
accept full responsibility for them.

CONTENTS

CONTRIBUTORS

R. L. Borthwick is Senior Lecturer in Politics at the University of Leicester.

Mark Franklin is Professor of Political Science at the University of Houston, Texas.

Philip Giddings is Lecturer in Politics at the University of Reading.

Helen Irwin is a Deputy Principal Clerk, House of Commons.

Andrew Kennon is a Deputy Principal Clerk, House of Commons.

David Natzler is a Deputy Principal Clerk, House of Commons.

Philip Norton is Professor of Government at the University of Hull.

Robert Rogers is a Deputy Principal Clerk, House of Commons.

Donald Shell is Senior Lecturer in Politics at the University of Bristol.

TABLES

1

Introduction: Parliament since 1960

Philip Norton

Question Time is a remarkable feature of the British House of Commons. It is certainly a popular one. Tickets for the Strangers' Gallery are particularly difficult to obtain for the beginning of a day's sitting, when Question Time is taken. Members of Parliament are more likely to make an effort to be present in the chamber for questions than they are for the rest of the day's business. The introduction of the television cameras has added to the attraction. The cut and thrust of Question Time, especially between the two front benches, is highly televisual. It is difficult to think of the House of Commons without thinking of Question Time.

Adding to the attraction of Question Time is the fact that it is, in the eyes of many observers, a unique institution of ancient lineage. 'I do not think there is anything like it in the world', declared A. P. Herbert in 1947; 'it is a unique and wonderful safety-valve, forum, and democratic hoo-ha.'[1] In any discussion of parliamentary scrutiny in plenary session, comparative works will often single out Question Time in the British House of Commons.[2]

The reality, in fact, does not quite match the popular perception. The British House of Commons is not alone in having a procedure for asking questions on the Floor of the House. Some legislatures lack the feature. Most, however, do not. 'In almost all parliamentary assemblies', according to Gaston Bruyneel, 'it is possible to ask oral questions which are either introduced by written notice and then sometimes are read out, or put orally by means of an organised procedure, or by using a point of order. In general, these questions receive an oral reply, which is given at a public

---

[1] A. P. Herbert, *The Point of Parliament*, 2nd edn. (London: Methuen & Co., 1947), 24.
[2] For an illustrative example, see D. M. Olson, *The Legislative Process: A Comparative Approach* (New York: Harper & Row, 1980), 201–4. For an exception, see G. Loewenberg and S. C. Patterson, *Comparing Legislatures* (Lanham, Md.: University Press of America, 1979), 148–54.

sitting by the appropriate member of the government.'[3] A fixed
period for questions—Question Time—is a feature of many
European parliaments. In some countries, such as Austria and
Finland, the procedure for asking questions is even enshrined in
the constitution. Nor is the practice confined to national legislatures. Both the Council of Europe and the European Parliament
instituted a procedure for asking questions when they were
established. A Question Time, allowing members to ask questions
in plenary session, was introduced in the European Parliament in
1973.[4]

What distinguishes the British Question Time from the others,
attracting the more extensive attention, is essentially the fact that
it pre-dates them. Yet in terms of the history of Parliament, the
development of a Question Time in the parliamentary day is of
relatively recent origin. The House of Commons was using select
committees as tools of scrutiny decades—indeed centuries—before
the use of parliamentary questions developed. Select committees
were well in evidence in the sixteenth and seventeenth centuries.
By contrast, Question Time in the House dates back, as we shall
see, to shortly before the nineteenth century.

Question Time is thus not quite as old or as distinctive as
popularly portrayed. Nor is it the sole mechanism in the House of
Commons for asking questions of ministers. Parliamentary questions and Question Time are not synonymous terms. Oral
questions—that is, those asked during Question Time—constitute
just one form of parliamentary questions (PQs). There are also
questions tabled for written answer. The answers to these are sent
direct to the Members tabling them, and are also published in
Hansard. Not surprisingly, it is Question Time that attracts the
most attention. It involves observable human behaviour. It is
watched from the Strangers' Gallery and from the Press Gallery.
There is always the chance that a minister may be caught out by a
clever question. There is less attraction to poring over the pages of
Hansard to read often factual answers.

[3] G. Bruyneel, *Interpellations, Questions and Analogous Procedures for the
Control of Government Actions and Challenging the Responsibility of the
Government*, Report adopted by the Association of Secretaries General of
Parliaments, March 1978, p. 84.
[4] See M. Westlake, The Origin and Development of the Question Time
Procedure in the European Parliament, *EUI Working Paper EPU 90/4* (Florence:
European University Institute, 1990).

There is thus, in popular coverage of parliamentary questions, a skewed focus. In academic study, there is a problem not of focus but of extent. PQs—oral and written—have received relatively limited attention in scholarly literature. Before the 1950s, parliamentary questions received coverage in standard works on Parliament, but were not singled out for particular analysis. In 1956, the first book on the subject appeared: *Questions in the House* by Patrick Howarth.[5] Though a scholarly study, it was not in the field normally covered by the author, who was a novelist and social historian. It was followed in 1962 by a work which has received far more attention: *Questions in Parliament* by Norman Chester and Nona Bowring.[6] Chester (later Sir Norman) was Warden of Nuffield College, Oxford, and subsequently a founder member of the Study of Parliament Group; Bowring was his research assistant. The book established itself as the standard work on the subject. Since 1962, various articles and chapters—including some in the works published under the aegis of the Study of Parliament Group—have provided more material on parliamentary questions,[7] but there has been no latter-day 'Chester and Bowring'.

The purpose of this volume is to provide the first book-length study of parliamentary questions since the period covered by Chester and Bowring. *Questions in Parliament*, after sketching the origins of parliamentary questions, focused on the first sixty years of this century. In this book we consider the subsequent three decades. In that period, major changes have occurred. The nature of Question Time has changed; the number of questions tabled has increased enormously; the fixed, twice-weekly slot for Prime Minister's questions has been introduced; and the rules governing questions have been variously—sometimes substantially—

---

[5] P. Howarth, *Questions in the House: The History of a Unique British Institution* (London: Bodley Head, 1956).

[6] D. N. Chester and N. Bowring, *Questions in Parliament* (Oxford: Clarendon Press, 1962).

[7] See especially the chapters penned by Chester himself: 'Questions in Parliament', in A. H. Hanson and B. Crick (eds.), *The Commons in Transition* (London: Fontana, 1970), 93–113; and 'Questions in the House', in S. A. Walkland and M. Ryle (eds.), *The Commons in the Seventies* (London: Fontana, 1977), 149–74. See also R. Borthwick, 'Questions and Debates', in S. A. Walkland (ed.), *The House of Commons in the Twentieth Century* (Oxford: Clarendon Press, 1979), 476–526.

amended, not least in the last Parliament under review. These changes have taken place against the backdrop—and indeed are largely the consequence—of a changing parliamentary environment. To explain the changes which are the subject of the subsequent chapters, it is necessary first to sketch the essential features of that wider environment.

The House of Commons before 1960

Chester and Bowring studied what is best described as the pre-reform House of Commons. The House had changed little for half a century: the last significant procedural reforms had taken place in the first decade of the century. The nineteenth-century emphasis on the amateur—on what Anthony King has portrayed as the 'spectator' politician[8]—was still embodied in the way the House conducted itself. The emphasis was on the Floor of the House, on subjecting the government and its measures to scrutiny through general debate. The MP who was a generalist with outside interests, able to weigh in measured terms the case put by government, was preferred to the full-time Member keen to generate and work through the mechanism of specialist committees. It was a preference held by many Members, among them Michael Foot and Enoch Powell.[9] It was also a view favoured by government. Specialist committees were potentially troublesome intrusions. To encourage a more specialized House was not worth the expense, politically or financially.

The resources available to Members reflected this approach. Any contact with constituents was at the Members' expense. There was no postage allowance. There was no provision for secretarial or research support, or even for offices. Members were allocated lockers, and for seating space had to use corridor benches or seats in the library. Each Member had a salary of £1,250. That was essentially all the MP had. The conditions were not conducive to spending the whole working week confined to the

---

[8] A. King, 'The Rise of the Career Politician in Britain—and its Consequences', *British Journal of Political Science*, 11 (1981), 249–85.

[9] Powell remained of this view throughout his period of service in the House. See E. Powell, 'Parliament and the Question of Reform', *Teaching Politics*, 11 2 (May 1982), 167–76, for a succinct expression of his viewpoint.

Palace of Westminster. And when Members did attend, it was in order to support their own side. Party cohesiveness in the division lobbies reached its peak in the 1950s.[10] For the backbencher, the corridors of the Palace of Westminster constituted what one of their number, Sir William Teeling, was to characterize as 'corridors of frustration'.[11]

It was within the context of this chamber-oriented and party-dominated body that Chester and Bowring studied parliamentary questions. Question Time stood out as a rare example of a mechanism utilized by backbenchers: they tabled the questions, and interventions from the opposition front bench were infrequent. Reflecting the nature of the House and the fact that it had changed relatively little compared with changes in the nature of government, it was not an extensively used mechanism. As Chester and Bowring noted, there were some fluctuations in the number of questions tabled each session. There was an increase in the number of questions tabled for oral answer, but the number tabled in sessions in the 1950s did not deviate much from the number tabled in the years of Liberal Government from 1906 to the outbreak of the First World War. As the authors observed, what was remarkable was the fact that what increase there had been over the years was so small.[12] Throughout the 1950s, the daily average of questions tabled for oral answer never—with the exception of the long session of 1950–51—exceeded one hundred, and the daily average of those tabled for written answer never exceeded twenty-one. An increase in the use of oral questions was not matched by an increased use of written questions. When Members had constituency matters they wished to pursue with ministers, they appeared content to correspond with them.[13] Tabling questions was seen as a last, rather than a first, resort.

So much for the position existing when Chester and Bowring undertook their research. Since then, the political environment has changed significantly. There have been major changes in the nature of government, in the nature of the electorate, in the composition, attitude, and resources of Members of Parliament, and in the nature and extent of parliamentary business.

---

[10] See P. Norton, *Dissension in the House of Commons 1945–74* (London: Macmillan, 1975).
[11] Sir W. Teeling, *Corridors of Frustration* (London: Johnson, 1970), see ch. 14.
[12] Chester and Bowring, 89–92.   [13] Ibid. 96–108.

6 *Philip Norton*

Government since 1960

Industrialization in the nineteenth century generated a more specialized society; the growth of a mass franchise facilitated a greater range of demands on government. Determination of general issues of public policy by government gave way, especially in the twentieth century, to consideration of more complex, technical, and specific issues. The increasing specificity of government decisions necessitated consultation with affected groups.[14] The co-operation of a party-dominated Parliament could largely be taken for granted by government; that of interest groups could not. Consultation with groups became more extensive and institutionalized. That was a feature of the period covered by Chester and Bowring. What has been marked since 1960 has been the embodiment of tripartism in institutional form and the attempt by government since 1979 to dismantle that form and reduce the realm of the public sector.

At the time that *Questions in Parliament* was published, the Macmillan government was about to utilize indicative planning and create the National Economic Development Council (NEDC). Subsequent years saw the tripartite relationship of government, the Trades Union Congress, and the Federation (later the Confederation) of British Industries extend to other institutional forms. In 1966, Harold Wilson told the House of Commons that it was the government's *duty* to consult with such groups. By 1979, the interlinkage of government with outside groups was a well-established feature of policy making, not least economic policy—what may be termed 'high policy'.

The premiership of Margaret Thatcher from 1979 to 1990 witnessed a deliberate attempt to scale the ramparts of tripartism and carve out for government an autonomous role in policy making. The disengagement was marked at the level of high policy making. Informal contacts and institutional structures—such as the NEDC and the Manpower Services Commission—were downgraded or done away with altogether. Privatization became a central feature of government policy, resulting in a significant reduction in the

---

[14] See J. J. Richardson and A. G. Jordan, *Governing Under Pressure* (Oxford: Martin Robertson, 1979), 44–5.

number of industries in the public sector. Though contact with groups remained extensive at the level of incremental policy making, a new attitude pervaded government. Awareness of that attitude influenced the perceptions and hence actions of interest groups. They perceived a less congenial environment for influencing public policy. They had to consider supplementary or alternative ways to those used previously to influence ministers. Professional lobbying became a more observable feature of political life.[15]

These developments affected the relationship of Parliament to government. Under tripartism (or more often, in practice, bipartism) and under the Thatcherite reaction, the latter necessitating a strong state,[16] Parliament was distanced from the locus of policy making. The developments affected also what Parliament did. They encouraged a change in institutional structures. As we shall see in Chapter 2, they had some effect on the content of parliamentary questions. They may also constitute a partial explanation for the increase in the number of questions tabled.

The Electorate since 1960

Chester and Bowring wrote at a time when the Conservative and Labour Parties were dominant at both the mass (electoral) and élite (parliamentary) levels. In the three general elections of the 1950s, the proportion of voters casting their ballots for one or other of the two principal parties never fell below 93 per cent; the proportion of seats held by the two parties never fell below 98 per cent. The pattern appeared fairly consistent, with a close relationship between class and voting. The middle class mostly voted Conservative; the working class mainly voted Labour. Party support was most marked at the two extremes of the social scale: the upper middle class overwhelmingly voted Conservative, the 'very poor' strongly voted Labour.[17] Class was not the exclusive

---

[15] P. Norton, *The British Polity*, 2nd edn. (New York: Longman, 1990), ch. 7; M. Rush (ed.), *Parliament and Pressure Politics* (Oxford: Clarendon Press, 1990).

[16] See A. Gamble, *The Free Economy and the Strong State* (London: Macmillan, 1988).

[17] B. Sarlvik and I. Crewe, *Decade of Dealignment* (Cambridge: Cambridge University Press, 1983); The Gallup Poll, 'Voting Behaviour in Britain, 1945–74', in R. Rose (ed.), *Studies in British Politics*, 3rd edn. (London: Macmillan, 1976), 206.

predictor of voting behaviour, but it was the most important—so much so that as late as 1967 Peter Pulzer was able to declare that 'class is the basis of British party politics: all else is embellishment and detail'.[18]

The decades since *Questions in Parliament* was published have seen major changes in the nature of the electorate. Developments taking place in post-war decades—notably in education and in the media of mass communication—have produced new generations of electors less wedded to traditional patterns of political thinking and support. There has been the phenomenon identified by Inglehart and Dalton of the 'cognitive mobilisation' of citizens.[19] There is a greater awareness of issues not encompassed within the confines of the traditional party divide. The class–party nexus has waned as an increase in issue awareness has taken place.

A consequence has been a less predictable electoral environment for the two major parties. They no longer have to compete only with one another but with other parties for the votes of a more volatile electorate. For the Conservative Party in the south of England, the Liberal Democrats—successors to the Alliance parties—constitute the biggest challenge. For the Labour Party in Scotland, the Scottish National Party constitutes the biggest threat, though in a country where there is now four-party electoral competition.

Parties now have to be more sensitive to new issues that have come on to the political agenda. This greater issue sensitivity has facilitated an increase in issue voting.[20] It has also had a wider impact on political activity. Greater issue sensitivity and a desire to influence the political system have resulted in more and more pressure groups being formed. Of the groups listed in one 1979 directory of pressure groups and representative organizations, more than 42 per cent had come into existence since 1960.[21] The number has continued to grow since then.

[18] P. Pulzer, *Political Representation and Elections in Britain* (London: Macmillan, 1967), 98.
[19] R. Inglehart, *The Silent Revolution* (Princeton, NJ: Princeton University Press, 1977); R. Dalton, *Citizen Politics in Western Democracies* (Chatham, NJ: Chatham House, 1988).
[20] M. Franklin, *The Decline of Class Voting in Britain* (Oxford: Clarendon Press, 1985).
[21] P. Shipley, *Directory of Pressure Groups and Representative Organizations*, 2nd edn. (Sevenoaks: Bowker, 1979).

These groups have added considerably to a crowded political environment, seeking to influence government and—increasingly since 1979—Parliament itself. Lobbying of government has become more overt, and lobbying of Parliament—starting from a relatively modest basis—more extensive. The 1980s witnessed a burgeoning of professional lobbying firms, known as political consultancies, as well as growing concern at the number of MPs who acted for or as consultants.[22]

The greater political awareness of citizens, generating group activity, is allied with the development of a post-industrial society. Increased political lobbying may also be associated with de-industrialization, as areas of traditional manufacturing industry seek support, thus adding to the crowded political environment. Consequently, MPs are lobbied not only on particular sectoral issues but on behalf of constituency or regional interests.[23] Such lobbying, though, is not confined to group or regional interests.

Constituents have increasingly come to expect more of their MP. The cognitive mobilization appears to have affected MPs both in terms of composition—new opportunities and attitudes producing a greater pool of aspiring candidates—and in terms of constituents' willingness to contact them and make use of them as 'grievance chasers'.[24]

The result for MPs has been a less certain environment. Though the number of marginal seats is fewer now than it was in the 1950s, the perception of electoral vulnerability by MPs appears greater. The waning of the class–party nexus has produced, according to Mark Franklin, 'an era of uncertainty in electoral outcomes unparalleled in fifty years'.[25] Party is no longer the exclusive protector that it used to be. Expectations have increased, and MPs, especially those new to the House, have been increasingly responsive to such expectations as a means of bolstering their electoral—and local political—base.[26] They have done so in a

---

[22] See esp. C. Grantham and C. Seymour-Ure, 'Political Consultants', in Rush (ed.), *Parliament and Pressure Politics*, 45–84.

[23] See D. M. Wood, 'The Conservative Member of Parliament as Lobbyist for Constituency Economic Interests', *Political Studies*, 35 3 (1987), 393–409.

[24] See P. Norton and D. M. Wood, *Back from Westminster: The Politics of Constituency Service* (Lexington, Ky.: Kentucky University Press, forthcoming). The term 'grievance chaser' comes from A. Beith, MP, 'The MP as a Grievance Chaser', *Public Administration Bulletin*, August 1976.

[25] Franklin, *Decline of Class Voting*, 176.

[26] Norton and Wood, *Back from Westminster*.

more partisan atmosphere, in which parties have had to compete more fiercely for less certain votes.

The political environment, in short, has changed fundamentally since the days of Chester and Bowring. As is clear already, from our brief review, the House of Commons has been dramatically affected by that change. The House in the 1990s is a very different institution from that which Chester and Bowring observed in the 1950s.

The House of Commons since 1960

The House of Commons has experienced major changes since 1960. Most can be seen to flow from, or have been facilitated by, changes in the wider political environment.

The number of spectator Members has continued to decline, giving way to Members for whom membership of the House is a full-time—and long-term—career. In the era of Chester and Bowring, it was still possible for a Member to accept a ministerial appointment under Harold Macmillan on condition that he could still go hunting two days a week. Those days are now gone. MPs are more likely to devote themselves to Westminster, with little interest in being torn away by independent pursuits that they would consider just as worthy as sitting in Parliament.[27]

There has been a convergence of Labour and Conservative Members in terms of their socio-economic characteristics. They are increasingly likely to be graduates drawn from business or professional backgrounds.[28] They have entered the House as the pay and resources of Members have improved; and, indeed, they may have been a creative force in their improvement. Members drawn from professional backgrounds and intent on playing an active role in the House are less likely to tolerate meagre resources and low pay levels (relative to the private sector and to other legislatures) than Members of independent means sitting in the House as a public duty. By the 1980s, service as a Member was the principal activity for the vast majority of MPs. A more professional House has marched hand in hand with more full-time Members.[29]

[27] See King, 'Rise of the Career Politician in Britain'.
[28] M. Rush, 'The Members of Parliament', in M. Ryle and P. G. Richards (eds.), *The Commons under Scrutiny* (London: Routledge, 1988), 22–8.
[29] Ibid. 28–33.

The improvements in resources are relative. Compared with other major Western legislatures, the House remains a poorly resourced institution. However, compared with what MPs had at their disposal in 1960, the improvements have been significant. Office space has expanded. By the end of the 1970s, there was desk space for all Members. For most Members, the desks were in shared rooms, but at least they now had somewhere to work. The secretarial and research allowance was increased, sufficient for Members to employ secretaries. The use of full-time secretaries increased rapidly in the 1970s: at the beginning of the decade, only a minority of MPs employed a secretary for more than thirty hours a week; by the end of the decade, more than two-thirds did so. The use of researchers increased at the same time: less than 10 per cent of MPs hired researchers at the beginning of the decade; by the end of the decade, about 40 per cent did so. By the mid-1980s, the figure had increased to just over half. In the latter half of the decade, Members proved willing to consolidate the position. In 1986, against government advice, they voted to increase the allowance (now known as the office cost allowance) by 50 per cent. At the beginning of 1992, an MP had a salary of £30,854 and an office cost allowance of almost the same amount.

The revolution in information technology has also had an impact on the House and Members. The Commons Library has introduced a computerized classification index, POLIS (Parliamentary On-Line Information Service), which allows considerable cross-referencing. Members have increasingly made use of personal computers and, more recently, facsimile (fax) machines. One survey reported a threefold increase in computer or word processor ownership by MPs between 1985 and 1990.[30]

Improvements in pay and resources have taken place at the same time as a behavioural change in the House. The former may have facilitated the latter, though greater political independence of MPs appears to have been a significant force in the 1970s and 1980s in achieving changes in structures and resources. In the Parliaments of the 1970s, starting with the 1970–74 Parliament, when the Conservative government enjoyed an overall working majority, government backbenchers demonstrated a greater independence in

[30] *Computer Services for Members: Fourth Report from the Select Committee on House of Commons (Services)*, HC (1989–90) 614 (London: HMSO, 1990), p. viii.

the divison lobbies, they voted against their own side more often, in greater numbers, and with more effect than before. This independence was carried on by Labour backbenchers during the period of Labour government from 1974 to 1979, and has been continued by Conservative backbenchers in the periods of Conservative government since 1979.[31] The sudden change in voting behaviour appears to have been triggered by the poor leadership of Edward Heath; his unwillingness to listen to backbenchers in particular motivated them to take their disagreements into the division lobbies.[32] This thesis has generated considerable academic discussion.[33] The essential point for our purposes is that it took place, generating on the part of many Members a greater awareness of what they could achieve in seeking to influence public policy. As a result, a number discarded their old deferential attitude toward government in favour of what Samuel Beer has termed a more participant attitude.[34] They wanted to be more involved in influencing government and public policy.

This change in attitude appears to have underpinned the pressure for a change in structure, for moving away from a chamber-oriented assembly to a more specialized, committee-oriented institution. The change in the nature of MPs—from spectator to 'professional' politicians—may have fostered a desire for change, but it was MPs' willingness to use their new-found political muscle that helped achieve it. Pressure from backbenchers on both sides of the House, coupled with a reform-minded Leader of the House (Norman St John-Stevas), was largely responsible for the establishment of the departmental select committees in 1979; the Cabinet was not prepared to challenge the wishes of the House.[35] The select

[31] P. Norton, *Dissension in the House of Commons 1974–1979* (Oxford: Oxford University Press, 1980); *idem*, 'The House of Commons: Behavioural Changes', in P. Norton (ed.), *Parliament in the 1980s* (Oxford: Basil Blackwell, 1985), 22–47.

[32] P. Norton, *Conservative Dissidents* (London: Temple Smith, 1978), ch. 9.

[33] See J. E. Schwarz, 'Exploring a New Role in Policy Making: The British House of Commons in the 1970s', *American Political Science Review*, 74 1 (1980), 23–37; M. Franklin, A. Baxter, and M. Jordan, 'Who Were the Rebels? Dissent in the House of Commons 1970–1974', *Legislative Studies Quarterly* 11 2 (1986), 143–59; P. Norton, 'Dissent in the House of Commons: Rejoinder to Franklin, Baxter, Jordan', *Legislative Studies Quarterly*, 12 1 (1987), 143–52.

[34] S. H. Beer, *Britain Against Itself* (London: Faber, 1982), 190.

[35] When the proposal came before the Cabinet, ministers were essentially silent rather than supportive. The PM had previously made known her opposition. Only two ministers spoke in support of St John-Stevas.

committees themselves have provided a major new dimension to the work of the House.[36] They have proved remarkably active, as well as prolific. They have also acted as magnets for interest groups.[37]

The select committees are not the only changes introduced since the 1970s. Other significant changes have included the creation in 1983 of the National Audit Office—the product of a Private Member's Bill introduced, after his return to the back benches, by Norman St John-Stevas—and the admission in 1989 of television cameras to cover the proceedings of the chamber and of committees. The latter development proved more successful than both broadcasters and many MPs expected, attracting more viewers than expected and providing much greater coverage of committee work than MPs had envisaged.[38] In the first six months of broadcasting, ninety-three select committee meetings and thirty-six standing committee meetings were televised. The House had become not only a more specialized but also a far more open institution.

MPs were generally very different from those who had sat in the Parliaments of the 1950s and before: they came from more solidly middle-class backgrounds; they had a different attitude towards the job of MP; they were relatively more independent in their voting behaviour; they faced more extensive demands on their time and parliamentary activity; and they had far more extensive resources, individually as well as collectively, to undertake the tasks expected of them.

Parliamentary Questions

Not surprisingly, Question Time and the use of parliamentary questions have not remained untouched by these developments.

[36] See G. Drewry (ed.), *The New Select Committees*, 2nd edn. (Oxford: Clarendon Press, 1989); and *The Working of the Select Committee System: Second Report from the Select Committee on Procedure*, HC (1989–90 19–I (London: HMSO, 1990).
[37] See P. Norton, 'The Changing Face of Parliament: Lobbying and its Consequences', in P. Norton (ed.), *New Directions in British Politics?* (Aldershot: Edward Elgar, 1991), 73–5.
[38] See A. Hetherington, K. Weaver, and M. Ryle, *Cameras in the Commons* (London: Hansard Society, 1990); and *Review of the Experiment in Televising the Proceedings of The House: First Report from the Select Committee on Televising the Proceedings of the House*, HC (1989–90) 265-I (London: HMSO, 1990).

Parliamentary questions have changed significantly in nature, in number, and in the uses to which they are put. A number of distinct pressures can be drawn out from the developments we have sketched. Three in particular deserve emphasis.

Partisanship. The first has been the greater partisanship on the Floor of the House. The parties have competed more vigorously with one another, and the Floor of the House of Commons has been the central arena for this competition. This partisanship has, as we shall see, been marked at Question Time; it is apparent especially to all those who watch the televised broadcasts of Prime Minister's Question Time.

The use of parliamentary questions for partisan purposes was far from unknown in Chester and Bowring's day. However, *Questions in Parliament* emphasized the extent to which the party clash was most evident in debates:

There is much less political content in the majority of Questions. Many are asked purely for the sake of obtaining information and a good proportion of the remainder are about constituency matters or concern interests with which the Member is associated. Some will bring into play the political attitude of the Member; some he will be inclined to take up with more enthusiasm than others for reasons of personal rather than of Party interest; but a great many he will deal with just as any other Member would deal with them.[39]

Opposition MPs, it was noted, asked more questions—both oral and written—than government supporters; but this was ascribed not just to the party struggle but to the fact that government supporters were likely to have closer personal contact with ministers, and hence could employ more informal methods.[40] And in so far as Question Time was employed as part of the party battle, it was used principally by backbenchers. Questions, declared Chester and Bowring, 'are not a major Front Bench activity. The leading opposition Members make their main contributions during the major debates and get sufficient opportunity to do this. They are unlikely, therefore, to wish to expand Question Time at the expense of the time available for debates.'[41]

Chester and Bowring did note the existence of the 'inspired

[39] Chester and Bowring, 216.   [40] Ibid.   [41] Ibid. 274.

question', which took the form of a minister arranging for the tabling of a friendly question. It did not appear to impinge greatly on Question Time itself, though, since 'quite often . . . such Questions are not starred [that is, not tabled for an oral answer]'.[42]

The contrast with the use of PQs today is stark. Participation by opposition front benchers is routine. The main media interest in Prime Minister's Question Time is the clash between the Prime Minister and the Leader of the Opposition. Greater participation by opposition front benchers has been supplemented by group organization, or 'syndication', of questions by both the main parties (discussed in Chapter 2). The practice developed in the 1970s,[43] and burgeoned in the 1980s as each side felt obliged to respond to the other. 'What is undeniable', declared the Procedure Committee in 1990, 'is that syndication has now very nearly taken over Question Time, turning it into yet another area of the house's activities which is organized—some would say manipulated—by the business managers.'[44] The proposals made by the Committee and accepted by the House in October 1990 were in large part designed to reduce this practice, though more recent evidence suggests that it remains a significant feature of Question Time.[45]

Ministers also appear increasingly to be encouraging the 'inspired answer'. Planted supplementary—that is, follow-up—questions have become an important component of the partisan battle. On 16 October 1990, Labour MP Michael Meacher drew attention to a set of papers he had found that contained not only the questions to be asked of ministers but also their proposed answers. 'In addition, there were 16 pages of briefing . . . putting substantial defensive arguments in favour of the Government's case.'[46] For many government backbenchers, Question Time provides an opportunity not only to defend the government but also to attack the opposition. They approach the occasion as part of the established partisan battleground.

---

[42] Ibid. 222.

[43] H. Wilson, *The Governance of Britain* (London: Sphere Books, 1977), 174–6.

[44] *Oral Questions: First Report from the Select Committee on Procedure*, HC (1989–90) 379 (London: HMSO, 1990), p. vii, para. 11.

[45] *Parliamentary Questions: Third Report from the Select Committee on Procedure*, HC (1990–91) 178 (London: HMSO, 1991), p. viii, paras. 8–9, and Appendix 3, p. 45.

[46] *HC Deb.* (1989–90), 177, col. 1055.

16 *Philip Norton*

Attention seeking. The second development has been the battle among Members themselves for parliamentary—and public— attention. Question Time is held in prime parliamentary time, and, following the introduction of the cameras, at a time fortuitously convenient for broadcasters. For politicians keen for office, it is an important medium for gaining the attention of the whips and in the front bench; and it is a widely used one.

It was not always such. At the time that Chester and Bowring wrote, PQs were still used infrequently or not at all by many Members. In pre-war years, a few Members were responsible for the majority of the questions tabled. One—Labour MP Colonel Harry Day—made himself unpopular by having questions down usually every day, 'usually going to the limit allowed'.[47] When he rose, Members used to shout 'Another Day'. In the 1940s and 1950s, more Members tended to table questions. 'Most back benchers now put at least one or two Questions on the Paper each Session.'[48] Chester and Bowring did note that some MPs might use questions for the purpose of personal publicity, but went on to comment that persistent questioners did not usually gain promotion to office and those new Members seeking advice on ways to make a mark would be told to concentrate on debates.[49]

The picture bears little resemblance to that of recent years. Backbenchers have competed vigorously with one another to achieve success in the daily ballot (see Chapter 2). In the 1980s, with large government majorities, the greater was the competition for attention among the large number of backbenchers on the government side of the House. For Members nursing marginal seats, it provides also a mechanism for local publicity. A number of Members, notably newer ones, table the maximum number of starred questions permissible under the rules of the House. For some Members, the facility of research assistants has proved especially useful. Instead of the greater facilities for research reducing the information sought of government, they are used instead to provide the material for asking questions.[50] Some research assistants have standing orders from their Members to draft up to the maximum number of oral questions permissible,

---

[47] Chester and Bowring, 195.
[48] Ibid.
[49] Ibid. 22–7.
[50] See *Parliamentary Questions* HC (1990–91) 178, p. xix, para. 76.

the goal being to maximize the opportunity for the Member to get to his or her feet during Question Time.

The extent to which parliamentary questions constitute a means of achieving publicity for backbenchers is not only recognized but also acknowledged by Members. For the purposes of this volume, a questionnaire was administered to a selected number of MPs. The results are detailed in Chapter 4. What is especially notable about respondents' evaluation of the effectiveness of PQs is that the function that questions were deemed to fulfil especially well—more so than any other—was that of 'publicising backbench MPs and their concerns'.

Constituents and pressure groups. The third development has been the increasing demands made of MPs by constituents and pressure groups. The typical MP now receives in one day the amount of correspondence he or she used to receive in one week in the 1960s. Most Members still prefer to write to ministers on constituency matters—anything between 150,000 and 250,000 letters a year now passing between Members and ministers[51]—but PQs are held in reserve as weapons to be used if letter writing fails to produce the desired response. That in itself is not a great change from the period covered by Chester and Bowring; the big change is in the volume, rather than the approach taken by Members. Virtually all the respondents to our questionnaire said that they used questions for 'defending or promoting constituency interests', though fewer than a third judged an oral question to be more effective than a letter to a minister.

What has probably had a more profound effect on the nature of questions has been lobbying by pressure groups. Though Chester and Bowring noted briefly that a question might be asked on behalf of a particular group with which a Member was associated, this did not figure prominently as a motivation for Members tabling questions.[52] Since 1979, pressure groups have, in effect, 'discovered' Parliament, with the growth in lobbying to which we have called attention. Tabling questions to elicit information or, in effect, raise a matter on behalf of an outside group has become a significant consequence of much of that lobbying. In our survey of

[51] See T. Elms and T. Terry, *Scrutiny of Ministerial Correspondence* (London: Cabinet Office Efficiency Unit, 1990).

[52] Chester and Bowring, 202.

Members (see Chapter 4), almost half admitted that one of the
reasons for tabling questions was 'because I was asked to'; the
proportion giving a similar answer for written questions was more
than 80 per cent. Syndication and inspired questions account for
some of this, but far more Members mentioned interest groups
than approaches by colleagues. More than two-thirds of the
Members conceded that written questions were sometimes drafted
for them by lobbying organizations. The Select Committee on
Procedure noted in its 1991 report on parliamentary questions that
there was nothing illegitimate in such activity as long as Members
were an active party to the proceedings and not acting in 'the role
of a postman for outside . . . bodies'.[53] As it then went on to observe,
it would be idle to pretend 'that the use made of parliamentary
questions by certain Members can or should be immune from
criticism'. Some MPs are known in the House for tabling questions
without clearly understanding what the questions actually mean.

Prior to the autumn of 1990, all questions that were tabled
received ministerial answers, and were printed in *Hansard*. For
groups, PQs provided a means of acquiring information and
publicity. It was a means at the disposal of the ordinary
backbencher—hence the attraction of seeking out a sympathetic
Member. New (1990) rules limiting the number of oral questions
that are printed each day on the order paper (with those not
printed not being eligible for a written answer) have not
necessarily diminished the attractiveness of oral questions as a
means of raising an issue. The attractiveness of seeking to get a
question raised during Question Time has been enhanced by the
presence of the cameras. The attractiveness of written questions as
a means of obtaining information from departments remains
largely unchanged: there is no limit on the number of questions for
written answer that a Member can table. On one occasion, though,
the Table Office took clear umbrage when an MP's research
assistant tabled no less than 122 at one go, a large proportion of
which were out of order and all of which—according to the Table
Office—appeared to emanate from the research assistant.[54]
Exasperation, though, was insufficient to bar those that were in
order from going down on the Order Paper.

---

[53] *Parliamentary Questions* HC (1990–91) 178, p. xxiii, para. 103.
[54] Ibid., Annex to Appendix 13, p. 55.

The nature of Question Time has changed significantly. By 1989, the number of oral questions tabled and their nature (notably syndication) were such as to be the cause of an inquiry by the Commons Procedure Committee. Questions, though, were not the only aspect of parliamentary activity to be affected by the changed political environment. The greater career activity of Members, the large number of government backbenchers, the extensive parliamentary programmes of government, and business emanating from the European Community increased the pressures on the timetable of the House. So too, extending beyond PQs, did the demands of constituents and pressure groups. Question Time became a problem in itself, as well as part of a wider problem of Parliamentary overload.[55] It was a problem that was not apparent in 1960.

The House of Lords since 1960

The House of Lords did not figure prominently in writings on the political system in the 1960s. It was a subordinate, unelected chamber, mentioned more often in tracts on reform than in analyses of policy-making power. Even though Chester and Bowring titled their work *Questions in Parliament*, the focus of their research was the Lower House, 'Questions in the House of Lords' being included as an appendix covering little more than a page.

That this should have been so is not surprising. Despite a membership in the early 1950s of about 800, the active membership of the House of Lords was less than 100. Votes were rare, especially in the period from 1951 to 1955, and when they were held, party determined the outcome. The House met at a leisurely pace. It rarely met for more than three days a week, and on those days would often meet for little more than three hours. When a debate was not being continued after dinner, it was not unusual for a peer rising after 5.30 p.m. to apologize for detaining peers 'at this late hour'.[56] The House had limited powers, and was conscious of its

---

[55] See P. Norton, 'The House of Commons: From Overlooked to Overworked', in B. Jones and L. Robins (eds.), *Two Decades in British Politics* (Manchester: Manchester University Press, 1992).

[56] P. A. Bromhead, *The House of Lords and Contemporary Politics 1911–1957* (London: Routledge & Kegan Paul), 86.

unelected nature. Many members were not young in years. There was little incentive to be involved.

Question Time reflected the nature of the House. More time than in the Commons was given over to each oral question, with more supplementary questions being asked; but there was a limit of four questions that could be asked at any one sitting. (Until 1954, questions could only be asked—and even then only a maximum of three—on Tuesdays and Wednesdays.) As Chester and Bowring recorded, 'Very few Questions are asked. . . . Each year only about 200 Questions are put down for oral answer'[57]— hence the limited attention given the subject in their work.

Like the Commons, the House of Lords has changed significantly since *Questions in Parliament* was published. The House now sits more often, for longer hours, and with more peers attending than was the case in the 1950s. Each session, more than 700 peers attend one or more sittings and more than 500 contribute to debate.[58] The average daily attendance exceeds 300. Votes are also more frequent, and peers more independent in their voting behaviour. The Labour government of 1974–79 suffered 347 defeats in the Upper House. Given the Conservative preponderance in the House, this is perhaps not surprising. What has been remarkable has been the number of defeats suffered by a Conservative government since 1979. By February 1991, the government had suffered more than 150 defeats at their Lordships' hands.

The behavioural change has also been accompanied by some degree of specialization. In the 1970s the House appointed two sessional committees: one on the European Communities, the other on Science and Technology. Both have proved authoritative and influential bodies.[59] They have variously been supplemented by *ad hoc* select committees.[60]

The explanations for these changes have been variously explored.

[57] Chester and Bowring, 314.

[58] D. Shell, *The House of Lords* (Oxford: Philip Allan, 1988), 41.

[59] See e.g. P. D. G. Hayter, 'The Parliamentary Monitoring of Science and Technology in Britain', *Government and Opposition*, 26 2 (1991), 147–66; C. Grantham and C. M. Hodgson, 'The House of Lords: Structural Changes', in Norton (ed.), *Parliament in the 1980s*, 114–35; C. M. Grantham, 'Select Committees', in D. Shell and D. Beamish (eds.), *The House of Lords At Work*; and Shell, *House of Lords*, 185–95.

[60] See Shell, *House of Lords*, 195–8.

According to the analysis of Nicholas Baldwin, they have been the result of two developments. The first is the introduction of life peers, allowing new blood to be brought into the House. Life peers (there are now more than 300) form the backbone of much of the active membership, especially on the opposition benches. Second, the failure of the Parliament (No. 2) Bill in 1969—designed to reform the House, phasing out the hereditary element—led many peers to realize that reform was not likely in the foreseeable future. Consequently, they might as well make the existing institution work. And that, according to Baldwin, is what they have done.[61]

This more active and independent House has not been immune from the wider political pressures that we have identified. Indeed, its very activity and independence have made it a target of lobbying by outside groups. The committees have built up a substantial body of attentive publics. Evidence submitted to Lords committees is often extensive, the number of submissions on occasion running into three figures. Individual peers are also often the recipients of literature from interest groups. Of just over 250 organized groups surveyed by the Study of Parliament Group in 1986, more than 70 per cent said that they had used the House of Lords to make representations or to influence public policy.[62]

The Upper House is thus very different from the cobwebbed institution that Chester and Bowring observed and then largely ignored. The change has been sufficient to justify a more extensive study of questions in the Upper House—hence its inclusion as a chapter in this volume.

Conclusion

Both Houses of Parliament are very different bodies from those which existed when Chester and Bowring were studying Question Time. A consequence of these changes has been a change in the form and nature of questions—and of Question Time—in both Houses. The remaining chapters in this volume identify and

---

[61] N. D. J. Baldwin, 'The House of Lords: Behavioural Changes', in Norton (ed.), *Parliament in the 1980s*, 96–113.

[62] N. D. J. Baldwin, 'The House of Lords', in Rush (ed.), *Parliament and Pressure Politics*, 160.

analyse the nature and extent of that change. Chapter 2 looks at the rules governing PQs and the changes that have taken place in those rules. Given the pressures we have identified, there have been significant changes, most recently—as we have seen—in 1990. Chapter 3 focuses on what happens on the Floor of the House itself. Chapter 4 looks at why Members actually table questions and what they do with them. Chapter 5 looks at how questions are dealt with in departments. Chapter 6 considers questions in 'the other place', the House of Lords. Chapter 7 looks at the use made of questions by bodies outside Parliament. We have already seen that many questions are tabled by MPs on behalf of particular groups. To what use are the answers put? What use is made of questions by the media and groups other than those who may have inspired them? In the concluding chapter we look at the present state of questions in the House of Commons and consider the essential question: where to from here?

2

Evolving Rules

*Helen Irwin, Andrew Kennon, David Natzler,
and Robert Rogers*

Very little is known about the earliest origins of parliamentary questions. These are probably to be found in the desire of Members to ask about future business of the House and of government spokesmen to announce it. The earliest parliamentary question of which there is a record was, however, overtly political, and was put in the House of Lords in 1721 by Earl Cowper.[1] On 9 February, he 'took notice to the House of the report of Mr. Knight's being taken and in custody, which being a matter in which the public was highly concerned, he desired those in the administration to acquaint the House, whether there was any ground for that report'. In light of the answer from the Earl of Sunderland—to the effect that Mr Knight, the absconding chief cashier of the South Sea Company, had been arrested in Brussels—a motion was made for an address to the King. In that respect this famous question was at least, unlike its myriad successors, a prelude to substantive debate.

Gilbert Campion stated that 'for more than a century [from 1721] Questions were infrequent and looked at somewhat askance as an irregular form of debate'.[2] The first recorded ruling about questions in the Commons dates from 1783. Following a lengthy speech by Edmund Burke in response to questions about two officials, the Speaker said that he had often repeated and wished to impress on the mind of the House, that conversations were disorderly; but any Member had in his opinion a right to put a question to a minister or person in office and that person had a right to answer or not answer, as he thought proper.[3]

[1] *Parl. Hist.* 7. col. 709.
[2] Lord Campion, *An Introduction to the Procedure of the House of Commons* (London: Macmillan, 1958), 46.
[3] *Parl. Hist.* 23. cols. 915–31; quoted in P. Howarth, *Questions in the House* (London: Bodley Head, 1956), 56. William Pitt announced his resignation in Mar. 1783 in answer to a question (ibid. 42 and *Parl. Hist.* 23, cols. 687–8).

This ruling suggests that parliamentary questions were at least no novelty in the latter part of the eighteenth century. It also demonstrates their principal procedural characteristic. Most of the business of Parliament, in both Houses, is directed towards eliciting a decision of the House. Decisions can only be reached if there is a motion before the House. Parliamentary questions do not—or should not—involve any debate, and no decision can be reached by the House in the course of Question Time, because no motion is before the House. They are thus an exception to the fundamental rules which govern virtually all parliamentary business.

Other such exceptions are statements by ministers, which are closely related to parliamentary questions; personal statements by Members, which are by their nature exceptional, and statements by the Speaker; and formal events such as the introduction and swearing-in of new Members or the receipt of Messages from the Sovereign or from the other House. Like parliamentary questions, none of these events is listed in the Orders of the Day. Unlike these other occasions when no motion is before the House, however, formal notice is required of PQs, and their texts are published in the Order Paper of the House.[4]

The History of Parliamentary Questions

Chester and Bowring described three stages in the development of parliamentary questions after the right of Members to put questions to ministers had been recognized.

1832–1990. Between 1832 and 1900 the rules requiring notice to be given in advance of the exact question to be asked were set in place.[5] Also during this period a comprehensive set of rules was established defining the permitted scope and content of questions, and oral Question Time, defined as a fixed opportunity in the daily timetable when ministers were expected to be in the House to answer questions, came to have a regular place in the timetable. Other developments in this period were the recognition of

[4] The only PQs whose texts are not published in advance are urgent questions asked by private notice to the Speaker (PNQs).

[5] Notice of a PQ was first printed in 1835, and a special position on the Order Paper was given to PQs from 1849.

Members' rights to ask, and have answered, supplementary questions and a steady increase in the number of questions asked.

Chester and Bowring attributed this increase to the 'Irish question' (to which the origins of many of the present Standing Orders can be traced), the steady growth in the powers of government during the century, Members' desires to give public illustration of their work (questions and answers were reported in some detail in the press), and changes in parliamentary procedures which had the effect of restricting Members' other opportunities to initiate proceedings on the Floor of the House.

1900–1906. The next stage completed this latter process. Faced with long delays at the start of the day's business while private business, questions, and urgent motions for the adjournment of the House were dealt with, the government set about amending the Standing Orders to provide sufficient time for public (mainly government) business. After a number of piecemeal changes, in 1901 Mr Balfour, then Leader of the House, put together a set of proposals for arranging the distribution of time between private business, other matters (including questions), and public business. In 1902 these proposals were debated and amended, and a set of Standing Orders was put in place which regulated the opportunities in the parliamentary day for conducting certain sorts of business. With relatively minor modifications, the timetable then established has governed the pattern of the parliamentary day's business ever since.

The exact time for taking questions was modified in 1906, as part of the final stage in this process, when the House abandoned the practice of taking a fixed dinner break. Since 24 April 1906 Question Time has begun very shortly after the House meets in the afternoon (when Prayers and unopposed private business have been disposed of, which usually takes less than five minutes), and has concluded at the end of the first hour of the day's sitting.[6]

The first written answers to questions also date from the 1902 reforms, as a result of the proposal that questions could be tabled for written answer, a proposal intended particularly for questions of a parochial rather than an 'Imperial' character. The answers were circulated with the daily Votes and Proceedings as well as

---

[6] See Standing Order (S.O.) No. 17.

eventually printed in *Hansard*. The first such answers were given on 5 May 1902 to two questions: one was about compulsory registration of title; the other concerned the possibility of a retrospective grant of a bounty of £10 to shoeing smiths enlisting in the Imperial Yeomanry for South African service—a good mixture of the parochial and the Imperial.[7]

1906–1960.   The principal characteristics of the third stage in the development of questions, from 1906 to the mid-1960s, were further increases in numbers of oral questions and, as a consequence, progressively more restrictions on the times when they could be tabled and answered. A rota determining the order in which ministers answered was established, and first minimum, and later maximum, periods of notice were laid down. Discussing the growth in numbers, Chester and Bowring noted that it was not steady, but fluctuated from session to session, and that, given the huge extension in the powers and activities of the government during the period, the increase in the number of questions asked was not really very great. In particular, there had been no increase of any significance in the use of written questions, which had continued at a daily average of around twenty ever since 1902.

1960–1990.   Between 1960 and 1990 there was a dramatic change. The number of oral questions on the Order Paper had increased from 13,778 in 1960–61 to 24,687 in 1989–90. By 1990 it had become common for well over 400 (and sometimes over 500) questions for oral answer to be tabled for the two busiest days of the week, when the Prime Minister, as well as departmental ministers, answered questions. The use of written questions increased even more markedly. In 1989–90, 41,358 questions were tabled for written answer, compared with 3,369 in 1958–59 (a session of comparable length).[8]

   In 1989–90 and 1990–91 there were two inquiries by the Procedure Committee into questions. The first led to recommendations about the arrangements for the tabling of oral questions and about ways of improving the effectiveness of Question Time which were speedily implemented. The second was a much wider

---

[7] *Parl. Deb.* (1902), 107, cols. 611–12.
[8] See *Parliamentary Questions*, HC (1990–91) 178, Evidence, p. 11, Appendix A.

investigation. It reviewed the changes resulting from the earlier inquiry, and went on to recommend abandoning the 'ration' for oral questions (see p. 45 below) and to reject the idea of a ration for written questions. Significantly, it recommended the abolition or relaxation of seven restrictive rules of order for questions, but sought stricter rules against campaigns and against questions designed to elicit lists of government achievements. Overall, the

Table 2.1. *Number of questions asked*

Session	Number on Paper for oral answer			Number on Paper for written answer	Number of PNQs asked[a]
	Reached for oral answer	Received written answer	Total		
1946–47	6,795	6,702	13,497	3,525	42
1956–57	5,151	6,617	11,768	6,020	33
1966–67[b]	8,464	8,850	17,314	16,951	39
1976–77	2,488	3,975	6,463	25,076	23
1977–78	2,648	5,034	7,682	28,739	14
1978–79[c]	1,272	1,368	2,640	13,152	23
1979–80[b]	3,787	8,881	12,668	39,912	40
1980–81	2,532	8,472	11,004	22,688	8
1981–82	2,554	6,202	8,756	23,439	9
1982–83[c]	1,793	4,833	6,626	17,095	7
1983–84[b]	3,226	10,650	13,876	40,119	48
1984–85	2,393	12,398	14,791	31,523	26
1985–86	2,480	14,852	17,332	31,808	43
1986–87[c]	1,484	11,722	13,206	21,331	19
1987–88	3,035	21,005	24,040	47,726	39
1988–89	2,417	21,515	23,932	39,540	35
1989–90	2,297	22,390	24,687	41,358	26

Note: There are some variations between different sources for number of questions asked, and methods of recording have changed over the years.
[a] Excluding the weekly Business Question.
[b] Unusually long session.
[c] Unusually short session.
Source: Sessional Returns.

Table 2.2. Number of parliamentary questions to each government department (excluding Private Notice Questions)

Department	1980–81		1984–85		1985–86		1988–89	
	Oral	Written	Oral	Written	Oral	Written	Oral	Written
Agriculture, Fisheries, and Food	331	1,113	327	1,515	369	1,426	311	2,712
Attorney-General	63	555	102	298	114	384	92	401
Church Commissioners	1	1	43	21	61	35	58	10
Defence	348	1,098	388	2,233	441	2,096	367	3,426
Duchy of Lancaster	4	7	0	0	16	9	12	8
Education and Science	380	1,276	367	1,727	381	2,185	318	2,052
Employment	325	2,017	336	2,343	315	2,261	362	3,004
Energy	360	810	468	791	426	1,008	280	1,444
Health and Social Security	322	3,174	338	5,385	381	5,675	552	6,871
Environment	449	2,034	370	3,344	415	3,624	423	4,947
Foreign and Commonwealth Office	541	1,243	576	2,318	607	2,271	495	2,552
Home Office	281	2,009	367	3,112	325	3,466	274	3,577
House of Commons Commission	13	25	1	27	6	27	4	38
Leader of the House of Commons	70	99	133	199	92	162	96	168
Minister for the Civil Service	77	413	9	2	99	51	98	96
Northern Ireland Office	336	926	314	1,265	332	1,089	264	1,277
Office of Arts and Libraries	79	84	119	146	111	247	85	377
Prime Minister	849	3,005	820	1,282	968	1,307	835	1,643
Public Accounts Commission	0	0	0	3	2	0	17	2
Scottish Office	392	1,445	340	1,932	391	2,014	437	2,972
Solicitor-General for Scotland	71	33	67	83	80	83	0	0
Trade and Industry	762	2,133	500	2,055	531	1,979	432	2,189
Transport	390	1,128	385	1,909	400	2,196	304	2,673
Treasury	339	1,658	498	2,232	381	1,680	330	2,720
Welsh Office	319	936	413	1,030	358	1,211	258	1,554

Committee continued its earlier approach: giving priority to the assiduous individual Member, giving the benefit of the doubt to Members as against ministers, and encouraging questions as a means of seeking information or pressing for action rather than simply a continuation of the debate betweeen the parties by another means.

Although, formally, PQs are questions to Members, almost all PQs are in fact asked of ministers.[9] They form today the most frequent and arguably the most important opportunity for ordinary Members (backbenchers on both sides of the House) to raise issues on the Floor of the House.

Types of Parliamentary Question

There are now several different types of parliamentary question. All have their origins in oral questions asked of ministers on the Floor of the House. The most direct successors of the first PQs are questions to the Leader of the House about the business of the House for the coming week (**Business Questions**). These now follow a short business announcement made, usually, on Thursdays in answer to a question by private notice to the Speaker from the shadow Leader of the House.[10] They do not form part of Question Time *per se*.[11]

---

[9] Among private Members to whom questions may be addressed are the Member who answers on behalf of the Church Commissioners, the Member who answers on behalf of the House of Commons Commission, and the Chairman of the Public Accounts Commission. The Leader of the House used also to answer questions in his capacity as Chairman of the House of Commons (Services) Committee. The Services Committee was abolished with effect from the end of the 1990–91 session, and was replaced by the Finance and Services Committee and four domestic committees. Questions concerning the exercise of the responsibilities of these committees may be tabled to the chairmen of the committees. It is currently the practice to provide a place on the rota of oral questions for Members answering on behalf of the Church Commissioners, the House of Commons Commission, and the Public Accounts Commission. An oral slot is also being provided for questions to the Chairman of the Finance and Services Committee; see *HC Deb*. (1991–92) 203, col. 452w.

[10] Until Feb. 1988, such questions were customarily asked by the Leader of the Opposition.

[11] Occasionally the business for the following week is announced in the form of a Business Statement (rather than in response to a PNQ), usually in order to permit a senior member of the government to precede it with another statement immediately after Question Time; see e.g. *HC Deb*. (1990–91) 189, cols. 584 ff.

Other **Private Notice Questions** (PNQs) on urgent matters may, at the Speaker's discretion, be asked on any day, either before the main business of the day, when they are in effect an extension of Question Time, or, on Fridays, at 11.00 a.m.; and they may be followed by a limited period of supplementary questions and answers. PNQs are asked on subjects ranging from the local (for example, the Rose Theatre, Southwark, or the Severn Tunnel rail crash[12]) to matters of high politics (for example, the situation in the Gulf or the situation in Yugoslavia[13]). The Speaker will only consider allowing a PNQ to be asked if the matter is urgent.[14] PNQs are frequently sought by the opposition in order to extract a response from the government if the latter is unwilling to make a ministerial statement to the House.

Slightly longer question and answer sessions follow **Ministerial Statements** announcing new policies or arising out of new political developments. Statements take place before the commencement of public business, after any Private Notice Questions (or at 11.00 a.m. on Fridays). Incidentally, the hallowed opening phrase used by ministers: 'With permission, Mr Speaker, I shall make a statement'—is meaningless. The making of statements is entirely within the control of the government.[15]

Question Time is the period between about 2.35 p.m. and 3.30 p.m. on Monday to Thursday when **oral questions** (sometimes known as 'starred' questions because they are distinguished by an asterisk on the printed Order Paper), of which notice has been given, are replied to by ministers (and certain other Members[16]), after which the Speaker allows a limited number of supplementary questions and answers. Questions tabled for oral answer which are not reached during Question Time receive written answers which are published in *Hansard* next morning, and are available from 3.30 p.m. onwards on the day they are due for answer, in the Library of the House. Copies of such written answers are sent by departments to the Members who tabled the questions, and are also placed in the Press Gallery. The majority of PQs, however,

[12] *HC Deb.* (1990–91) 153, cols. 21–5; *HC Deb.* (1991–92) 200, cols. 609–14.

[13] *HC Deb.* (1990–91) 186, cols. 797–806; *HC Deb.* (1990–91) 193, cols. 1137–40.

[14] *Erskine May's Treatise on the Law, Privileges, Proceedings and Usage of Parliament*, 21st edn. (London: Butterworths, 1989), 296. Hereafter designated *Erskine May*.

[15] See e.g. *HC Deb.* (1985–86) 91, cols. 305–6, and *HC Deb.* (1990–91) 190, col. 628.   [16] See n. 9 above.

are written questions tabled by Members for **written answer**. Answers to these questions are similarly published in *Hansard*.

Scope and Content

The Standing Orders of the House of Commons make no reference to the scope or content of PQs. There is, however, a comprehensive set of rules set out in *Erskine May* regarding the form and content of questions (see Appendix).[17] These embody rulings made by successive Speakers, and apply equally to oral questions, supplementary questions arising therefrom, and written questions. Control over the form and content of PQs rests with the Speaker, and the rules are administered on his behalf by Clerks of the House.

Most of the Speakers' rulings have their origins in the nineteenth century, and derive from decisions given by successive Speakers in relation to individual questions; most are to be found in the reports of parliamentary debates,[18] but some were private rulings given by the Speaker. Since 5 November 1981, following pressure from Conservative backbencher Sir Robin Maxwell-Hyslop, the Speaker has directed that the substance of any private ruling which in his judgement was of general interest or could serve as a precedent should be published in *Hansard*.[19]

Between 1844 (the date of the first edition of *Erskine May*) and the end of the nineteenth century, a steady stream of Speakers' rulings laid down regulations about the content of questions. The earliest rulings followed Mr Speaker Cornwall's lead in 1783, and sought to limit the possibility of questions leading to 'conversations'—disorderly debates taking place without a motion being before the House. These led to the present rules, which prohibit the inclusion in the text of a question or 'argument'. In 1861 the Select Committee on the Business of the House said

[17] *Erskine May* is a handbook of parliamentary rules and precedent. The 1st edn. was written by Sir Thomas Erskine May, later Clerk of the House of Commons, and was published in 1844. May was responsible for a further 8 editions. The Clerk of the House of Commons is the editor of the work, which is now in its 21st edn.

[18] The reports were at first known simply as Parliamentary Debates, Official Report. In 1943 the word *Hansard* was added to the title.

[19] *HC Deb.* (1981–82) 12, col. 113; *Erskine May*, 21st edn. p. 5.

that both the questions and the answers should not be 'sustained by reasoning, which might give rise to debate'.[20] Other rules applied the conventions of the House governing speech and behaviour to questions; thus offensive references to or aspersions on the Sovereign and certain other categories of individuals are prohibited in questions. Still others defined the issues on which questions could be asked, which had to be limited to matters for which ministers were in some degree responsible, while other rules required that Members assume responsibility for the facts set out in a question; thus 'fishing' questions asking if a rumour or report in a newspaper is true are not allowed.

Despite the substantial body of 'case law' governing the scope and content of questions, the basic rules are very simple, and have operated unchanged since the end of the nineteenth century. These are:

> A question must:
> *either* seek, rather than give, information
> *or* press for action;
> A question must relate to a matter for which a minister is responsible;
> A question must not be fully covered by an answer (or a refusal to answer) given in the same session.[21]

The rules concerning content were examined by the Procedure Committee in 1966–67 and 1969–70 and by a Select Committee on Parliamentary Questions in 1971–72. The Committees in 1966–67 and 1969–70 examined the rule about questions relating to nationalized industries and the extent to which the rule concerning the admissibility of questions to which an answer had been refused could be invoked to prevent further questions being asked. Both Committees also considered the rule prohibiting questions suggesting amendments to Bills and the extent of ministerial responsibility for issues in Commonwealth or foreign countries. In 1969–70 the Committee also examined the operation of the rule prohibiting questions citing individual incidents as the basis for a request for

---

[20] *Report from the Select Committee on the Business of the House*,1861, HC 173, para. 56.

[21] See *Parliamentary Questions*, HC (1990–91), 178, Evidence, p. 6.

new legislation and the rule relating to questions repeating in substance those already answered in the same session.[22]

The 1971–72 report reaffirmed the principal rules as set out in *Erskine May*. It expressed concern, however, that the cumulative effect of previous decisions relating to the orderliness of questions should not be allowed to become unduly restrictive, and recommended that, while the Speaker should continue to have regard to the basic rules concerning the form and content of questions listed in *Erskine May*, he should not consider himself bound, when interpreting the rules, to disallow a question solely on the grounds that it conflicted with any previous individual ruling.[23]

The Procedure Committee re-examined the rules for questions in 1990–91. In a memorandum to the Committee, the Principal Clerk of the Table Office suggested a number of relaxations to the rules. In particular, he made the following suggestions:

(1) The distinction between speeches outside Parliament by ministers of Cabinet rank or with particular responsibilities (about which questions were in order) and those by other ministers (about which questions might not be asked) should be abolished.

(2) Following the giving of ministerial answers on, for example, human rights issues, the rule against asking questions about the internal affairs of foreign countries should be relaxed.

(3) Members should be allowed to ask ministers to interpret the law in respect of ministerial power or responsibility (rather than seeking advice on a particular case).

(4) Questions suggesting or seeking amendments to Bills before the House should be allowed.

(5) Partly because of the inconsistency of certain ministerial replies, ministerial 'blocking answers' should lose their ability to block (that is, prevent) the asking of questions on a particular subject over a long period, and should be treated as no more than 'previous answers' to be taken into account when the orderliness of a new question was being considered.

[22] *Fifth Report from the Select Committee on Procedure*, HC (1966–67) 410; *Second Report from the Select Committee on Procedure*, HC (1969–70) 198; *Report from the Select Committee on Parliamentary Questions*, HC (1971–72) 393. See also *First Report from the Select Committee on Nationalized Industries*, HC (1967–68) 371.

[23] *Parliamentary Questions*, HC (1971–72), 393, para. 10.

The Committee endorsed almost all these suggestions. The only exception was that concerning questions seeking an interpretation of the law, upon which the Committee recommended no change. As noted above, the Committee's recommendations sought to give the benefit of the doubt to Members rather than to ministers, who had profited from the accumulated restrictions which decades of case law had placed upon questioners.[24]

Regulation of Question Time

By contrast with the rules concerning the content of PQs, the rules of the House governing the structure of Question Time have been frequently reviewed and modified. The increasing number of rules was mainly a consequence of the increase in numbers of questions. As Chester and Bowring explained, by 1900, more PQs were asked in one day than were asked in the whole of the session of 1830. At the same time, as Chester and Bowring show, the increasingly tight restrictions on other forms of procedure led Members to make greater use of PQs. That process continued into the twentieth century.

By 1832 the right of Members to ask questions of ministers had been clearly established, and the basic structure of Question Time as we know it today was set in place by 1906. The two principal developments after 1832 were the formalization of the giving of notice in advance of PQs and the fixing of a regular place for questions in the daily parliamentary timetable.

Notice of Questions

Prior to 1835 Members appear to have given notice of their question to ministers either by sending the minister a note in advance or by indicating orally in the House that they intended to ask such and such a question on a subsequent day. Between 1835 and 1849 some questions were printed on the Notice Paper, along with motions of which notice had been given.[25] From 1849 to 1869 notices of questions in the Notice Paper were grouped together,

---

[24] *Parliamentary Questions*, HC (1990–91) 178, Evidence, p. 6, paras. 41–9.
[25] *Erskine May*, 9th edn. p. 355 n. The first printing of a notice of a question (see n. 5 above) was on 27 Feb. 1835.

and from 27 April 1869 a separate list of questions was published immediately before Notices of Motions. However, during this period there was no consistent practice of giving notice of questions, and some Members continued to give notice orally or privately by letter.

As a pattern of Speakers' rulings on the content of questions grew up, so the Clerk of the House took on a role in editing the texts of questions. The then Clerk, Sir Thomas Erskine May, told the Select Committee on Public Business in 1878: 'Before questions appear, they are most carefully revised, and objectionable parts removed, generally with the consent of the Member and under the direction of the Speaker.'[26] Such preliminary vetting of questions was obviously not possible so long as oral notice persisted. The absence of a rule requiring written notice of the text of questions enabled Members to ask disorderly questions. In 1886 Mr Speaker Brand suggested that the House give the Speaker powers to prevent disorderly questions being asked. On 12 March of that year the House agreed 'That Notices of Questions be given by Members in writing to the Clerk at the Table, without reading them *viva voce* in the House, unless the consent of the Speaker to any particular Question has been previously obtained'.[27] This became part of the first Standing Order of the House governing PQs, which was agreed to on 7 March 1888.

Even where written notice had been given, on the day they were answered, questions were read out *in extenso* before they were answered until nearly the end of the nineteenth century. Sometimes questions were very long (one read out in 1880 contained nearly 500 words[28]), and there were complaints by Members during the 1880s about the amount of time taken simply by the reading of questions. With the encouragement of Mr Speaker Brand, during the 1880s the practice was discouraged. In his memoirs published in 1925, Mr Speaker Lowther wrote;

When I first entered the House [in 1883] every Member who had a question on the notice paper read the whole of his question aloud before the Minister answered it. . . . It was Sir Charles Dilke who first set the example of calling out the number of his question. To ears accustomed to

---

[26] *Report of a Select Committee on Public Business*, 1878, HC 268, q. 82.
[27] *Parl. Deb.* (1886) 303, cols. 697–702.
[28] D. N. Chester and N. Bowring, *Questions in Parliament* (Oxford: Clarendon Press, 1962), 19.

the more lengthy process, this procedure seemed somewhat bald, but the House soon adopted it and saved much time thereby.[29]

The system of giving notice in writing, to the Clerks, of the text of questions has continued ever since. The Clerks in the Table Office, under the authority of the Speaker, vet questions to ensure that they comply with the rules governing scope and content, and if necessary assist Members in the drafting of orderly questions. Once accepted by the Table Office, until very recently, all questions were then printed and circulated the following morning as Notices of Questions to be asked on a particular date.

Increases in the number of questions tabled for oral answer, with an accompanying diminution in a Member's chances of obtaining an oral answer on the Floor of the House about which supplementaries could be asked, led to a number of changes in the period of notice required for questions for oral answer and subsequently to the arrangements for printing the texts of questions.

Period of Notice Required

Until 1902 the only requirement about notice was that a question had to appear on the Notice Paper; thus a question could be tabled as late as midnight one day and a minister be expected to provide an oral answer the following day. During consideration of the package of proposals put forward by Mr Balfour in 1902 for changes in the hours of business of the House of Commons, the House agreed to limit the answering of starred (that is, oral) questions to those which appeared on the Notice Paper the day before. The reason given for this proposal still sounds familiar: 'The extraordinary pressure thrown upon some of those heavily worked departments by the modern increase of Questions is so great that some precaution must be taken with a view to mitigating the burden which would be placed upon them'.[30] The new rule applied only to questions for oral answer.

The formal rule about the **minimum notice** required for an oral question in 1990 was not very different from that introduced in 1902. In respect of oral questions to all but the smallest

---

[29] Viscount Ullswater (Mr Speaker Lowther), *A Speaker's Commentaries*, (1925), ii. 299–300, quoted in Chester and Bowring, 19.

[30] *Parl. Deb.* (1902) 105, col. 1267.

departments, however, the minimum notice rule became progressively less relevant. As the number of questions for oral answer
increased, the chances of getting an oral answer to a question only
two days after tabling the question became negligible.

The Rota

The introduction of a single fixed opportunity on each of four days
each week when oral questions could be asked and answered,
coupled with the rise in the numbers of oral questions of which
notice was given, led, in the period after 1902, to a rota system,
whereby individual ministers had fixed slots in the parliamentary
timetable when they were expected to be in the House to answer
questions. Prior to 1902, questions were taken in the order in
which notice had been given to the Clerk, with the exception of
questions to the Prime Minister, which since 1881 had been
grouped together at the end of the day's list. Mr Balfour proposed
in 1902, just before the new Standing Orders (including the fixed
period for questions) came into operation, that the first fifty oral
questions should be arranged so that those addressed to the same
minister were grouped together. This, he said, would be 'convenient
to Ministers of hard-worked Departments' and also 'to the
convenience . . . of members asking questions'.[31] Soon thereafter,
the practice of grouping was extended to all questions on the list.

Following complaints that questions to the Prime Minister,
grouped at the end of the list, were being squeezed out, in 1904 the
Speaker directed that questions to the Prime Minister would begin
not later than, initially, question 51 on the list. When there proved
still to be difficulty in ensuring that PM's questions were reached
within the time available for questions, this direction was amended
so that questions to the Prime Minister began after question 45 on
the list. This remained the case until 1959. After a Procedure
Committee investigation demonstrated that the time available for
PM's questions was again being squeezed by the number and
length of other questions and supplementaries, for a brief period
PM's questions began after question 40, on Tuesdays and
Thursdays and after question 45 on other days. Finally, in 1959 the
Prime Minister agreed to a recommendation made by the

---

[31] *Parl. Deb.* (1902) 107, col. 572.

Procedure Committee that there should be a separate fixed slot for Prime Minister's questions at 3.15 p.m. on Tuesdays and Thursdays only.[32] That system continues today.

So long as all questions tabled for oral answer on a given day could be answered within the time allowed for questions, the order in which they were asked does not seem to have mattered (apart from the grouping referred to above). Already by 1905, however, there were complaints that not all questions tabled for oral answer were reached, and, first informally and subsequently formally, a rota system was introduced whereby each day questions to some ministers were high on the list for answering and questions to others at the end of the list (and thus liable not to be reached). Chester and Bowring traced the various stages in the development of the rota over the next forty years.[33] Two points in this process may be particularly stressed. First, it was established early on that the order for answering questions was determined not by the Speaker, but by the government, after consultations through the 'usual channels'—that is, between the whips of the main parties.[34] That remains the position today.

Secondly, it became much more complicated for Members to ensure that their questions would be listed high enough in the list to receive an oral answer. Chester and Bowring stated: 'Increasingly in recent years finding the right day has become one of the arts of the questioner.'[35] The development of the rota meant that Members' opportunities to ask questions of ministers were progressively restricted to certain days. Ostensibly the rota still provided for oral questions to an individual minister in each of the main departments on at least one day each week, as the example of the rota for the four weeks before Christmas 1990 shows. In practice, however, it has long been the case that the number of questions tabled to the department first for answering on a given day will take up the whole of the time available, and it is not now the practice for Members to bother to table questions to ministers lower down the list for answer. Indeed, it has long been rare for there to be sufficient time for all the questions to the minister top

[32] *HC Deb.* (1958–59) 609, col. 49.

[33] Chester and Bowring, ch. 6.

[34] See Chester and Bowring, 132–3; *Parliamentary Questions*, HC (1971–72), 393.

[35] Chester and Bowring, 152.

for answering to be reached. The only exceptions occur on some Mondays, when questions to some of the small 'departments' (which include questions to certain Members who are not ministers, such as the Member answering for the House of Commons Commission) are sometimes exhausted within the time available, in which case the House reverts to questions tabled to the larger department whose minister answered earlier that day. From January 1990 the rota was amended to reflect what was happening in practice. It now lists only those departments or ministers who will actually be answering questions each day.

Adaptations to the rota have been made by the government from time to time. Sometimes such adaptations have followed changes in the structure of government: for example, in 1988, after the [then] Prime Minister had split the former Department of Health and Social Security into two new departments, each with its own Secretary of State, separate provision was made in the rota for health questions on one day and social security questions on another, with consequential changes to the times for taking questions to other departments.[36] The separate slot for questions to the Scottish law officer, the Solicitor-General for Scotland, was discontinued in 1987, when no MP was available to take that office; such questions were instead tabled in the Commons to the Secretary of State for Scotland.[37]

Other amendments to the rota have followed pressure within the House for a change. The separate slot within questions to the Foreign Secretary for questions about the EEC was abandoned, for an experimental period, from 20 April 1985. That decision was taken by the 'usual channels', and announced on 22 March 1985.[38] The arrangement was subsequently made permanent. In 1991, the Procedure Committee reported that it had received representations that there should be a separate period allocated for questions relating to sport (then part of the responsibilities of the Secretary of State for Education and Science). The Committee concluded that any such changes 'are best discussed through the usual channels'.[39]

---

[36] Further changes were made to the rota in 1992 to reflect changes in the structure of government departments following the 1992 general election.

[37] e.g. *HC Deb.* (1987–88) 125, col. 515w.

[38] *HC Deb.* (1984–85) 75, cols. 622–3w.

[39] *Parliamentary Questions*, HC (1990–91) 178, pp. xiv–xv, paras. 49 and 50.

ORDER OF QUESTIONS
Monday 26 November–Thursday 20 December 1990

(The rota is printed on wallsheets which are displayed in lobbies of the House.
Footnotes given are printed on these wallsheets for the information of Members.)

Mon. 26 Nov.	Tues. 27 Nov.	Wed. 28 Nov.	Thurs. 29 Nov.
Transport	**Educ. & Science**	**Foreign & Commonwealth**	**Ag. Fish & Food**
Wales	Defence	(other than Overseas Development Questions)	Treasury
Energy	Employment	Trade & Industry	Home Office
Social Security	Health	Environment	Northern Ireland
Arts[1]		Scotland	
Civil Service[3]			
At 3.15 p.m.		At 3.15 p.m.	
Prime Minister		**Prime Minister**	

Mon. 3 Dec.	Tues. 4 Dec.	Wed. 5 Dec.	Thurs. 6 Dec.
Wales	**Defence**	**Trade & Industry**	**Treasury**
Energy	Employment	Environment	Home Office
Social Security	Health	Scotland	Northern Ireland
Transport	Educ. & Science	Foreign & Commonwealth	Ag. Fish & Food
Attorney General[1]			
Foreign & Commonwealth (Overseas Development Questions)[1]			
At 3.15 p.m.	At 3.15 p.m.	At 3.15 p.m.	At 3.15 p.m.
	Prime Minister		**Prime Minister**

Mon. 17 Dec.	Tues. 18 Dec.	Wed. 19 Dec.	Thurs. 20 Dec.
Social Security	**Health**	**Scotland**[6]	**Northern Ireland**
Transport	Educ. & Science	Foreign & Commonwealth	Ag. Fish & Food
Wales	Defence	Trade & Industry	Treasury
Energy	Employment	Environment	Home Office
Arts[1]			
Civil Service[3]			
	At 3.15 p.m.		At 3.15 p.m.
	Prime Minister		**Prime Minister**

Mon. 10 Dec.	Tues. 11 Dec.	Wed. 12 Dec.	Thurs. 13 Dec.
Energy	**Employment**	**Environment**	**Home Office**
Social Security	Health	Scotland	Northern Ireland
Transport	Educ. & Science	Foreign & Commonwealth	Ag. Fish & Food
Wales	Defence	Trade & Industry	Treasury
Chancellor of the Duchy of Lancaster[1]			
Church Commissioners[5]			
Public Accounts Commission[2]			
Lord President of the Council[3,4]			
	At 3.15 p.m.		At 3.15 p.m.
	Prime Minister		**Prime Minister**

[1] Starting not later than 3.10 p.m.

[2] Starting not later than 3.15 p.m.

[3] Starting not later than 3.20 p.m.

[4] Also answers as Leader of the House and Chairman of the Select Committee on House of Commons (Services).

[5] Starting not later than 3.10 p.m., Questions to the Chancellor of the Duchy of Lancaster have precedence.

[6] Also answers on behalf of Lord Advocate.

Note: For the Departments shown in bold type, Questions for oral answers should be submitted between 10 a.m. and the time set by Mr Speaker, exactly ten *sitting* days before the date of answer, in order to be included in the random shuffle to determine the order of questions.

ORDER OF QUESTIONS
Monday 13th January–Thursday 6 February 1992

(The rota is printed on wallsheets which are displayed in lobbies of the House.
Footnotes given are printed on these wallsheets for the information of Members.)

Mon. 13 Jan.	Tues. 14 Jan.	Wed. 15 Jan.	Thurs. 16 Jan.
Transport Arts[1] Civil Service[3]	Employment	Trade & Industry	Treasury
	At 3.15 p.m.		At 3.15 p.m.
	Prime Minister		**Prime Minister**

Mon. 20 Jan.	Tues. 21 Jan.	Wed. 22 Jan.	Thurs. 23 Jan.
Wales Attorney-General Foreign & Common-Wealth (Overseas Development Questions)[3]	Health	Environment	Home Office
	At 3.15 p.m.		At 3.15 p.m.
	Prime Minister		**Prime Minister**

Mon. 27 Jan.	Tues. 28 Jan.	Wed. 29 Jan.	Thurs. 30 Jan.
Energy Chancellor of the Duchy of Lancaster[1] Church Commissioners[5] Public Accounts Commission[2] Lord President of the Council[3,4]	Education & Science	Scotland[4]	Northern Ireland
	At 3.15 p.m. **Prime Minister**		At 3.15 p.m. **Prime Minister**

Mon. 3 Feb.	Tues. 4 Feb.	Wed. 5 Feb.	Thurs. 6 Feb.
Social Security[1] Arts[1] Civil Service[3]	Defence	Foreign & Commonwealth (other than Overseas Development Questions)	Agriculture, Fisheries & Food
	At 3.15 p.m. **Prime Minister**		At 3.15 p.m. **Prime Minister**

[1] Starting not later than 3.10 p.m.
[2] Starting not later than 3.15 p.m.
[3] Starting not later than 3.20 p.m.
[4] Also answers as Leader of the House.
[5] Starting not later than 3.10 p.m., Questions to the Chancellor of the Duchy of Lancaster have precedence.
[6] Also answers on behalf of Lord Advocate.

Note: Questions for oral answer should usually be submitted between 10 a.m. and 5 p.m., exactly ten *sitting* days before the date of answer, in order to be included in the random shuffle to determine the order of questions. Where the House is adjourned for more than two days, tabling dates are in accordance with paras. 7 and 8 of Standing Order No. 18.

The existence of a fixed period of just under an hour for oral
questions and answers, the rota which establishes the day on which
a particular minister will be answering, and above all the
increasing numbers of questions tabled for oral answer meant that
the order in which questions were answered was of crucial
importance. As the Procedure Committee stated in 1975–76:

Since the value of an oral Question lies largely in the opportunity to ask
supplementary Questions, Members attach importance to the order in
which the notices of Questions appear, and it is clearly desirable that this
order should be determined according to well understood principles and
by a method in which Members have confidence.[40]

Two developments are relevant: the coming of rules governing the
maximum notice which could be given of an oral question and the
invention of the '**shuffle**' to decide the order in which questions are
printed and asked.

Maximum Period of Notice

Two linked rules were introduced after a Report in 1958–59 from
the Procedure Committee.[41] First, no Member was allowed more
than two oral questions per day (or for answer on a particular
day), and secondly, the maximum period of notice for an oral
question was set at twenty-one days. Any excess over two oral
questions was removed by the Table Office two days before they
were due to be answered. These rules were modified in 1971, when
the maximum notice period was reduced to ten sitting days after
the Procedure Committee had concluded that the existing rule
meant that some questions would be stale by the time they were
reached.[42]

The rules were changed again in 1971–72, after which Members
were allowed to table no more than two oral questions for answer
on any day and no more than one to any one minister or other

[40] *First Report from the Select Committee on Procedure*, HC (1975–76) 618, para.
1; see also *Procedure Committee Reports*, 1966–67 and 1969–70, and *Parliamentary
Questions*, HC (1971–72) 393.
[41] *Report from the Select Committee on Procedure*, HC (1958–59) 92, para. 40.
The 3-week rule came into operation on 27 Oct. 1965.
[42] *Second Report from the Select Committee on Procedure*, HC (1969–70) 198,
para. 13; the Standing Orders were amended on 7 Apr. 1971, CJ 226 (1970–71),
p. 380.

Member answering and, in addition, could have outstanding no more than eight oral questions on the Notice Paper awaiting answer in a period of ten sitting days.[43] The 1971–72 Select Committee set out its reasons for suggesting this latter change:

The purpose of such a limit would be to discourage Members from tabling large numbers of Questions that have little chance of being reached, and which because of the indiscriminate way in which they are tabled, often prevent other Members from having their Questions answered orally.[44]

To keep within their permitted 'ration' of eight questions, Members whose questions were listed too low in the list for the day they were due for answer could withdraw the question or 'unstar' it (that is, convert it into a question for written answer), and thus have an opportunity to table oral questions to other ministers on other days.[45]

The consequence of these two rules governing notice of questions was to introduce effective ballots for the opportunity to ask oral questions, which replaced the earlier first-come, first-served system. Because on practically every occasion the number of questions tabled for oral answer on a given day exceeded the number likely to be reached within the time allowed for questions, oral questions tabled less than the maximum permitted period in advance have for many years stood no practical chance of receiving an oral answer. Thus the maximum period of notice became the minimum.

In 1990 the Procedure Committee commented that the reasoning behind the precise period of notice required had 'more to do with the convenience of Government Departments than with that of Members or the House authorities'.[46] In 1991 the Committee considered a proposal from the Principal Clerk in the Table Office to reduce the period of notice from ten to five sitting days, to reduce printing costs and make questions more topical.[47] After taking evidence from ministers, the Committee reported:

---

[43] CJ 228 (1972–73), p. 84.

[44] *Parliamentary Questions*. HC (1971–72) 393, para. 18.

[45] See ibid., Appendix, p. xvi.

[46] *Oral Questions*, HC (1989–90) 379, para. 21.

[47] It was estimated that such a change would save £317,000 in printing costs per session. See *Parliamentary Questions*, HC (1990–91) 178, para. 18, and Evidence, pp. 2–3.

We certainly would not regard the convenience of Departments—even if it could be clearly demonstrated that some difficulty would be caused—as an overriding consideration in weighing the merits of any shortening of the period of notice.[48]

and recommended that the maximum period of notice be reduced to five sitting days.[49]

Order in which Questions are Answered: The Shuffle

In 1902 the suggestion was made that questions should be listed in their order of importance, which would be determined by the Clerks under Mr Speaker's authority. Not surprisingly, the proposal was rejected.[50] For many years, when there was no maximum period of notice, questions were listed on the Order Paper according to the day on which they were tabled.

The determination of the order in which questions tabled on the same day were listed took place at the printers, under the supervision of the Editorial Supervisor of the Vote, a member of the Clerk's Department's staff.[51] When the maximum of twenty-one days notice was introduced in 1965, this system continued.[52] At 4.00 p.m. on the first day on which notice could be given of questions for oral answer, pieces of paper bearing the text of each question tabled were sent in a pouch to the printers, where they were picked from a table in random order and printed. Further pouches were sent in the course of that day's sitting, but, in order to have any chance of an oral answer from a minister in a major department, a question had to be tabled early enough to be in the four o'clock pouch.[53] That system was modified in 1967, after what the Speaker described as 'the supererogatory practice of an enthusiastic printer', when questions were listed in alphabetical order of the Member asking the question.[54] Thereafter, the rule was introduced that the papers bearing the questions had to be turned out on to a table at the printers and shuffled (like a pack of

---

[48] Ibid., p. x, para. 21.
[49] Ibid.
[50] See Chester and Bowring, 72 and 81–2.
[51] Formerly known as the Superintendent of Printing the Votes and Proceedings.
[52] *Fifth Report from the Select Committee on Procedure*, HC (1966–67) 410, p. v, para. 2.
[53] See *Parliamentary Questions*, HC (1971–72) 393, p. 49, para. 9.
[54] See *HC Deb.* (1967–68) 755, cols. 807, 966.

cards), and then printed in the random order resulting from the shuffling process.[55]

This was examined by the Procedure Committee in 1975–76, which confirmed conclusions of previous committees, that, partly for practical reasons and partly because 'the present system makes it less easy for a number of Members to concert the tabling of Questions so that they appear to the exclusion of others (which a priority system would facilitate), Your Committee have concluded . . . that a random system has fewer objections than one designed to establish priorities'.[56]

The Committee decided, however, that although they had 'no doubt that this shuffling has been carried out responsibly . . . they attach importance to Members having confidence in the system', and recommended that the shuffle should in future be carried out in the House itself, at the Clerk's Department, at a set time, 'so that any Member who so wished might see it being done'. Thereafter the shuffle (occasionally attended by a Member and also, latterly, from time to time by television cameras) took place in an office above the Chamber at 4.05 p.m. on each day on which a maximum notice period for oral questions began. In 1990 the cumbersome physical shuffling of papers was partially replaced by a system of electronic random numbering again open to Members who wished to verify its fairness.

Despite occasional suggestions that the randomness of the system may not be total, the House seems broadly satisfied with this arrangement.[57] The Procedure Committee looked at it in 1990 and again in 1991. As part of its package of changes which were introduced in October 1990 (see below), it recommended that the timing of the shuffle be deferred till later than 4.00 p.m., to allow Members longer each day to hand in their questions.[58] In 1991 it considered, and rejected, a plea from a Welsh Member that the

---

[55] This random system of establishing priorities is a well-established feature of the practice of the House. It is used also in the ballot for Private Members' Bills each session (where more than 400 Members normally compete for 20 places), for the ballots for Private Members' Motions each session, and for 4 of the 5 half-hour adjournment debates each week.

[56] See *The Procedure for Establishing the Order of Oral Questions*, HC (1975–76) 618, para. 3.

[57] See *HC Deb.* (1989–90) 160, col. 356; D. Davis, *BBC's Viewer's Guide to Parliament* (London: BBC, 1989), 62.

[58] *Oral Questions*, HC (1989–90) 379, para. 9.

shuffle take place substantially later on Mondays because of the distance Welsh Members had to travel from their constituencies.[59] A single 'shuffle' is held of all questions tabled for oral answer on the day concerned;[60] questions are then printed, grouped, in the order determined by the shuffle, by minister answering. The same arrangements apply to the shuffle from Prime Minister's questions as for all other ministers.

Supplementary Questions

The origins of most of the changes to the arrangements for oral questions lie in the increase in the number of questions tabled for oral answer and in the limited time available for them to be answered. Supplementary questions date back at least as far as the mid-nineteenth century. In 1873 *Erskine May* noted the practice of further questions being addressed to the minister on the same subject as the original question, but without 'observations or comments'.[61] In the 1880s supplementary questions came to be used by some Members to harass ministers and to air grievances, and were asked by Members other than those who had asked the original question.[62] The resolution passed in 1886 requiring formal notice of questions also permitted questions put for the elucidation of former answers to be asked without notice, and so enshrined the supplementary question.[63]

As the number and length of supplementaries increased, so the number of questions tabled for oral answer which actually received an oral answer diminished. Since 1906, questions not answered orally have received a written answer which is published at the back of the daily volume of *Hansard*. A written answer, of course, provides no opportunity for a Member to probe the reply given or for other Members to join in the questioning. Mr Speaker Lloyd wrote:

---

[59] *Parliamentary Questions*, HC (1990–91) 178, paras. 13–15. See *HC Deb.* (1989–90) 178, col. 728, for a similar complaint from a Scottish Member, and EDM 361 of 1991–92 requesting postponement of Monday Question Time until the evening.

[60] Since the beginning of the 1990–91 session the shuffle has taken place at 5.00 p.m.

[61] *Erskine May*, 4th edn. (1873), 321.

[62] Chester and Bowring, 29, 43–8.

[63] Ibid.

The Speaker has to strike a balance between reaching a reasonable number of questions in the time available and permitting reasonable probing of the Minister's position. I took the view that the number of questions reached was less important than a searching examination of a Minister's conduct. . . . I knew which gave less trouble to the Minister.[64]

He quoted Richard Crossman's view: 'Life is too easy for Ministers in our Parliament. Take Question Time. Now that Questions have been speeded up, the last anxiety has been removed.'

Successive reports from the Procedure Committee described, but perhaps did little to alleviate, the difficulties faced by the Speaker in attempting to increase the number of questions reached and maintain the orderliness of supplementaries while at the same time allowing a sufficient cross-examination of ministers. In 1958–59 the then Clerk of the House (Sir Edward Fellowes) suggested that questions might be taken on two days a week in three Grand Committees 'upstairs' rather on the Floor of the House, and in 1964–65 Richard Barlas, then Second Clerk Assistant, made a similar proposal in relation to Scottish questions.[65] Neither suggestion found favour with the Committee to which it was put.

Some observers believed that the setting up of a systematic set of departmental select committees might allow more intensive cross-examination of ministers in committee than was possible at Question Time, where questions can range from subject to subject across the whole of a minister's responsibilities.[66] The new committees, set up in 1979 (See Chapter 1), may perhaps have added to the Speaker's difficulties at Question Time. In a memorandum to the Procedure Committee in 1989–90, the Clerk of the House drew attention to the Chair's desire to strike a balance in calling Members between due acknowledgement of the particular role and expertise of select committee chairmen and members, on the one hand, and the need 'not to let [them] swamp proceedings with their special knowledge' on the other.[67] 'Ordinary'

---

[64] S. Lloyd, *Mr Speaker, Sir* (London: Jonathan Cape, 1976), 87.

[65] See HC (1958–59) 92, paras. 38–43; *Question Time*, HC (1964–65) 188, Evidence, p. 7.

[66] See e.g. *Parliamentary Questions*, HC (1990–91) 178. Evidence, p. 9, paras. 58–9.

[67] *Second Report from the Committee on Procedure. The Working of the Select Committee System*, HC (1989–90) 19, para. 18.

backbenchers seeking to be called to ask a supplementary question may thus now have to compete with 'specialist' members of select committees wishing to intervene as well as with opposition and minority party front bench spokesmen anxious to ask supplementaries.

In 1990 the Procedure Committee recommended:

> Accepting that there will always be some subjects of topical interest or controversy on which an extended line of questioning would be appropriate, Mr Speaker should nevertheless have the full support of the House in seeking to increase the number of tabled questions reached, by curbing the length of both Ministerial replies and supplementaries; and in particular by trying to ensure that supplementaries consist of a single question rather than a dialogue of queries.[68]

Reporting on the progress of its recommendations a year later, it recorded a very slight increase in the number of questions reached.[69] The regular participation in supplementary questions by opposition front bench spokesmen and women may make it difficult for the number (or length) of supplementaries to be substantially reduced.

Syndication and Changes Made in 1990

In 1989–90, the Procedure Committee examined the growth in the number of questions tabled for oral answer and the rules about the tabling of such questions. Its recommendations, which were accepted by the House on 24 October 1990 and put into effect at the start of the 1990–91 session, were designed generally to enhance the effectiveness of Question Time and particularly to put an end to one practice which had developed during the 1980s which was widely recognized to be an abuse of the rules.

The 'abuse' described by the Committee had become generally known as 'syndication', which the Committee identified as 'one of the prime factors behind the sharp rise in the number of oral questions', which doubled in the period from 1980–81 to 1988–89.[70]

---

[68] *Oral Questions*, HC (1989–90) 379, para. 35(v).

[69] *Parliamentary Questions*, HC (1990–91) 178, paras. 10–11.

[70] *Oral Questions*, HC (1989–90) 379, para. 10. As the Procedure Committee pointed out, the totals themselves understate the size of the problem, since they exclude questions unstarred or withdrawn. Since Members usually unstarred or

The Committee defined 'syndication' as 'the practice adopted by PPSs [Parliamentary Private Secretaries] . . . of farming out pre-arranged groups of identical (or nearly identical) and often vague texts to a large number of individual Members, with a view to increasing the probability of "desirable" subjects dominating Question Time'.[71] Syndication had come to be practised by both the main parties; it began with Prime Minister's questions, but quickly spread to questions to all the major departments and some of the smaller ones.[72]

The Committee considered two changes in response to the growth of syndication. The more radical suggestion, put forward by the Principal Clerk in the Table Office, took for granted that Members (or parties) would continue to try to orchestrate Question Time. Given that it is now regularly televised live, it is possible that this will indeed be the case. His memorandum proposed moving instead to a system of explicit ballots for the opportunity to table oral questions to each minister, the texts of which would be tabled on a subsequent day.[73] The Committee, however, after extensive consultations, decided to adopt a different approach.

It recommended two changes: first, that all questions for oral answer should be handed in to the Table Office *in person* by a Member, and that no Member should be able to table more than two oral questions to a single minister, one on behalf of him or herself and one on behalf of another Member. Its other recommendation was concerned with printing. Principally in order to save money, it recommended that only a specified number of the highest-placed questions in the shuffle should be treated as valid

withdrew questions only because they were placed too low in the list to have a chance of an oral answer, it is likely that many more questions were so removed from the list of oral questions in the latter year than in the former (ibid., Appendix 1, para. 6).

[71] Ibid., para. 10.

[72] The syndication which concerned the Procedure Committee in 1989–90 and 1990–91 was different in form (but not in effect) from the practice which had been examined by the Select Committee on Parliamentary Questions in 1971–72. In that case, civil servants had been asked by ministers to maintain a 'bank' of questions friendly to the government in order to redress the party balance in questions on the Order Paper. Modern syndication does not fall foul of the 1971–72 Committee's prohibition on the formal involvement of officials.

[73] *Oral Questions*, HC (1989–90) 379, Appendix 1, paras. 35–42, and Appendix 7, paras. 13–16.

notices of questions and printed (the precise number, to be
determined by Mr Speaker, would vary according to the time
allotted to the answering department). All notices of questions
which were not printed would thus fall.[74] It was estimated that this
second change would save up to £750,000 in a full session.[75] The
Report of the Procedure Committee was debated and approved by
the House on 24 October 1990. Both proposals were put into effect
at the beginning of the 1990–91 session.

These changes had the immediate effect of a dramatically
shorter Order Paper and consequently fewer pages of written
answers published in *Hansard* in answer to questions which had
not been reached at Question Time. The Committee assumed that
they would reduce the workload on departments drafting ministers'
replies.[76] The Principal Clerk told the Committee during its
subsequent wider examination of Parliamentary Questions in
1990–91 that the new system had worked 'extraordinarily smoothly
from an administrative point of view',[77] and the Committee itself
concluded that the new system was proving a success.[78] Initially, in
the first nine weeks of the new system, the number of oral
questions tabled fell by 39 per cent, and oral questions to the
Prime Minister by 51 per cent.[79] Three months later the number of
oral questions had risen again, and stood at 29 per cent fewer than
in a comparable period in the previous session, and Prime
Minister's questions were 43 per cent fewer than before. The
Principal Clerk of the Table Office commented: 'The decline in
the reduction in the numbers tabled reflects principally the re-
emergence, as the new Session had gone on, of the practice of
syndication'.[80] He illustrated this with some figures about oral
questions tabled in the first weeks of the new system (See Table 2.3).

Questions to the Prime Minister: The Open Question

Over the years, the style and content of oral questions to the Prime
Minister have changed very considerably. In theory, as head of the
government, the PM can be asked about virtually any aspect of

---

[74] Ibid., para. 8.   [75] Ibid., Appendix 1, paras. 21–2.
[76] Cf. Ch. 5. See also *Oral Questions*, HC (1989–90) 379, p. vi, paras. 7 and 9.
[77] *Parliamentary Questions*, HC (1990–91) 178, q. 12.
[78] Ibid., para. 5.   [79] Ibid., q. 2.
[80] Ibid., Appendix 16, p. 57.

Table 2.3. *Oral questions tabled in February 1991*

Department	Number Tabled	Number Syndicated	% Syndicated
Trade & Industry	127	59	46.4
MAFF	99	26	26.2
Energy	77	46	59.7
Environment	118	24	20.3
Treasury	154	75	48.7
Social Security	105	64	60.9
Health	146	27	18.4
Arts	25	13	52.0
Education	139	49	35.0

Source: *Parliamentary Questions*, Appendix 3, p. 45.

government responsibility. All ministers, including the PM, answer questions as members of the government, and have generally transferred questions to other ministers if the matter of the question lay more appropriately within the responsibility of another department.[81] Ministers have always refused to answer questions designed to set one minister against another and thus breach the principle of collective responsibility.[82] Although PMs have always answered some detailed policy questions, most have made it a practice to transfer many to the most appropriate departmental minister.

Transfer of a written question to another minister did not make much difference, seen from the perspective of the Member asking the question, nor, in the days when ministers and PMs were frequently available to answer oral questions in the House, did the transfer of a question from the PM to another minister necessarily prevent the Member from getting an oral answer in the House.

Increased pressure on Question Time and, in particular, the growth of, in effect, ballots for the opportunity to question the PM, meant that if a question to the PM drawn high in the shuffle

[81] But see the examples of substantive questions not transferred in the period 1946–83 in the memorandum by the Table Office (*Fifth Report from the Select Committee on Procedure* (Sessional Committee), HC (1976–77) 320, pp. xxvi ff.

[82] For more discussion of the rule relating to the 'internal workings of government', see *Parliamentary Questions*, HC (1990–91) 178, para. 86, and Evidence, pp. 7 and 29.

was subsequently transferred to another minister for answer, the Member lost the opportunity to ask it on the Floor of the House and, of course, the chance to pursue the issue with the PM through a supplementary question (with the attendant publicity for the Member and the issue). The same considerations also applied, though to a much lesser extent, to oral questions to other ministers, but the application by the Table Office of the rule requiring that questions should be tabled to the minister primarily responsible has meant that it is relatively unusual for other oral questions to be transferred.

Concern about the possibility of transfer led Members to attempt to devise 'transfer-proof' questions to the Prime Minister. Three types of question came to be asked.

(1) The first concerned **visits**: 'If he will make an official visit to (an overseas country)' or 'If he will make an official visit to (a town or village within, usually, the constituency of the Member asking the question or to a more general area)'. One early such 'open' visits question—that is, without defining the purpose of the proposed visit (and thus rendering the question liable to be transferred to another minister)—was asked in 1963–64.[83] Such questions are still asked, but infrequently. From the point of view of other Members wishing to ask additional supplementaries, questions about an area have the disadvantage that any supplementary question has to relate to that area. If the question is even narrower, referring perhaps only to a single constituency, the Speaker may well not call for a supplementary from any Member other than the one asking the question.[84]

(2) A more flexible open question, on which further supplementaries could be asked, concerned **meetings**. The usual form of such questions is: 'When he last met representatives of the TUC (or the CBI) and what matters were discussed' or 'If he will seek a meeting with the TUC/CBI'. Such a question could lead to a topical series of exchanges on the state of the economy or industrial relations. The first such questions seem to have been asked in 1968–69, and grew out of questions about meeting the TUC to discuss unemployment or economic affairs.[85] On 5 May

[83] *HC Deb.* (1963–64) 698, cols. 619–20w.
[84] See e.g. *HC Deb.* (1991–92) 199, cols. 1064–6; *HC Deb.* (1991–92) 202, cols. 485–6.
[85] *HC Deb.* (1968–69) 785, cols. 247–55. See also *HC Deb.* (1967–68) 758, col. 84.

1970 an open question to the PM about meeting the National Economic Development Office (NEDO) developed into supplementary exchanges on the state of the economy.[86] Perhaps because 'beer and sandwiches' lunches at No. 10 became less prominent after the Conservative government came to power in 1979; perhaps because, although open, such a question did not permit supplementaries on each and every issue of the moment, this open question came, during the 1980s, to be much less used. When the Procedure Committee looked at questions to the PM in 1976–77, however, TUC/CBI questions were as frequent as visits questions and the third type of open question, about engagements.[87]

(3) **Engagements** questions take the form: 'If he will list his official engagements for (the date on which the question is to be answered)'. Such a question to the PM has proved to be totally transfer-proof, and permits an almost infinite variety of supplementaries so long as the supplementary covers a matter for which government is in some way responsible; supplementaries—for example, asking the PM to comment on the policies of the opposition—which are not in order, have not been permitted.[88] Supplementaries in theory take the form, after the PM has read out a list of meetings scheduled for that day, 'If, in his busy day, the Prime Minister will . . .'.

The first engagements question appears to have been asked in 1964–65, though unlike the current formulation, if referred to the PM's future engagements. This was followed by questions about past engagements. The first engagements question in the present form was asked in 1974–75.[89] By 1976–77 such questions had become a regular feature of PM's questions. Engagements questions (rather than visits or meetings questions) have dominated PM's Question Time since 1979. Substantive questions have become the exception. In recognition of this and in order to save money by reducing expenditure on printing, the Speaker authorized the first significant change in the way questions were laid out on the Order Paper this century. From 30 April 1985 until the procedure changed at the start of the 1990–91 session the Order

---

[86] *HC Deb.* (1970–71) 807, cols. 613–16.
[87] *Fifth Report, HC* (1976–77) 320.
[88] See e.g. *HC Deb.* (1991–92) 202, cols. 178–82.
[89] *HC Deb.* (1964–65) 710, col. 101w; *HC Deb.* (1970–71) 815, cols. 240–1; *HC Deb.* (1974–75) 891, col. 90w.

Paper listing questions to the PM read: '*The following Members have set down Questions for oral answer by the Prime Minister. With the exception of those set out in full after the Member's name the Questions take the form*: To ask the Prime Minister, if she will list her official engagements for [Tuesday 11th December].'

The use of open questions increased for four main reasons:

the low risk of transfer;

the minimal time needed to be spent on drafting a question which might be unsuccessful in the ballot;

the possible topicality of supplementaries; and

in the eyes of a Prime Minister's opponents, the difficulty of predicting supplementaries.

But the open question had its disadvantages. The Prime Minister began to group similar questions for answer together, and this encouraged Members to table similar or identical questions in the hope of getting some priority in the asking of a supplementary. In 1965 Speaker Hylton-Foster decided to give no such priority to Members whose questions were grouped.[90] Nevertheless, the grouping of questions continued (a group of a dozen or more being not unusual.)[91]

In 1972 the Select Committee on Parliamentary Questions considered that the use of 'meaningless' open questions had led to 'a general feeling in the House that such a situation is unsatisfactory'. The Committee was unable to suggest any solution; it rejected a move to the Canadian system of 'Questions without notice', and its recommendation of a fifteen-minute extension of Prime Minister's Question Time was not implemented.

The use of open questions, particularly engagements questions, continued to increase, and by 1977 the then Prime Minister, James Callaghan, regarded the process as a 'charade'. The matter was referred to the Sessional Committee on Procedure, which reported in April 1977. The Committee's recommendations demonstrated how difficult it would be to frame any rule and the extent to which the matter was one of practice. It recommended that the Prime Minister should transfer fewer questions, that Members should put down fewer open questions, that open or 'indirect' questions

[90] *HC Deb.* (1964–65) 708, col. 1281.
[91] The Select Committee on Parliamentary Questions noted a group of 18 on 15 June 1972; *Parliamentary Questions*, HC (1971–72) 393, para. 25.

should not be grouped for answer, and that the Speaker should enforce stricter rules of relevance on supplementaries to open questions.[92]

The first and third of these recommendations were broadly followed, and the fourth had intrinsic difficulties; but the second was frustrated by the fact that Members continued to put down open questions. The four reasons quoted above for the popularity of open questions were still valid, and the growth of syndication meant that a Member tabling a question for a colleague or colleagues found it much more convenient to put down formulaic questions.

Shortly after taking office in 1979 Margaret Thatcher noted 'dissatisfaction' on both sides of the House with the number of open questions tabled. While she reserved the right to transfer a question 'if it seems to me appropriate to do so', she made it clear that she was prepared to answer 'substantive questions that raise issues of general significance and national interest, if hon Members wish to ask them'.[93] The qualification was prophetic; so well established had the open question become that Mrs Thatcher's willingness to answer substantive questions had no appreciable effect on the numbers of open questions tabled, which were actually increasing rapidly. Eighteen months later she noted that of more than 5,000 oral questions tabled to her, she had transferred none;[94] but the overwhelming majority of those questions were open.[95]

Mrs Thatcher in fact turned the continuing extensive use of open questions to her advantage. It became observable that very precise supplementaries from backbenchers on the government side frequently called forth equally precise answers from the Prime Minister; and this stage-management of oral questions drew some criticism from the opposition.[96]

During the 1980s, the main reason for the growth in the use of the open question was probably the growth of syndicates.[97] While

---

[92] *Fifth Report*, HC (1976–77) 320, para. 11.
[93] *HC Deb.* (1979–80) 970, col. 663.
[94] *HC Deb.* (1980–81) 997, col. 494w.
[95] But by Dec. 1989, in answering a question on the cost of answering questions, she said: 'As many questions have to be transferred, we do not calculate the items specifically here' (*HC Deb.* (1989–90) 162, col. 446w).
[96] e.g. *HC Deb.* (1989–90) 174, col. 1111. See also *HC Deb.* (1989–90) 177, col. 1055. [97] See above, p. 50.

it might have been difficult to arrange for hundreds of separate
substantive questions to the PM to be drafted for tabling on behalf
of Members, and indeed, Members might not have been willing for
a substantive question to be tabled in their name without knowing
the terms of the question, regular tabling twice a week of the
simple engagements question was very straightforward and could
be easily arranged. The extent of the increase in the numbers of
questions tabled and of the reduction in the percentage which were
substantive is striking. In February 1982, for eight PM's Question
Times, a total of 450 oral questions stood on the paper. Of these
52, or 11.6 per cent, were substantive. In February 1989, during
which there were also eight PM's Question Times, a total of 1,430
oral questions stood on the paper. Of these, only 34 or 2.4 per cent
of the total, were substantive.

Since 1990, as described above, all oral questions have had to be
tabled in the Table Office by a Member in person, and only a
limited number of questions tabled for oral answer are printed.
There were some initial problems about the number of questions
printed. The Speaker had decided that only the top ten PM's
questions in the shuffle should be printed.[98] After John Major
became Prime Minister on 28 November 1990, his brief style of
answering questions meant that the Speaker was able to speed up
Question Time. On 11 December the Member who had tabled
question 9 was not present, another question had been withdrawn,
and the House thus ran out of questions. On that occasion
the Speaker allowed supplementary questions on the previous
question to recommence.[99]

Another consequence of the change in the arrangements for
tabling oral questions made in 1990 might have been a renewal of
popularity for substantive questions to the PM. However, this has
not been the case. Although a few Members, notably Labour
backbencher Tam Dalyell, remain passionately of the view that
substantive questions should be tabled to the PM, the majority of
Members seem to prefer the open question. As the Procedure
Committee put it in 1991, the system is:

bizarre . . . difficult to explain rationally to outsiders. . . . But, like many
of the quainter aspects of the House's procedures, it serves a purpose and

---

[98] *HC Deb.* (1989–90) 178, cols. 727–8.
[99] *HC Deb.* (1990–91) 182, cols. 818–19; see also *Parliamentary Questions*, HC
(1990–91) 178, para. 11.

responds to a particular need—in this case the desire of the House to be able to question the Prime Minister across the whole range of Government policy and actions, whilst preserving last-minute topicality in the choice of subject.[100]

Questions to Other Ministers

Open questions to other ministers have been actively discouraged. In his memoirs Mr Speaker Thomas wrote:

The House thought open questions were a marvellous idea and tried to put them to other ministers who did not have the Prime Minister's right to transfer questions to the relevant department. I felt I had to protect Question Time and made a statement to the House, which I had to repeat a few months later, that I would not allow any open question to any other minister because it would alter completely the character of Question Time. I also believed the House had the right to know the real nature of the question being asked; after all, that is what the notice on the order paper is all about. Without this ruling, I am convinced that Question Time would have degenerated into an uncontrollable classroom brawl. It is bad enough as it is.[101]

Some questions to other ministers were very specific. Two tendencies can be identified from a study of the Order Papers of the 1980s as compared with those of the 1960s. First, questions are now, in general, shorter. The average length of the first ten oral questions on 18 November 1963 was between twenty-seven and twenty-eight words; on 12 November 1990 the first ten oral questions averaged eighteen words. Questions for written answer which were answered on the same days showed little change, and averaged about thirty words.

Secondly, although not 'open' in the sense of open questions to the Prime Minister, syndicated questions in particular came to be very short and relatively 'open', although usually confined to one particular aspect of a minister's responsibilities. On 19 July 1989 groups of three or four opposition Members had almost identical questions down for oral answer by the Secretary of State for Trade and Industry about consumer credit, competitiveness, and investment, respectively, while four government backbenchers had very similar questions down about trade with Japan.

---

[100] *Parliamantary Questions*, HC (1990–91) 178, para. 32.
[101] G. Thomas (Lord Tonypandy), *Mr Speaker* (London: Century Publishing, 1985), 141–2.

The recommendations of the Procedure Committee in 1990 for discouraging syndication and enhancing the effectiveness of Question Time were intended to encourage a return to more specific, substantive oral questions and to make questions tabled more than simply a series of pegs on which Members, including the front benches, could hang a series of exchanges. In its 1990–91 Report the Committee returned to the subject of the 'stage-management of Question Time for public relations purposes', the most obvious symptom of which was 'syndication—which has itself, by provoking retaliation in kind, contributed to the further entrenchment of the trend towards the greater politicisation of Question Time'.[102] The Committee considered the increase in the number of open questions to departmental ministers. It endorsed the practice which had been developed by the Speaker, which he had described to the House in May 1989:

There has been a resurgence in the number of open questions being tabled to departmental Ministers. The practice has been that the Chair will not call supplementaries to questions to a departmental Minister about that Minister's meetings or visits which do not state their purpose reasonably precisely.[103]

Members wishing to table open questions to departmental ministers are now advised by the Table Office, acting on his authority, that the Speaker will not call them to ask a supplementary to such a question. In 1991 the Procedure Committee recommended that such questions should not be allowed to be tabled.[104] The recommendation has not yet been put to the House for a decision.[105]

Development of Written Questions

Questions which receive a written answer can be divided into four groups:

    questions originally tabled for oral answer, which were not reached at question time;
    'ordinary' written questions;
    'priority' written questions;
    'planted' or 'inspired' questions.

[102] *Parliamentary Questions*, HC (1990–91) 178, para. 29.
[103] *HC Deb.* (1988–89) 152, col. 360.
[104] *Parliamentary Questions*, HC (1990–91) 178, paras. 42–3.
[105] *HC Deb.* (1991–92), 199, cols. 287–8.

The rules governing the content of questions have never distinguished between written and oral questions.

Questions which receive a written answer because they were not reached during Question Time are almost certainly the earliest type of 'written question'. Written answers have been published in *Hansard* since 1901, as 'written questions and answers circulated with the Vote'. As the number of questions tabled for oral answer came to far exceed the numbers which had any chance of receiving an oral answer, this category of 'question' (or more properly, answer) grew dramatically. A major consequence of the 1990 change limiting the number of oral questions to the number likely to be answered during Question Time has been an immediate fall in the number of written answers given to questions originally tabled for oral answer and consequential savings in departmental costs and time and in printing costs.

The other categories of written questions listed above are all questions originally tabled with the intention of receiving a written reply from the minister. Most of the restrictions introduced providing for a minimum period of notice for questions for oral answer did not apply to questions for written answer. Members can still table a question for written answer the next day but, with the exception of 'inspired questions' (see below), such questions are very unlikely to be answered on the next day. There have been no changes in the system of and rules for written questions this century, except the introdution of a category of 'priority written' questions (see below).

Apart from a rule against 'campaigns' on the Order Paper, designed to prevent Members from flooding the Order Paper with identical or near-identical questions, there are no limits on the number of written questions a Member may table. A few Members table a large proportion of the total: in 1989–90, 9,999 questions receiving written answers (27 per cent of the total) were tabled by just twenty Members.[106] In 1990–91, twenty-eight Members each asked more than 200 written questions. Of these, seven Members asked more than 400, two of them, Labour backbenchers Paul Flynn and Martin Redmond, asking 928 and 646 respectively.[107] There is no rule about when an answer must be given to an

---

[106] *Parliamentary Questions*, HC (1990–91) 178, Evidence, p. 5; *HC Deb.* (1991–92) 201, cols. 378–9w.
[107] *HC Deb.* (1991–92) 201, cols. 378–9w.

ordinary written question although the 1972 Committee on Parliamentary Questions considered that 'Ministers should endeavour to answer ordinary written Questions within a working week of their being tabled, and in any case, provide a holding answer within that period'.[108] Successive governments have given undertakings that they will aim to answer within a working week.[109]

Priority written questions date from 1972. They were introduced to permit Members to obtain an answer on the day they chose, rather than when government decided, and to permit Members to insist on a speedy answer. The minimum period of notice was fixed as the same as the minimum period for oral questions (roughly two sitting days). Figures prepared for the Procedure Committee in 1990 show that up to the end of the first decade of the use of such questions, roughly equal numbers of 'ordinary' and 'priority' written questions were tabled. During the 1980s priority writtens exceeded ordinary writtens.[110] When priority written questions were first introduced, the Procedure Committee expressed the hope that Members would not abuse the new system. By 1990 some Members and ministers and government departments believed that the high numbers of priority writtens were indeed an abuse, attributable in part to the large number of research assistants employed by Members.[111] By contrast, some Members felt that the system could be easily circumvented by the government, which can give a holding answer on the date the question is due for answer and then produce a substantive reply when it chooses. Some minor recent changes have been made: to save printing costs, holding replies are not now printed; the minimum period of notice required was amended in 1990 to three sitting days to bring it into line with the new minimum period of notice for oral questions; and, to make sure Members and their staff always understand what sort of answer they are seeking, the printed forms on which most questions are tabled have been redesigned.[112] In 1991 the Procedure Committee rejected suggestions for a limit on the number of priority written questions a Member may table, although it took the opportunity to remind the government of the

---

[108] *Parliamentary Questions*, HC (1971–72) 393, para. 28.
[109] See *HC Deb.* (1988–89) 147, col. 81w.
[110] *Parliamentary Questions*, HC (1990–91) 178, Evidence, p. 11.
[111] Ibid., p. xv, paras. 53–8.   [112] Ibid., p. xviii, para. 73.

convention that ordinary written questions should be answered within a working week of their being tabled.[113]

'Inspired', or 'planted', questions are included in the category of ordinary written questions. They have probably existed as long as there have been written questions. In 1987 the Speaker commented that 'the parliamentary undergrowth is strewn with planted Questions and has been so over the decades'.[114] They are usually tabled by government backbenchers the day before they are due for answer.[115] They usually ask for a statement from the government, and provide a useful way whereby the government may make an announcement to the House without taking up time on the Floor of the House. If the subject is very controversial, making an announcement in this way can lead to protests in the House because there is no opportunity to cross-question ministers about it. In 1985 the announcement in a written answer of a change to the Immigration Rules to comply with a recent judgment of the European Court of Human Rights led to a lengthy series of points of order.[116] In general, however, the system is well understood and accepted.

Few distinctions can be made between the types of questions tabled for written rather than oral answer or between different categories of written questions. Of the two purposes of parliamentary questions set out above, a logical proposition could be made that questions tabled for written answer are more likely to 'seek information' and those for oral answer to 'press for action'. It is true that far more questions for written answer do seek information, but many others call upon the government to do something. Equally, many questions for oral answer seek (often detailed) information. The minister, rather than read out lengthy details, then tells the House that the full details will be given in the Official Report.

Perhaps the most significant characteristic of written questions is that they represent a good and relatively quick way for a Member to get authoritative information or a formal, on the record statement of government policy. The massive increase in the

[113] Ibid., p. xix, para. 75.
[114] *HC Deb.* (1986–87) 113, cols. 1250–1.
[115] Questions tabled the day before they are due for answer are distinguished on the Order Paper by the symbol ¶. See below.
[116] *HC Deb.* (1985–86) 82, col. 1085.

number of written questions and the huge quantity and variety of official publications means that the rule designed to prevent questions from asking for 'information which is readily available' cannot easily be enforced.[117] There have been attempts by the government to restrict questions seeking certain categories of information, such as detailed employment or unemployment statistics, by placing the information in the library (often latterly on computer disc).[118] As more information becomes accessible to Members in electronic form, it may be that some types of questions seeking data will become obsolete. However, it will no doubt continue, in some circumstances, to suit the Member asking the awkward question to oblige the minister to set out the information in the Official Report. Since the establishment of 'Next Steps' executive agencies, the chief executives of such agencies have replied by letter to written parliamentary questions about operational matters, and such letters have been placed in the House of Commons library and the Public Information Office. In response to pressure for those replies to be more widely available, the government has agreed that such replies should also be published on a regular basis.[119]

Written questions can also signal a Member's interest in a subject and ensure that the issue is brought on to a minister's desk. Chester and Bowring thought one reason for the small increase in the number of written questions up to 1960 was that letters to ministers got quicker results. The massive increase in the number of written questions since then may suggest otherwise.

One reason for the growth in the number of written questions has been referred to in Chapter 1: the advent of paid research assistants for Members. Mr Speaker Thomas wrote:

Their presence was felt in the number of parliamentary questions, as the research assistants spend their time delving into all sorts of subjects to provide questions for people who until then had not been asking any at all. None of this does anything for our democracy and is only a cheap publicity stunt which has lowered the order paper of the House of Commons and lowered the prestige and dignity of the members. . . . Most

[117] See Appendix to this chapter.
[118] See *HC Deb*. (1989–90) 177, col. 945w.
[119] See *HC Deb*. (1991–92) 199, cols. 558–9w. Exact arrangements for their publication had not been announced by the end of the 1987–92 Parliament.

of them are questions just for the sake of it and are not intended to provide real knowledge.[120]

However the increase in the number of written questions shows the potential of this device for obtaining information and especially for making the government publish that information. The rule prohibiting questions seeking information already given in reply to a recent question is perhaps the major limitation on the number of written questions tabled.

The other significant limitation on written questions as a device for obtaining information concerns costs (see Chapter 5). Governments may refuse to provide an answer to a question if obtaining the necessary information would give rise to 'disproportionate cost' (although ministers may still decide to answer a question irrespective of cost if they so choose). The advisory limit applied by ministers when deciding whether an answer concerned would involve disproportionate cost is revised from time to time. It is set at roughly eight times the average cost of answering a question.[121]

Conclusion

The Procedure Committee concluded in May 1991 that 'with a few isolated exceptions, there is no dissatisfaction [among Members of Parliament] with the way in which parliamentary questions currently operate' and recommended only modest changes to the rules governing their operation.[122] It also took the opportunity to remind the House

that the *content* of answers is entirely the responsibility of Ministers . . . It follows therefore that no changes to the rules governing the admissibility of questions, or to the practice with regard to their tabling, will ever guarantee *answers* of model clarity, nor banish completely the occasional lapse into replies containing obfuscation, deliberate ambiguity, and evasion. . . . It remains a truism that the failure to answer a question directly, or a refusal to reply at all, can, in their own way, shed just as much light on Government policy (or the lack of it) in a particular area as a full and detailed response, which in practice may conceal more than it reveals.[123]

[120] Thomas, *Mr Speaker*, 207.
[121] See *HC Deb.* (1991–92) 201, col. 546w, which sets out the limits in use, and *HC Deb.* (1991–92) 201, col. 4w, which gives the cost of answering a question about the achievements of the government in 1990 as £1,520.
[122] *Parliamentary Questions*, HC (1990–91) 178, para. 135.
[123] Ibid., para. 136.

The principal features of the period since 1960 have been a huge increase in the use of both oral and written questions by Members and increasing orchestration of oral question time by the parties. Changes introduced during the period to the rules governing the asking of questions have largely been made in response to these two developments.

Appendix[a]

Rules of Order Regarding Form and Contents of Questions

The purpose of a question is to obtain information or press for action; it should not be framed primarily so as to convey information, or so as to suggest its own answer or convey a particular point of view, and it should not be in effect a short speech. Questions of excessive length have not been permitted.

The content of a question must comply with the general rules which apply to the content of speeches (see pp. 372–384), and is subject to the more detailed limitations set out below.

The Select Committee on Parliamentary Questions of Session 1971–72 expressed its concern that the cumulative effect of previous decisions relating to the orderliness of questions should not be allowed to become unduly restrictive. It therefore recommended that, while the Speaker should continue to have regard to the basic rules concerning the form and content of questions which are set forth in the pages which follow, he should not consider himself bound, when interpreting these rules, to disallow a question solely on the ground that it conflicted with any previous individual ruling.

(i) Argument and disorderly expressions. Questions which seek an expression of an opinion, or which contain arguments, expressions of opinion, inferences or imputations, unnecessary epithets, or rhetorical, controversial, ironical or offensive expressions, are not in order.

(ii) Factual basis. The facts on which a question is based may be set out as briefly as practicable within the framework of a question, provided that the Member asking it makes himself responsible for their accuracy, but extracts from newspapers or books, and paraphrases of or quotations

from speeches, etc, are not admissible. Where the facts are of sufficient moment the Speaker has required prima facie proof of their authenticity.

(iii) Personal reflections. It is not in order in a question to reflect on the character or conduct of those persons whose conduct may only be challenged on a substantive motion (see pp. 325–326), nor is it permissible to reflect on the conduct of other persons otherwise than in their official or public capacity. Moreover, a question introducing names (whether or persons or of bodies) invidiously or for advertisement or in any way not strictly necessary to render the question intelligible is not in order. The Speaker has ruled that questions referring to communications between an individual Member (other than the Member asking the question) and a Minister should not be allowed on the notice paper and that discourteous references to a friendly foreign country, or the head of State of such a country, are inadmissible.

(iv) Royal Family. No question can be put which brings the name of the Sovereign or the influence of the Crown directly before Parliament, or which casts reflections upon the Sovereign or the royal family. A question has been altered by the Speaker's direction on the ground that the name of the Sovereign should not be introduced to affect the views of the House.

(v) Royal Prerogative. Questions may be asked of the Ministers who are the confidential advisers of the Crown regarding matters relating to those public duties for which the sovereign is responsible. It has been ruled that the Prime Minister cannot be interrogated as to the advice that he may have given to the sovereign with regard to the grant of honours, or the ecclesiastical patronage of the Crown or the appointment and dismissal of Privy Councillors or the dissolution of Parliament.

In any case involving a capital sentence the circumstances on which the exercise of the prerogative of mercy depends should not be made the subject of a question while the sentence is pending nor may the sentence itself be raised in a question while it is pending.

This rule applies to sentences imposed by courts in Colonies as well as those in the United Kingdom. However, the Speaker has allowed a question about the exercise of the Prerogative in the case of death sentences imposed in a Colony whose authorities were in revolt.

(vi) Statements outside Parliament. The Prime Minister may be asked whether statements made outside Parliament by Ministers of Cabinet rank or Ministers with specific responsibilities on public occasions represent the policy of the Government, but questions about statements so made by

other Ministers are not in order. Questions about proposals or statements made by Ministers or Departmental Representatives attending conferences or negotiations on behalf of the Government should, however, be addressed to the Minister in charge of the Department concerned. Recently, questions have occasionally been allowed when Ministers have made statements elaborating new policies in public speeches outside the House, or in a broadcast or on the texts of such speeches when these have been officially distributed. When the Prime Minister has made a speech on a public occasion outside the House, a question may be asked in the form of asking for a copy of that speech to be placed in the Library; it has been ruled that questions in this particular form are *sui generis* and not capable of being 'blocked' by an answer of the sort which would normally be interpreted as a refusal to answer further questions.

(vii) Ministerial responsibility.   Questions to Ministers must relate to matters for which those Ministers are officially responsible. They may be asked for statements of their policy or intentions on such matters, or for administrative or legislative action. A number of decisions from the Chair have closely defined the interpretation of this rule of Ministerial responsibility. Among them are the following:

(1) Questions asking whether statements in the Press, or of private individuals, or unofficial bodies are accurate or asking for comment on statements made by persons in other countries (unless the statement is a message from another government to Her Majesty's Government) are not in order.

(2) Questions are not admissible which seek information about the internal affairs of foreign countries or an independent Commonwealth country. However, questions are allowed seeking information about the internal affairs of such countries if the information can be obtained by the Government from international organizations of which they are members. The Speaker has ordered the removal from the paper of a question referring to the speech of a Commonwealth Minister. Questions which ask Ministers to assist United Kingdom citizens coming before the courts or being subjected to arrest in foreign countries, or to protect United Kingdom citizens or companies who are being discriminated against by foreign authorities are allowed; but questions about the actions of independent states in refusing entry to United Kingdom citizens have not been allowed.

(3) It is not in order in a question to ask for action to deal with matters under the control of local or other statutory authorities, or of bodies or persons not responsible to the Government such as banks, the Stock Exchange, companies (except where there is a Government shareholding

in such companies), employers' organizations and trades unions; or to ask for action regarding or information about the activities of such persons or bodies which Ministers have no power to perform or obtain.

(4) Questions relating to nationalised industries, ie, industries or services placed by Parliament under the control of statutory bodies, are restricted to those matters for which a Minister is made responsible by the Statute concerned or by other legislation and to those matters in which Ministers are known to be involved. In general Ministers have powers, under the statutes, to make regulations concerning (or otherwise deal with) certain specific matters such as safety and to give directions to the industry, or part of it. They can therefore be asked about the use of these powers.

The statutes also confer on Ministers power to obtain information from the Boards or governing bodies concerned, but successive governments have refused, on grounds of public policy, to answer questions seeking information on the day to day administration of the industries or on administrative matters contained in the annual reports of the industries. Since the refusal to answer a class of questions prevents further questions dealing with that class of matters (see para. ix on p. 292) most questions asking for information on the working of the Boards are in practice inadmissible. There are however two general exceptions. Ministers have undertaken to answer questions asking for statistical information on a national basis; such question are therefore in order. The Speaker has also undertaken to allow questions on what might otherwise be called day to day administration provided that they raised matters of urgent public importance such as might in other circumstances fall within the meaning of Standing Order No. 20.

(5) Questions are inadmissible which refer to the evidence of witnesses or other matters before a royal commission or a parliamentary committee, or deal with matters within the jurisdiction of the chairman of a select committee or the authorities of the House. No question can be asked regarding proceedings in a committee which have not been placed before the House by a report from the committee. However, questions are regularly asked about the administrative decisions of the Select Committee on House of Commons (Services).

(6) Questions addressed to a court official or referring to the action of a court official are inadmissible.

(7) A question may not be asked which deals with the action of a Minister for which he is not responsible to Parliament. For example, in 1924 a question asking the Attorney General whether he had communicated with certain Members before deciding to withdraw a prosecution was disallowed privately by the Speaker.

(8) Questions seeking an expression of opinion on a question of law, such as the interpretation of a statute, or of an international document, a

Minister's own powers, etc., are not in order since the courts rather than Ministers are competent in such matters. Moreover, questions requiring information set forth in accessible documents (such as statutes, treaties, etc.) have not been allowed when the Member concerned could obtain the information of his own accord without difficulty. Ministers may however be asked by what statutory authority they have acted in a particular instance, and the Prime Minister may be asked to define a Minister's responsibilities.

(9) It is not in order to put to a Minister a question for which another Minister is more directly responsible, or ask one Minister to influence the action of another.

(10) Questions are out of order which seek legislation to deal with circumstances of a very restricted or particular character presently outside ministerial powers or responsibilities, and thus evade the rule that questions must relate to matters for which Ministers are officially responsible, as are those which cite individual incidents in relation to which the Minister has no administrative power or responsibilities when asking for general legislation.

(11) Questions which suggest amendments to bills before the House or in committee are inadmissible unless such amendments would only be in order if a financial resolution were first moved by a Minister.

(viii) Parliamentary business.   Limitations have been placed on the sort of question which may be asked about the conduct of public business in Parliament for which Ministers are responsible. The Speaker has refused to allow questions as to whether the government proposed by resolution to put a close to a stage of a bill, and as to the time at which a Minister would move the closure; and a question asking a Minister about a motion on the paper when under standing orders that motion must be decided without amendment or debate has been ruled out. Questions anticipating discussion upon an order of the day have also been disallowed. Questions about the day to day progress of the business of the House are not placed on the notice paper; such questions are asked as supplementaries to the weekly private notice question on business which the Leader of the Opposition customarily asks of the Leader of the House (see p. 296).

(ix) Questions already answered, or to which an answer has been refused, or on secret matters.   Questions are not in order which renew or repeat in substance questions already answered or to which an answer has been refused or which fall within a class of question which a Minister has refused to answer. Where, however, a Minister has refused to take the action or give the information asked for in a particular question, he may be asked the same question again after an interval of three months; and

where successive administrations have consistently refused to answer certain classes of questions, Ministers may be asked once a session whether they will now answer such questions. Similarly, where a Minister answers a question on a matter previously blocked, questions may be asked on that matter. Among the subjects on which successive administrations have refused to answer questions upon grounds of public policy are discussions between Ministers or between Ministers and their official advisers or the proceedings of Cabinet or Cabinet committees; security matters including the operation of the security services; operational defence matters including the location of particular units; and details of arms sales to particular countries. In addition to such classes of questions there are certain matters, of their nature secret, relating to the secret services and to security, and questions on these matters are not in order. A question which one Minister has refused to answer cannot be addressed to another Minister and a question answered by one Minister may not be put to another.

An answer to a question cannot be insisted upon, if the answer be refused by a Minister, and the Speaker has refused to allow supplementary questions in these circumstances. The refusal of a Minister to answer a question on the ground of public interest cannot be raised as a matter of privilege, nor should leave be sought to move the adjournment of the House under Standing Order No. 20 for this reason.

(x) Decisions of either House.   Questions which criticize the decisions of either House of Parliament are inadmissible; nor is it in order to refer to debates or questions and answers of the current session other than for the purpose of seeking further clarification of a previous answer. The Speaker has also ruled that questions referring to the time taken by individual speeches may not be asked.

(xi) Matters sub judice.   By a resolution of the House matters awaiting or under adjudication in a criminal court or a court martial, and matters set down for trial or otherwise brought before a civil court may not be referred to in any debate or question (see pp. 377–379); though the House has further resolved to give the Chair some discretion to allow reference to be made to matters awaiting or under jurisdiction in all civil courts in certain specified circumstances, provided that there is no real and substantial danger of prejudice to the proceedings. The 'sub-judice rule' as it is often called, also applies to matters before a coroner's court. If the subject matter of the question is found to be, or becomes, sub judice after notice of the question has been given, the Member is asked to withdraw it, or the Speaker may direct it to be removed from the notice paper or refuse to allow it to be asked if it is on the Order paper.

The rule does not apply to matters which are sub judice in courts of law outside Great Britain and Northern Ireland, nor to matters which are the subject of administrative enquiry.

Questions which reflect on the decision of a court of law are not in order. The Speaker has ruled privately that questions relating to a sentence passed by a judge, and to the circumstances under which rules of court were made and issued by the Lord Chancellor, were inadmissible.

(xii) Miscellaneous. Questions are also inadmissible which seek the solution of hypothetical propositions; raise questions of policy too large to be dealt with in an answer to a question; seek information on matters of past history for the purposes of argument; are multiplied with slight variations on the same point; or are trivial, vague or meaningless.

3

On the Floor of the House

R. L. Borthwick

In any account of the House of Commons, images of Question Time are never far from centre-stage. It has acquired an aura of drama, of governments being held to account, of the competence of ministers being tested, of the opposition making its criticisms and backbenchers their name. In the words of Geoffrey Smith and Nelson Polsby, 'among the few things that most foreigners know about the parliamentary system is that there is a question hour'.[1]

Opinions vary greatly as to the merits of Question Time. Phrases like 'the jewel in the parliamentary crown'[2] can be found in the literature to describe it. The opposite view tends to be put no less forcefully. Among its severest critics have been disillusioned former or current Members of Parliament. Writing in the early 1970s, Woodrow (now Lord) Wyatt, for example, described it as being 'hardly more useful than a Punch and Judy show' and 'a fake instrument of democracy'.[3] Two decades later, Michael Latham, who had already announced his intention to retire from the Commons described a situation where 'Virtually every question from every MP is a shamelessly party-line effort with the other side being devils and one's own side the angels'. Of Question Time he said, 'It has become ordeal by bellowing. It is the theatre of the absurd, devised as unremitting confrontation and ideal for television.'[4]

The setting is impressive: as the first substantial business on four days each week, it is one of what have been called the 'prime time opportunities' for backbenchers.[5] In total something like 8 per

---

[1] G. Smith and N. W. Polsby, *British Government and its Discontents* (London: Harper & Row, 1981), 126.

[2] Quoted in M. Rush, *Parliamentary Government in Britain* (London: Pitman, 1981), 206.

[3] W. Wyatt, *Turn Again, Westminster* (London: André Deutsch, 1973), 31.

[4] M. Latham, 'Sloggers in the House', *Leicester Mercury*, 4 July 1991.

[5] H. Irwin, 'Opportunities for Backbenchers', in M. Ryle and P. G. Richards (eds.), *The Commons under Scrutiny* (London: Routledge, 1988), 76–98.

cent of the time of the House is taken up by the oral answering of questions.

On this stage departmental ministers have to face their inquisitors. However well prepared ministers are (and sceptics suggest that the questioners are unlikely to be a match for the well-briefed minister), a banana skin may lurk. The position has been very fairly set out by Michael Rush:

The backbencher often asks what appears to be an innocuous Question, hoping to catch the minister unaware with a supplementary; the minister, however, armed with a comprehensive 'PQ file' prepared by his department, hopes to parry effectively, even wittily, the supplementary; and any others that may follow. There is no doubt that Question Time can be a very effective means of keeping a check on the government, but all too frequently it develops into a parliamentary game more impressive in the appearance than the substance.[6]

That aspect of Question Time has been described as the modern equivalent of the medieval tournament, 'an occasion not for the serious examination of the issues or for eliciting information in any depth from ministers, but displaying one's opponents to the greatest possible disadvantage'.[7] Those same observers see Question Time as having a second function: to enable governments to publicize information which is favourable to themselves. 'Friendly backbenchers are deputed to feed appropriate questions to hungry ministers. In doing so they both help the government to secure a little useful publicity and reduce the time available for critical examination'.[8]

Similar tactics were described by *The Times*'s sketch-writer in July 1991. He referred to pliant backbenchers as toads, and went on:

[T]he Government chief whip has been giving the toads ever simpler routines to perform. He used to prime each with a different question but, though Mr Major could remember the answers, the toads kept forgetting the questions. So this week he seemed to have given nearly *all* of them the same one: 'Invite the PM to condemn Labour's links with the unions or their minimum wage policy'.[9]

[6] Rush, *Parliamentary Government in Britain*, 207.
[7] Smith and Polsby, *British Government and its Discontents*, 126.
[8] Ibid.
[9] M. Parris, 'Toadying: The Art of Going Plonk', *The Times*, 10 July 1991.

The sense of drama which is always potentially there with Question Time has been highlighted in recent years, by the introduction first of sound broadcasting and more recently of television. In each case, for the broadcasters, Question Time has exercised its seductive charm. It offers for them the prospect of confrontation and political conflict and the clash of personalities. Whether this greater exposure has enhanced the reputation of the House is another matter.

Question Time

In *Questions in Parliament* Chester and Bowring began with a description of a typical Question Time of 1960. Thirty or so years later, the outward form remains the same: oral questions are still taken at the same times on each of the first four days of the parliamentary week and for the same length of time. Questioners still begin not by reading out their question (which has been printed on the Order Paper) but simply by standing and giving its number when called by the Speaker.

To this question a minister replies; the original questioner asks a single supplementary question, which in turn is answered. Further supplementary questions may be asked at the discretion of the Speaker. Members who want to ask a supplementary stand up to catch the Speaker's eye each time an opportunity arises. It is for the Speaker to judge how many supplementaries to allow and from whom. In making this judgement the Speaker will bear in mind the importance of the subject and the extent to which a relevant supplementary can be asked, the need to secure a balanced representation of views, how often particular Members have been called in the past, and which Members have questions lower down the Order Paper that are unlikely to be reached. Privy Councillors generally, and opposition spokesmen in particular, have a special status when it comes to catching the Speaker's eye.

This process of question and answer, followed by a variable number of supplementary questions each with its own answer, provides the staple content of Question Time. On Mondays one main department answers until about 3.10 p.m., thereafter a number of small departments have fixed slots at 3.10 p.m., 3.15 p.m., or 3.20 p.m. If questions to them do not fill all the available time, the House reverts to questioning the original

department. On Tuesdays and Thursdays questions to the department of the day last only until 3.15 p.m.; at that point questions to
the Prime Minister are taken for fifteen minutes. On Wednesdays
a single department is the subject of questions.

A minister may ask leave to answer a question at the end of
Question Time at 3.30 p.m., perhaps in order to avoid having to
make a statement with its much longer questioning period. That
apart, Question Time proper may be followed, as we have seen
(Chapter 2), by a Private Notice Question (PNQ) and then by
ministerial statements which strictly are not questions but proceed
in a similar way, with the Speaker calling individuals who seek to
catch his eye to ask a single question. There then follow requests
for emergency debates, applications to introduce Bills under the
ten-minute rule (on Tuesdays and Wednesdays), and points of
order which have been deferred at the Speaker's request to that
time.[10]

As described in the previous chapter, before Question Time
begins, MPs have competed for slots by entering what in effect is a
ballot for the right to ask a question for oral answer. Those whose
names are drawn first will be able to ask their questions; those
drawn much later will almost certainly not, unless an unusually
large number of Members with more favourable positions are
absent. Since November 1990 only the first thirty questions from
the ballot to main departments answering on Mondays, Tuesdays,
and Thursdays, forty to the department answering on Wednesdays,
and ten to the small departments and the Prime Minister are
printed. The Speaker will not call a question if she has been
informed in advance of a Member's absence; if she has not been
informed, the absence of the would-be questioner is likely to be
the subject of comment. Occasionally ministers and backbenchers
may be taken by surprise when questions reach further down the
Order Paper than was expected. In July 1983, for example, a
minister faced with question 29 on the Order Paper had to confess
to the House: 'The hon Member will have noticed that my brief
runs only up to question 28.'[11] Such a situation is, admittedly,
unusual. Slightly less unusual, particularly prior to November
1990, is the situation where backbenchers find themselves being

[10] See *HC Deb*. (1990–91) 194, cols. 647–8, for a description by the Speaker of
current practice.   [11] *HC Deb*. (1983–84) 45, col. 18.

called unexpectedly to ask a supplementary when their question has been reached because of a large number of absentees ahead of them and then having to do some quick thinking.

Normally, however, ministers come fully armed by their civil servants to answer not only a wide range of possible supplementaries to questions that are likely to be reached but also with answers for at least some of those questions that are unlikely to be reached. A minister is 'provided with a loose-leaf folder which contains the main answer, further pages suggesting answers to possible supplementary questions and background notes as well'.[12] Although in theory the supplementary may be the surprise element designed to get past a minister's defences, the reality is often less dramatic.

Civil servants will have briefed ministers extensively on likely supplementaries from both the opposition and the government's own backbenchers. As already pointed out in the preceding chapters, questions from the latter may have been inspired by the government itself, and a range of supplementaries suggested. Alternatively, a minister's Parliamentary Private Secretary (PPS) may have tried to find out what a questioner on his own side is likely to ask by way of a supplementary. It is quite possible for a degree of mutual benefit to accrue. A questioner may wish to portray the government in a good light or the opposition in a poor one or to help put some piece of information on the public record. For the backbencher there may be the additional satisfaction of a compliment from the minister. It will hardly be unwelcome to a backbencher to have an answer which leads to a headline in his local paper along the lines of: 'Minister congratulates local Member'.[13] It was reported in 1991 that this process had been carried a stage further:

At least one Secretary of State has revived a practice (which I never knew existed) of opening up his stall in the Aye lobby at 2 p.m. to meet his backbenchers informally before business gets under way. The idea is quite genuinely to hear problems and explain what is being done about them. . . . But, invariably, helpful backbenchers have tended to use the sessions to explain to the Secretary of State what their supplementary might be about.[14]

[12] G. Kaufman, *How to Be a Minister* (London: Sidgwick & Jackson, 1980), 92.
[13] Gerald Kaufman makes a similar point (ibid.).
[14] C. Brown, 'The Business of Brownie Points', in *The House Magazine*, 29 Apr. 1991, p. 5.

78 R. L. Borthwick

Questions from opposition Members pose potentially more
hazards for ministers, but even here a good deal can be anticipated
both by knowledge of particular Members' concerns, by the issues
of the day, and by awareness of campaigns being organized by the
opposition. Despite all this, it still remains possible for a minister
to be made decidedly uncomfortable by the unexpected supple
mentary. A good example of this occurred in June 1991 when
following an answer in which John Major attacked the idea of a
minimum wage, Andrew Bennett followed up a standard engage
ments question to the Prime Minister with the following supple
mentary: 'Why have not the problems of a minimum wage that the
Prime Minister just outlined caused difficulties in Germany?'[15] It
was apparent to all concerned that the Prime Minister and his
advisers had not anticipated such an angle of attack, and he was
left visibly struggling to answer.

In form, Question Time is an occasion for backbenchers and for
individual enterprise. It may, however, be more realistic to see it
as part of the battle between political parties; as John Griffith and
Michael Ryle put it: 'The true purpose of Members today when
tabling an oral Question is to secure an opportunity to make a
political point.'[16] It is not surprising, therefore, that Members
should take steps to try to improve the chances of their group or
their party securing as many good slots as possible in the ordering
of questions for oral answer. This practice of syndication was
discussed in the previous two chapters. In addition, Members
particularly on the opposition side, may organize 'campaigns' on
particular subjects. 'One of the purposes of such campaigns is to
give as much publicity as possible to an issue—and to the point of
view of the questioners on that issue—in order to influence the
Minister concerned or to impress various opinions or persons
outside the House (including constituents).'[17]

What takes place at Question Time is essentially an attempt to
secure favourable recognition for each party's point of view and
perhaps as important, favourable recognition for individuals, both
front benchers and backbenchers. Question Time has an important
place in the holding of governments to acccount. Governments
will be anxious to try to see that their record is placed in the best

[15] *HC Deb.* (1990–91) 192, col. 406.
[16] J. A. G. Griffith and M. Ryle, *Parliament* (London: Sweet & Maxwell, 1989)
369.   [17] Ibid. 370

light. Opposition parties will be equally anxious to secure the reverse. There has been, as is noted in the opening chapter, a great increase in partisanship at Question Time.

The rewards for this are both political and personal. At a general level there is no question that party morale is affected positively or negatively by the quality of front bench performance at Question Time. This applies particularly at Prime Minister's Question Time, but also at others. If questions are put to which the government does not seem to have satisfactory answers, then this not only has a damaging effect on the morale of government backbenchers, but is also likely to have an impact on party morale and standing outside the House.

For backbenchers and for ministers there are reputations to be made and, perhaps more significantly, lost at Question Time. Some ministers have never come to terms with the demands of Question Time. One notable example of this was Frank Cousins, who was translated by Harold Wilson in the 1960s straight from being a trade union leader to a Cabinet minister. A seat was found for him in the Commons, but the experience was not a happy one. Consider this description of his first Question Time:

[A] highly inexperienced and inarticulate Mr Cousins was called on to answer his first questions as Minister of Technology. He swayed backwards and forwards like an old bull in a ring, but there was very little in what was actually said, on either side, to convey a true impression of this lumbering incoherence subjected to a shower of light-hearted banderillos.[18]

More recently, as Andrew Adonis notes, it was their obvious unhappiness at the dispatch box that contributed to the political downfall of two of Mrs Thatcher's ministers, Paul Channon and John Moore.[19] Others were more successful in demonstrating that they could cope with the pressures. Likewise some members of the opposition front bench have been conspicuously successful in making their reputations as able performers in the Question Time theatre. Mrs Thatcher, on the other hand, was a more effective performer at Prime Minister's Question Time as Prime Minister than she had been as Leader of the Opposition.

[18] T. F. Lindsay, *Parliament from the Press Gallery* (London: Macmillan, 1967), 30.
[19] A. Adonis, *Parliament Today* (Manchester: Manchester University Press, 1990), 98.

Prime Minister's questions are considered in more detail in the next section, but at this stage it is perhaps worth noting that the sense of occasion and tension is undoubtedly greatest on those twice-weekly occasions. Harold Wilson pointed out that one of his predecessors, Harold Macmillan, 'a highly successful performer at Question time, used on occasion to be physically sick, or very near it, before Questions on Tuesdays and Thursdays'.[20] On the basis of his own experience, Wilson suggests that no prime minister views Prime Minister's Question Time 'with anything but apprehension; every prime minister works long into the night on his answers, and on all the notes available to help him anticipate the instant and unpredictable supplementary questions that follow his main prepared answer'.[21]

A view of Question Time for the departmental minister is given by Tony Benn. Of his first Question Time as a minister, he noted in his diary, 'I had a rough passage.'[22] A week later he recorded: 'The Tories were gunning for me and anything I said might have caused a riot. I did make a couple of slips which gave them their opportunity. It was a tough day but I stayed firm and found it quite bracing, though extremely exhausting.'[23]

As the quotation earlier about Frank Cousins indicates, it is difficult to get a feel for the atmosphere of Question Time from the written record in *Hansard*.[24] The mood of the House at Question Time varies enormously. In part the variation relates to the importance of the issues being raised, but in part it is also affected by the tone adopted by questioner and questioned. Gerald Kaufman quotes with approval Harold Wilson's advice to 'answer a question in the spirit in which it is asked', and goes on to say, 'I only occasionally departed from this and when I did, slapping down serious questions from Tory MPs like David Price and Peter Emery, I felt ashamed.'[25]

---

[20] H. Wilson, *The Governance of Britain* (London: Weidenfeld & Nicolson and Michael Joseph, 1976), 132.   [21] Ibid.

[22] T. Benn, *Out of the Wilderness: Diaries 1963–67* (London: Hutchinson, 1987), 182.   [23] Ibid.

[24] See Lindsay, *Parliament from the Press Gallery*, 29. The use by *Hansard* of 'Interruption' hardly conveys the variety of heckling and abuse that may be hurled across the Floor of the House. *Hansard* records only remarks made from a sedentary position if they are subsequently answered or referred to by a speaker.

[25] Kaufman, *How to Be a Minister*, 93.

Some ministers are emollient in their responses, others more abrasive. In 1990 one observer described questions to the Department of Trade and Industry while it was under the leadership of Nicholas Ridley:

The monthly sessions of DTI questions have become compulsive viewing for those who enjoy blood sports. . . . The four ministers go through their routine, smiling at each other in appreciation, as each in turn treats the enemy—usually but not exclusively on the Opposition benches—to a withering range of dismissive answers. Hansard records the words but cannot fully convey the impact of the Ridley boys let loose on the Opposition.[26]

This treatment eventually produced an angry outburst from one of the opposition spokesmen in June 1990.[27] Tam Dalyell drew from the incident the conclusion that while ministers were undoubtedly at fault, so too were questioners for the way in which many supplementaries were framed.[28]

Question Time is also an opportunity for Members to pursue individual campaigns. In the 1950s and 1960s Gerald Nabarro made himself into one of the best-known backbench MPs by his campaign against the anomalies of purchase tax, though in this he was assisted very considerably by a well-known parliamentary lobbyist, Commander Christopher Powell.[29] More self-sufficient as a one-man campaigner has been the backbench Labour MP Tam Dalyell. During his time in the Commons, he has mounted a number of campaigns in which PQs have played a prominent part. In the 1960s he campaigned successfully against the plan to build an airfield on the Indian Ocean island of Aldabra. The Labour Defence Secretary at the time, Denis Healey, records in his memoirs: 'We expected no political difficulties. We reckoned without the environmental lobby, which won its first great victory against us, aided by a brilliant campaign of parliamentary questions by the assiduous Tam Dalyell.'[30]

In the 1980s Mr Dalyell organized campaigns through questions (and other parliamentary devices) to seek to cast more light on the

[26] C. Brown, 'Ridley Boys Let Loose', in *The House Magazine*, 2 July 1990, p. 4.
[27] *HC Deb.* (1989–90) 174, col. 921.
[28] In a letter in *The House Magazine*, 2 July 1990, p. 25.
[29] 'All the questions [tabled by Nabarro] were drafted by Powell' (Obituary of Commander Powell, *The Times*, 4 May 1989).
[30] D. Healey, *The Time of My Life* (London: Michael Joseph, 1989), 292.

sinking of the Argentinian ship the *General Belgrano* during the Falklands War, the part played by Mrs Thatcher during the Westland affair, and most recently to oppose the war over Kuwait. He used substantive questions to the Prime Minister to pursue his campaigns, and had twelve oral questions answered by the Prime Minister in the 1983–87 Parliament.

Whether facing the individual MP with a bee in his bonnet or facing an organized party campaign, ministers and their civil servants are compelled by the existence of Question Time to address issues and to provide answers. Both groups will be concerned about how successfully criticism is dealt with at Question Time. Genuine public concern may become apparent (especially to the government's own supporters), and the opposition may discover it has an issue at which it can chip away. Peter Riddell notes an example of this: 'Repeated pressure by Neil Kinnock and the opposition at question time during the winter and spring of 1987–88 fed the demand from the Conservative benches for action on nurses' pay and for alleviating some of the impact of the April 1988 social security changes.'[31]

One factor affecting atmosphere at Question Time is attendance. It is difficult to say precisely how well attended Question Time is. Because no record is kept of attendance in the House, there are no official figures to refer to. There are occasions, notably at Prime Minister's questions, when the House is crowded and a large number of Members are pressing to ask a supplementary or merely enjoying the spectacle. At other Question Times attendance can be rather sparse, and largely confined to those hoping to ask questions.

For questions to other ministers a variety of factors is likely to have an effect on attendance. The first is simply the political visibility of the department at the time. During military crises like the Falklands War in 1982 and the Gulf War in 1991, questions to the Ministry of Defence were of more than usual interest. When the government seemed to be struggling to find a replacement for its community charge in 1989/1990, questions to the Environment Department drew many.

---

[31] P. Riddell, 'In Defence of Parliament', in *Contemporary Record*, 3 1 (Autumn 1989), 8.

A second factor is the popularity of the minister concerned. PPSs will work to secure the attendance of backbenchers for particular Question Times. If the minister is popular, their task will be easier, or even unnecessary. In some cases there may be special difficulties: for example, during the 1987–92 Parliament there were so few Scottish Conservative MPs that Scottish questions were poorly attended on the government side.

Some MPs will make a point of trying to attend Question Time regularly. For some new Members, it is a quick way of acquiring a feel for the moods of the House and its characters. For a new Member, attendance at Question Time represents an effective way of being seen by party leaders as a diligent and promising backbencher and by constituents as an assiduous constituency Member—part of what Philip Norton in the opening chapter calls attention-seeking behaviour. With the advent of the televised House, being seen is perhaps more important than being heard. Pressure is greatest at Prime Minister's questions, where the prospect of being able to ask a question on live television and certainly of having it replayed on regional television is a strong inducement for those who wish to make their name and face well known to their constituents.

Some evidence about attendance at Question Time is provided by the results of a survey of MPs undertaken by the editors of the present volume. Ninety per cent of the respondents in the survey suggested that there were particular departments whose Question Times they tried to attend regularly. There was, however, considerable variation in the drawing power of departments. On this evidence, Question Times involving the Departments of Education, Employment, Health, and Transport are likely to be the best attended. The day of the week also has a bearing on attendance: those departments which answer on a Tuesday or a Thursday are likely to have better attendances simply because of the proximity to Prime Minister's Question Time. At the other end of the spectrum, questions to the Welsh Secretary or the Attorney-General would get regular attendance from only 3 per cent of the respondents in the survey.

Towards the end of their book, Chester and Bowring looked at possible changes that might occur in questions. As Norton noted earlier, at the time they wrote, they could speak of Question Time as 'primarily a backbencher activity' and one where ' "individual grievances" are largely constituency matters'.[32] By 1990 front benchers were much more prepared to join in on backbenchers' questions, and the questions themselves had lost a good deal of their constituency content.

Chester and Bowring were certainly prescient in their observation that 'step by inevitable step there may come a time when only one Minister will be reached at most sittings'.[33] If for 'minister' we read 'department', then that situation can be said to have arrived well before 1990. Apart from Mondays, when a more than usually complicated rota system ensures that certain small departments get their turn, it is, as shown in the previous chapter, now normal for only a single department to be covered at Question Time. However, this does not mean that a single minister has to face the House alone. In the 1960 example with which Chester and Bowring began their study, questions were addressed to the Board of Trade. On that occasion, the President of the Board, Mr Maudling, answered them all himself. So in effect he carried the burden of the Question Time on his own shoulders, apart from three questions to the Prime Minister. In all, Reginald Maudling that day handled thirty-seven questions (including, admittedly, sixteen which he answered together, something that would be unlikely to be tolerated today). Compare that with the modern format where the style is for a squad of ministers to answer. Normally, all the Commons ministers of a department share the load. The questions will be shared out according to the subject responsibilities of the ministers, with some regard also to the general distribution of the load. The Secretary of State would be expected to answer those questions deemed most important.

Chester and Bowring predicted also that in future there might be fewer questions answered orally. This, they suggested, 'would not turn Question time into a series of short debates but it would allow for greater cross-examination of Ministers'.[34] To a considerable extent this is what has happened. Thirty years ago the House got through forty to forty-five questions at each Question Time.[35] The number that are got through today varies somewhat according to the day of the week. Mondays consistently see more questions reached than other days. This is largely because of the presence on

---

[32] D. N. Chester and N. Bowring, *Questions in Parliament* (Oxford: Clarendon Press, 1962), 271.   [33] Ibid. 281.   [34] Ibid. 283.
[35] Ibid. 127.

the Monday rota of some low-key departments. Although Monday questions begin with one mainstream department, the presence there of such 'departments' as the Attorney-General's Department, the Office of Arts and Libraries, or the Church Commissioners makes it more difficult to generate the passionate supplementaries or noisy interruptions which can slow down progress on other days.

For a sample period of the first thirteen weeks of the 1989–90 session, (covering in all fifty-one Question Times) on Mondays on average 20.9 questions were answered orally, while on Wednesdays the average was 15.2. Figures on the other two days are complicated by Prime Minister's questions. Excluding them, the average figure was 12.6 on both Tuesdays and Thursdays. To this should be added a figure of 5.7 for Prime Minister's questions on Tuesdays and 6.0 on Thursdays. That produces average totals for those two days of 18.3 and 18.6 respectively. Overall, the average number of questions answered per day in this period was 18.2. This is only very slightly less than the figure of 19 per day for four years earlier (admittedly for a shorter sample period).[36]

Chester and Bowring coupled their prediction about fewer questions being answered orally with the suggestion that in that event there would be more supplementaries asked. Evidence here is harder to come by for earlier periods. For our sample of fifty-one Question Times at the start of the 1989–90 session, the average number of supplementaries asked on Mondays was 49.8, on Wednesdays 44.5, on Tuesdays 36.5 plus 12.2 to the Prime Minister, and on Thursdays 36.0 plus a further 12.1 to the Prime Minister. The overall average, therefore, was 47.7.

Prime Minister's Question Time

It will be clear from the previous chapter that Prime Minister's Question Time has changed a great deal over the past thirty years. Virtually all attempt at asking specific questions of the Prime Minister has been abandoned. As Helen Irwin and her colleagues indicate in Chapter 2, this is partly to reduce any risk of questions

[36] For figures comparing the numbers reached in sample periods at 10–year intervals from 1946 onwards, see 'Parliamentary Report', *Social Studies Review*, Jan. 1987, pp. 29–30.

being transferred to other ministers and partly to permit the widest
possible scope for topicality in supplementaries when a question is
eventually reached.

Deserved or not, Prime Minister's Question Time has acquired
a considerable reputation as a twice-weekly gladiatorial contest.
Richard Crossman described this twice-weekly encounter as 'the
essence of our Prime Ministerial system'. Addressing an American
audience, he went on to say:

The whole of British politics is centred here. The man that's running the
Executive has to be there at the dispatch-box, has to present himself, has
to fight the contender for power, and the whole press and television will
report that evening on what happened to him. He's being tested and the
House of Commons feels itself to be participating in the test.[37]

Prime Minister's Question Time is an opportunity for government backbenchers both to show loyalty by the wording of their
supplementary questions and to occupy space that might otherwise
be taken up with more hostile questions. According to one former
Conservative MP who is now a journalist:

Government whips find out which Tory MPs are well-placed on the list of
questioners, enquire of No. 10 what Mrs Thatcher would like to be asked,
and then give the backbencher the appropriate Question. This excellent
procedure ensures that nothing unexpected or embarrassing comes up,
that the PM is able to give a series of mini-statements on subjects of her
choice, and that she is always copiously briefed with just the facts and
quotations she needs, to fit the enquiry.[38]

At the end of one Prime Minister's Question Time in 1990, Bruce
Grocott, the opposition deputy shadow Leader of the House,
asked the Business Question in this way: 'Having heard the Prime
Minister read so many answers to planted questions may we now
have the business for next week?'[39] It was reported in late 1990
that Conservative MPs were being encouraged to table more
questions to the new Prime Minister because the new restrictions
which obliged MPs to hand in their own questions was having the
effect of possibly allowing Labour to have too much of the
limelight on television at Prime Minister's Question Time.[40] On

[37] R. Crossman, *Inside View* (London: Jonathan Cape, 1972), 34–5.
[38] M. Parris, 'Primed Minister's Question Time', *The Times*, 28 Apr. 1989.
[39] *HC Deb.* (1989–90) 174, col. 1111.
[40] *The Times*, 14 Dec 1990.

the opposition side there is the opportunity to score points at the government's expense and to demonstrate support of their own parties' policies and attitudes.

The occasion is partly a personal test: the Leader of the Opposition is as much under scrutiny as the Prime Minister of the day. (It was suggested during 1990 that Neil Kinnock had become more effective as his questions had become shorter.) It is also partly spectator sport. For the immediate audience of backbenchers on both sides, there is the chance to demonstrate noisily their support or antagonism as the case may be. In a wider sense, too, it has become a spectator sport, first for the radio and now for the television audience. Live broadcasts and, perhaps even more, extracts for the evening national news bulletins are now an accepted feature of coverage of the House's activities.

The timing of Prime Minister's Question Time is, from that point of view, immensely convenient: the 3.15–3.30 p.m. slot could hardly be better placed both for that evening's radio and television news bulletins and for the needs of national newspapers, both in the form of parliamentary reports and the increasingly used 'sketch-writers' for whom Question Time forms part of the staple diet.

Evidence provided to the Procedure Committee in 1989–90 gives an indication of the growth of questions to the Prime Minister. According to this, in 1988–89 over 13,000 questions were tabled for answer by the Prime Minister, over half the total of oral questions tabled during the session. The average number of questions on the Order Paper to the Prime Minister had moved from 16.5 in early 1971 to about 200 in recent sessions.[41] In the first twenty-five Prime Minister's Question Times of the 1989–90 session, a total of 146 questions on the Order Paper was reached. Of these, 138 (or 94.5 per cent) were of the engagement type. Several of the others were of the older visit type. Those 146 questions produced 304 supplementaries; a ratio, perhaps surprisingly, only just over 1:2.

The atmosphere at Prime Minister's Question Time is usually noisier and more tense than at other Question Times. For the Speaker the problems are considerable, and her requests for order frequent. It is not necessarily the case, however, that the worst

[41] *Oral Questions*, HC (1989–90), 379, Appendix 1, paras. 8–9.

problems of disorder arise with questions to the Prime Minister. In June 1989, for example, the Speaker had to appeal for MPs to stop making 'really unseemly animal noises' during questions to the Secretary of State for the Environment. Mr Tam Dalyell, who has been suspended from the House several times for outbursts at Question Time, incurred his suspensions during questions to the Minister for the Civil Service in July 1988 and to the Attorney-General in July 1989, neither normally among the more boisterous Question Times. Although separated by a year, his offence was the same in each case: the refusal to withdraw an accusation that the then Prime Minister was a liar.[42]

Nevertheless, questions to, and answers from, the Prime Minister are in general likely to generate stronger passions than those to other ministers. A good example of the kind of noise produced and the level of insult traded was the first Prime Minister's Question Time after the release from prison of Nelson Mandela. In the course of answering questions, Mrs Thatcher accused the Leader of the Opposition, Neil Kinnock, of taking his orders from the African National Congress, while a supplementary question from Joan Ruddock which began 'If the Prime Minister had just spent 27 years in prison' produced the intervention from Gerald Kaufman 'As she should'.[43] So heated were the exchanges on this occasion that the Speaker was moved to observe, 'I have never heard the House behave in this way at Prime Minister's Question Time.'[44]

It may be that to some extent the tone of Prime Minister's Question Time is set by the main participants; though it is more likely that it is an institutionalized part of the Westminster culture. It will be interesting to see, therefore, whether John Major's observation at one of his first Question Times as Prime Minister that the chamber 'need not necessarily be a perpetual cockpit of confrontation' bears any fruit.[45] There is some evidence that Mr Major may be disappointed in his hopes. In July 1991, for example, there were acrimonious exchanges at Prime Minister's questions over the BCCI affair. Mr Major challenged Mr Kinnock

---

[42] *HC Deb*. (1987–88) 138, cols. 17–20, and *HC Deb*. (1988–89) 157, cols. 729–30. [43] *HC Deb*. (1989–90) 167, col. 140.
[44] Ibid.
[45] *HC Deb*. (1990–91) 182, col. 449. See also 'Major's Men Ditch the Old Taboos', *The Times*, 17 Dec. 1990.

in these terms: 'If he is saying that I am a liar, he had better do so openly'; and a few moments later a furious Mr Major denounced his opposite number in the following terms: 'The right hon. Gentleman has just revealed to the House why he is unfit to be in government.'[46]

One consequence of Mr Major's generally less combative style and shorter replies is that more questions are reached than under his predecessor. Comparison of sample of ten Prime Minister's Question Times in February–March 1990 with the same number a year later shows that Mr Major dealt on average with 8 questions each time, whereas Mrs Thatcher managed an average of only 6.4. It is not unusual for 10 questions to be reached with Mr Major; an extremely rare event with his predecessor.

There is inevitably a conflict of interest at Prime Minister's Question Time between the legitimate expectations of the opposition, minor parties, and backbenchers. It is as Helen Irwin and others have pointed out elsewhere, not uncommon for the Leader of the Opposition to have as many as three supplementaries to the Prime Minister.[47] More than that may mean trouble. For example, on 15 December 1987 Mr Kinnock was allowed four supplementaries to the Prime Minister. Although the Speaker had stressed that this was exceptional, it raised objections from a Conservative backbencher who argued that nine of the fifteen minutes available had been taken up by Mr Kinnock's questions.[48] In the course of stressing that Mr Kinnock's share on this occasion was indeed exceptional, the Speaker indicated that his aim was to ensure that every Member on the backbenches who wished to be called was called at Prime Minister's Question Time in the course of a Parliament.[49]

Given the predominance of engagements questions to the Prime Minister on the Order Paper, MPs are in effect entering a raffle for the right to ask a topical supplementary to the Prime Minister if they are lucky enough to draw a low-numbered ticket. The range

---

[46] *HC Deb.* (1990–91) 195, col. 1032.
[47] Irwin, 'Opportunities for Backbenchers', 82.
[48] *HC Deb.* (1987–88) 124, col. 919.
[49] Ibid., col. 924. To one MP who complained about not being able to ask a supplementary question to the Prime Minister, the Speaker added, 'I carefully keep a list, so I am aware that the hon. Member has not asked a Question to the Prime Minister in this Session. I shall seek to make it up to him later' (col. 925).

of possibilities is almost unlimited. One small example may serve
to suggest the variety that is encountered. On 6 February 1990
there were two supplementaries to an engagements question. The
first was about cot-deaths, the second about the maintenance of
sanctions against South Africa. On the other hand, other types of
question are subject to the restriction that supplementaries must
relate to the subject of the original question. For example, in
November 1989 the Speaker refused to allow a supplementary
about Eastern Europe because the original question had asked
about the Prime Minister's plans to visit West Yorkshire.

The Questioners

It has often been remarked that MPs vary greatly in their degree of
participation in Question Time. Philip Norton, for example, draws
attention to Barker and Rush's study of 1970 which found that
about one-third of MPs surveyed did not table questions for oral
answer.[50] Norton goes on to point out that, 'In the 1977–8 session,
over 150 backbenchers failed to table starred questions'.[51] Our
focus here is not so much the tabling of questions as success in
having them answered. Of course, there is an element of luck
about the opportunity actually to have questions answered orally
in the House. A Member may table such questions (within the
limits allowed by the rules described in the previous chapter), but
then find him or herself unlucky in the shuffle, so that the
questions are too low on the list (or now, not listed at all) to have
any chance of securing oral answers to them.

With that substantial qualification, one can identify those who
ask a lot of questions, those who ask few, or those who ask none at
all. An additional complication, given the practice of syndicating,
is to know how much significance is to be attached to the fact that a
question appears in the name of a particular Member. Other MPs
may, of course, join in with supplementaries without having tabled
questions of their own (as is most obviously the case with some
senior opposition figures).

[50] A. Barker and M. Rush, *The Member of Parliament and his Information*
(London: Allen & Unwin, 1970), 141–2.
[51] P. Norton. *The Commons in Perspective* (Oxford: Martin Robertson, 1981),
113.

Table 3.1. *Number of MPs receiving answers to oral questions, grouped according to number asked, in 1988–89 session*

Party	Number of questions asked							
	0	1–5	6–10	11–15	16–20	21–25	26+	Total
Conservative	170[a]	130	48	12	7	5	3	375
Labour	47	111	47	15	6	2	2	230
SLD	2	9	5	1	2			19
SDP	2	1						3
PC	0	2	1					3
SNP	0	2	2					4
UU	3	6						9
UDUP	3							3
UPUP	0	1						1
SDLP	2	1						3
SF	1							1
Speakers[b]	4							4
TOTAL	234	263	103	28	15	7	5	655

[a] Includes 85 ministers who are answering, not asking questions.
[b] Includes Chairman of Ways and Means Committee and two deputies.

Some measure, albeit flawed, of the extent to which MPs used oral questions is given in Table 3.1, based on my research of *Hansard*. This covers one recent session of normal length. The table indicates that, apart from the Speaker and the three deputies, 230 MPs out of a total of 655 (the extra five being accounted for by by-elections during the session) did not have a starred question answered orally during the session. Of these, 170 were Conservative MPs, of whom at least 85 were members of the government, and therefore were replying to, rather than asking, questions. Many of the other 85 were senior backbenchers, including a former Prime Minister (Edward Heath) and other former ministers such as John Biffen, Michael Heseltine, and Michael Jopling, who may have regarded oral questions with a touch of disdain. At the other end of the spectrum, three backbenchers first elected in 1987 did not have any questions answered orally (Rupert Allason, Andrew Hargreaves, and John Redwood).

On the Labour side it is less easy to make a clear separation

between front and backbenchers. Of the forty-seven Labour MPs
who did not have an oral question answered in 1988–89, seventeen
were shadow cabinet members, and another ten were lesser front
bench spokesmen. So again, roughly half of those who did not
have an oral question answered can be accounted for in this way.
However, two shadow cabinet members, John Prescott and Stan
Orme, each had one tabled question answered. (The latter
admittedly had no shadow departmental duties, but owed his
membership to being chairman of the Parliamentary Labour
Party.) Of the non-shadow cabinet front bench spokesmen, many
did have questions answered.

Of the other Labour MPs who did not have an oral question
answered during that session, some were senior figures in the
party, like Michael Foot, a former leader, and other former
ministers such as Tony Benn, Denis Healey, Merlyn Rees, and
Peter Shore. Others were more junior, including Douglas Henderson,
first elected in 1987, and Kate Hoey, who was elected at a by-
election during the session.

At the other end of the scale are those MPs who had substantial
totals. On the Conservative side there were eight MPs who each
had more than twenty questions answered orally. They were Tony
Baldry (twenty-one), David Knox (twenty-two), James Cran and
John Marshall (each with twenty-four), Michael Jack (twenty-
five), Michael Stern (twenty-six), Peter Thurnham (thirty-three),
and Harry Greenway (forty-five). Of these only Mr Cran and Mr
Jack were first elected in 1987.

On the Labour side Graham Allen had forty-five questions
answered orally. The next highest total among opposition MPs was
thirty-two for Mr Dalyell, followed by twenty-five for Andrew
Bennett and twenty-two for Greville Janner. It is perhaps worth
noting that Mr Bennett's status as an opposition front bench
spokesman does not appear to have unduly inhibited his question-
asking activities. Other opposition front bench spokesmen with
starred questions answered in double figures were Tom Clarke,
Maria Fyfe, and Tony Lloyd, all with eleven. No MP from any of
the other parties exceeded twenty questions answered orally, the
highest totals being eighteen recorded by Simon Hughes and Jim
Wallace of the Liberal Democrats.

Overall, there was very little difference in the total number of
questions asked by Conservative and Labour MPs during 1988–89.

Table 3.2. *Number of oral questions answered in 1988–89 session, grouped according to MPs' frequency of asking*

Party	MPs asking						
	1–5	6–10	11–15	16–20	21–25	26+	Total
Conservative	333	365	152	119	116	104	1,189
Labour	332	353	179	106	47	77	1,094
SLD	34	40	11	36			121
SDP	2						2
PC	8	10					18
SNP	5	13					18
UU	15						15
UPUP	2						2
SDLP	3						3
TOTAL	734	781	342	261	163	181	2,462[a]

[a] This total differs somewhat from the figure given in Table 2.1. The figures used here have been derived from *Hansard*; they include questions answered together, which may account for the discrepancy.

As Table 3.2, based on my own research, indicates, each group accounted for over 1,000 of the 2,462 questions receiving oral answers during the session. On the Conservative side, 1,189 questions were shared among 205 questioners, while 187 Labour MPs asked 1,094 questions. In a sense it is misleading to focus on questions on the Order Paper, because this takes no account of supplementary questions.[52] Obviously there are some MPs who are inhibited by convention from tabling starred questions of their own, but who join in Question Time with supplementaries. The most obvious example is the Leader of the Opposition, who normally asks several supplementaries at each Prime Minister's Question Time. Shadow departmental ministers now frequently join in questions in their area of responsibility, and indeed have an expectation that they will be called.

Some backbenchers, too, seem to make frequent interventions by way of supplementary questions. Among Labour MPs during

[52] The index to *Hansard* is of little help here in calculating the numbers of these. Apart from the fact that it is greatly in arrears, it lists together under each MP starred questions, supplementaries, and questions for written answer.

1988–89 these included Dennis Skinner (though he also asked
twenty starred questions), Jeff Rooker, David Winnick, Dale
Campbell-Savours, and Ron Brown, the last named in particular
often incurring the displeasure of the Speaker for the irrelevance
of his interventions.[53]

Some Problems of Prime Time

In the previous chapters reference was made to the problem of
syndication of questions. We have already seen that this was a
feature of questions to the Prime Minister, where not only
questions on the Order Paper but also supplementaries were
organized. In this case, given the openness of the original
questions, it was very much the supplementaries which mattered.

Explicit evidence of the practice of syndication was offered to
the Committee on Procedure in 1990. For example, in a letter to
the Chairman of the Committee, the Labour backbencher Joe
Ashton had this to say:

You are no doubt aware of the growing practice of Whips of both sides,
PPS's, Shadow spokesmen, research assistants and others touting sheaves
of questions around the tearooms, etc., and handing them in batches to the
Table Office, simply to ensure that the other party gets crowded out in the
resulting raffle.[54]

The changes of late 1990 outlined in the previous chapter are
designed to make at least part of this more difficult. When the
changes were agreed to by the House, they were welcomed by the
shadow Leader of the House, Dr Jack Cunningham:

I am sure that they will be met with a sigh of relief—particularly by
members of Opposition Front Benches who have had to organise against
the fusillade organised by Government Whips in an attempt to pre-empt
Question Time. . . . I, as both a participant in and victim of that system,
know very well how it operates—and I for one will not be sorry to see it
come to an end.[55]

It remains to be seen, of course, to what extent the changes
introduced at the start of the 1990–91 session do mark the end of
the practices complained of.

[53] *HC Deb.* (1989–90) 162, cols. 570–1 and 583.
[54] See *Oral Questions*, Appendix 2, p. xix.
[55] *HC Deb.* (1989–90) 178, col. 379.

The initial impression of the Principal Clerk of the Table Office was given to the Procedure Committee in January 1991: 'It is our firm impression that perhaps for the first two weeks [after the changes] there was a pause while the syndicates were re-grouping and adopting new tactics, but since then there is no doubt that syndication is still alive and well.'[56] In a further memorandum to the Committee, the Clerk provided conservative estimates of the extent of the survival of syndication.[57] (These are given in Chapter 2.) In their Third Report the Procedure Committee drew attention to some decline in syndication compared with the previous session, but noted also, 'In the final analysis, the responsibility lies with individual Members; syndication could not survive without their acquiescence.'[58]

Syndication is one aspect of the growth in the volume of questions, but it is also an aspect of the struggle between government and opposition for which Question Time provides part of the stage. Another feature of this, remarked on earlier, is the extent to which in supplementary questions opposition front benchers encroach on what was formerly regarded as primarily backbench territory. We have already noted the pressures on the Leader of the Opposition to intervene consistently at Prime Minister's Question Time. Similar, if lesser, pressures are present at questions to departmental ministers. Failure to call an opposition front bencher may on occasion be taken badly, although rarely as badly as when in 1984 the shadow Foreign Secretary walked out of the chamber in protest at the Speaker's refusal to call him for a supplementary. The Speaker pointed out that slow progress was being made and that the opposition front bench had already had four interventions.[59]

The position of opposition front benchers was addressed by the Speaker in a letter to the Chairman of the 1989–90 Procedure Committee. 'This is obviously an issue of some delicacy; the Opposition Front Bench expects to have a chance at Question Time to challenge Ministers' policies and actions, and to canvass its own alternatives.' Pointing out that the opposition front bench had other procedural opportunities to make their points, he made a plea for a reduction in front bench interventions to allow more

---

[56] *Parliamentary Questions*, HC (1990–91) 178, 4.
[57] Ibid., Appendix 3.
[58] Ibid., p. viii, para. 9.
[59] *HC Deb*. (1983–84) 64, col. 978.

opportunities for backbenchers. He noted that in some subject areas, the shadow team was as large as eight, and suggested, 'It would be helpful to establish that not *every* member of the Front Bench Team would be called at every Question Time and that the most senior one would only be called *once*, rather than twice, which has become almost universal practice.'[60] This last comment provides interesting confirmation of the role of the shadow spokesmen. In their report, the Procedure Committee did not make a recommendation on the Speaker's suggestion that fewer opposition front bench spokesmen be called to ask supplementaries.[61]

In the previous chapter it was pointed out that there has been some change in the style of questions over the past thirty years. Tabled questions have become shorter, though the same may not be true of supplementaries. Helen Irwin and her collegues also discuss the opposition to the tendency towards more open questions to departmental ministers. However, in his evidence to the Procedure Committee, Philip Norton struck a different note, suggesting that, 'they may provide the only means for Members to raise an important issue and to make a point to Government that otherwise would not be possible'.[62]

Lying behind many of these arguments is the perennial problem of breadth versus depth at Question Time. In the previous chapter, the views of former Speakers, such as Selwyn Lloyd, were described. There is little likelihood today that any Speaker would seek to emulate Horace King and aim for a significantly greater number of questions being covered. Nevertheless, there has been concern about the length and number of supplementaries, and in the course of 1990, Mr Speaker Weatherill tried to speed up Question Time, as he pointed out to the Chairman of the Procedure Committee: 'Since the Christmas Recess I have in fact been attempting, with some success if I may say so, to speed up Question Time a little.'[63] The Committee endorsed these efforts,

accepting that there will always be some subjects of topical interest or controversy on which an extended line of questioning would be appropriate, Mr Speaker should nevertheless have the full support of the House in seeking to increase the number of tabled questions reached, by

---

[60] *Oral Questions*, Appendix 21.   [61] Ibid., p. x, para. 31.
[62] Ibid., Appendix 18.   [63] Ibid., Appendix 21.

curbing the length of both Ministerial replies and supplementaries; and in particular by trying to ensure that supplementaries consist of a single question rather than a dialogue of queries.[64]

Having secured Procedure Committee support for his efforts, the Speaker was then able to cite this in the House. For example, in March 1990 he put it this way, 'I should explain that I am being heavily urged by the Procedure Committee to speed up Question Time.'[65] How sucessful these efforts will be is something that remains to be seen.

The Impact of Television

Of all the changes that the House has seen in recent years, none is potentially more significant than the introduction of television cameras. What effect this has had on Question Time is a matter of some dispute. A major study of the first months of televising the House's proceedings pointed to one harmful effect:

the growing number of backbenchers who are entering questions in the daily ballot, in their endeavour to be seen on the screens, or to promote what their whips want. As a result, Question Times are losing their value. The extreme consequence is the decision of BBC Northern Ireland and Ulster Television to cancel their March [1990] live cover of NI questions, because their MPs have, in effect, been driven out by the mainlanders.[66]

The study found no evidence that behaviour in the House had been made worse by the advent of television. Indeed, one MP interviewed in the Hansard Society study suggested that TV had repaired some of the damage done earlier by sound broadcasting of Prime Minister's Question Time.[67] In other ways too, TV may have an impact. One is in the style of speaking; one observer has suggested that Mrs Thatcher while Prime Minister realized before Mr Kinnock that 'in the televised House the audience could not see the other side bellowing at you (the Member speaking) but can see you bellowing, and it doesn't go down at all well'.[68]

There seems to be some evidence that the arrival of the cameras

---

[64] Ibid., p. xi, para. 35(v).   [65] *HC Deb.* (1989–90), 168, col. 996.
[66] A. Hetherington, K. Weaver, and M. Ryle, *Cameras in the Commons* (London: Hansard Society, 1990), 2.   [67] Ibid. 70.
[68] Ibid. 32–3.

has increased pressures to participate at Question Time. One MP interviewed saw tabling a question for oral answer as 'a daily ballot for a TV slot'.[69] Apart from the pressure on Northern Ireland questions already mentioned, there was a suggestion that Scottish questions were also under heavier pressure. Such claims must be treated with caution, because before the arrival of the cameras there were already complaints about the number of questions from English Members at Scottish Question Time, as a result of there being very few Scottish Conservative MPs.[70]

What seems to be generally agreed is that the arrival of TV, and especially the live televising of the House between 3.05 p.m. and 4 p.m. on Tuesdays and Thursdays, has increased the pressures not only on Question Time, but also on the various activities which immediately follow it. Of particular concern here are things like the weekly Business Question, PNQs, and ministerial statements. The Hansard Society inquiry raised the issue of whether more ministerial statements were now being made, increasing pressure for PNQs and more Members being called to ask questions on statements and PNQs (including the weekly Business Question). On the basis of a small sample of evidence, the Report suggests that as far as the sample period is concerned (January to mid-February 1990) there is no evidence of more statements being made or PNQs being asked compared with a period of similar length in the 1985–86 session. However, there was some evidence that average length of time spent on statements, PNQs, and the weekly Business Question was longer than in 1985–86.[71] This seems a convenient point at which to move on to a discussion of those areas of the House's activity where questions may be asked but which are not part of Question Time.

Private Notice Questions

Question Time, as we have seen, is limited in duration by the 3.30 p.m. cut-off point. There are, however, a number of ways in which, in effect, it can be extended. The first of these is when a

[69] Ibid. 75.
[70] *HC Deb*. (1988–89) 154, col. 216.
[71] Hetherington, Weaver, and Ryle, *Cameras in the Commons*, 85.

minister decides to answer one or more questions at the end of Question Time rather than during it, as referred to above.

More important are questions asked by private notice. These provide the speediest way of securing an oral answer to a question. Requests for them must be made to the Speaker by noon (or 10 a.m. on Fridays) of the day they are to be asked. The Speaker has discretion as to whether to accept such requests. If granted, the question is asked immediately after Question Time (or at 11 a.m. on Fridays).

Table 2.1 gives details of the number of these questions asked in recent sessions. (Excluded from this is the weekly Business Question, in which each Thursday after Question Time the Leader of the House is asked about forthcoming business.) The table shows considerable variaton in the number of PNQs permitted: one important factor here is the attitude of the Speaker. In the last three sessions under Mr Speaker Thomas, for example, the number allowed was in single figures. Under his successor there was a much larger number, with, for example, forty-three granted in 1985–86, the largest for a normal-length session in recent years. In 1988–89, thirty-five such questions were asked.

In recent years a significant proportion of the successful requests (it is difficult to know about unsuccessful requests since, officially, no reference is made to them) have been made by opposition front bench spokesmen. According to a written answer from the then Leader of the House in March 1990, twenty-one of the thirty-five PNQs in 1988–89 were asked by opposition front benchers. The question had asked for comparable figures for 1977–78 and 1978–79. The reply indicated that it was not possible to say precisely how many in those sessions were asked by opposition front benchers, but suggested that the best estimate was six out of twenty in 1977–78 and thirteen out of twenty-nine in 1978–79.[72]

The topics covered by PNQs are matters of urgent concern: for example, accidents and disasters at home or crises abroad. In the 1989–90 session twenty-three PNQs were asked. Some dealt with problems like storm damage or an outbreak of football hooliganism in Bournemouth. Others concerned problem areas abroad: Panama, Iraq, South Africa, and Hong Kong. Fourteen of the twenty-three questions were asked by Labour front bench spokesmen, with the shadow Foreign Secretary, Mr Kaufman, asking

[72] *HC Deb*. (1989–90) 168, col. 403 w.

four and his deputy, George Robertson, one. Of the other
questions six (including three about storm damage) were asked by
Conservative backbenchers, two by Liberal Democrats, and one
by a Northern Ireland Member. The average length of time spent
on the questions in the sample was 23.5 minutes, so they
represented an appreciable extension of Question Time. The
average number of supplementary questions asked on each PNQ
was 12.6.

One unusual use of a PNQ occurred in March 1989, when the
Chancellor of the Exchequer made his Budget speech in response
to such a question. This reflected a degree of collusion between
government and opposition to deny the Scottish National Party an
opportunity for publicity.[73]

Ministerial Statements

Some PNQs—for example, one asking about an EC meeting of
ministers—differ little in substance from ministerial statements.
Although not technically a type of question, the ministerial
statement provides a further opportunity for questions outside the
restrictions of Question Time itself.

In 1989–90 there were sixty-six ministerial statements (excluding
business statements) occupying some fifty-five hours of the
House's time. (In the previous session statements had occupied
just over sixty hours.) On average in 1989–90 the time spent on
statements and the accompanying questions was just over twice
that spent on PNQs (50 minutes compared with 23.5 minutes).
Likewise, the number of questions asked was also about double:
24.5 per statement compared with 12.6 per PNQ.

Although the Hansard Society study on the effects of televising
the proceedings of the Commons suggested that the number of
ministerial statements had not grown in recent years, this
judgement was based on a relatively short sample period, and the
comparison was made with 1985–86. Over a longer time span,
different answers might be arrived at, depending on the periods
looked at, although comparisons are complicated by the tendency,
for example in the 1960s, for more statements to be made not as

[73] *HC Deb.* (1988–89) 149, cols. 289–93.

outright statements but as answers to private Notice Questions or to questions detached from their place in the Order Paper and answered at the end of Question Time. Statements, too, must be seen as one of the 'prime time' opportunities for government, opposition, and backbenchers to have maximum impact with the media.

Costs

Details were given in the previous chapter of the escalation in the number of questions tabled for written answer. Questions for written answer do not, by definition, occupy any time on the Floor of the House, but, like other questions, they incur costs. Questions about costs are of two kinds: the costs of preparing the answers and the costs of printing both questions and answers. (In addition, it could be argued there are the costs of running the Table Office, the staff costs in Hansard of editing the answers, and the library costs of indexing.)

Evidence presented to the Procedure Committee in 1989–90 provided some indication of printing costs. According to an estimate by the Principal Clerk of the Table Office, in the 1988–89 session the cost of printing questions was about £1.15 million, and the cost of printing answers perhaps £0.23 million.[74] As noted in the previous chapter, the changes introduced at the start of the 1990–91 session will result in some savings. Since only a limited number of questions for oral answer will now be printed and those that are not printed will not receive an answer unless they are retabled as questions for written answer, the savings should be substantial. The estimate given by the Procedure Committee, and repeated when the changes were agreed to by House, was £750,000.

The costs of answering questions have risen steadily over the years. The estimate of cost given at the end of 1989 was that the average cost of answering a written question was £53 and an oral question £87.[75] A year later the total cost of answering written questions in the 1989–90 session, when 41,371 such questions were asked, was said to be £3.7 million,[76] and the total cost of PQs in

[74] *Oral Questions*, Appendix 1, para. 22.
[75] *HC Deb* (1989–90) 163, cols. 579–80 w.   [76] Ibid. 178, col. 643 w.
[77] HC (1990–91) 178, Evidence, p. 8, para. 54.   [78] Ibid.

1989–90 was put at around £6 million.[77] However, it is worth noting that in his evidence to the 1991 Procedure Committee the Principal Clerk at the Table Office admitted: 'I confess that I cannot begin to understand how these figures are worked out.'[78] That there is a hypothetical element in them seemed to be conceded by the government in its evidence to the Committee: 'When considering costs and quoting a total cost of PQs in a session as being £6 million, it is important to recognise that a large proportion of this money will not be saved if the number of questions were reduced even substantially.'[79] In its Report the Procedure Committee was cautious about the figures, and indicated that they needed to be seen in context. 'Even taking the figures at face value, many would argue that the cost of parliamentary questions is a reasonable price to pay for their contribution towards ministerial accountability, representing as it does a minuscule fraction of the machinery of Government as a whole.'[80]

Conclusion

The 1990–91 review of questions by the House's Procedure Committee was a response to the sense that not all was well with the way questions were handled in the House. In its Report the Committee took a more optimistic view. 'The very small number of responses we have received to our invitation to Members to submit evidence suggests that, with a few isolated exceptions, there is no dissatisfaction with the way in which parliamentary questions currently operate.'[81]

As we have seen, Question Time has become to a considerable extent an orchestrated affair, with much less left to individual enterprise than used to be the case. Moreover, there are pressures towards the use of open questions which enable topical issues to be raised when questions are eventually asked. Evidence from ministers presented to the 1990–91 Procedure Committee revealed a variety of reactions to open questions. In its Report the Committee noted the attempt by the Speaker to discourage open questions by indicating that he would not allow supplementaries

---

[79] Ibid., Evidence, p. 31.   [80] Ibid., p. xvii, para. 65.
[81] Ibid., p. xxix, para. 135.

on questions to departmental ministers which did not have some indication of their purpose. The Committee also endorsed a suggestion from the Principal Clerk of the Table Office that 'in order to be admissible, an oral question (for instance, asking a Minister when he next expects to meet the Chairman of a nationalized industry or other public body) should be so worded as to indicate, within reasonably broad limits, a particular subject matter'.[82]

Part of the change in Question Time has been the decline in the traditional notion of questions for oral answer being concerned with obtaining information or pressing for action. Increasingly they are part of a political battle in which party points are scored and personal or party glory pursued. All this now has the added ingredient of being seen on television.

Of necessity, Question Time must be seen as part of the range of activities that occupies the House in the first two to two and a half hours of its sitting from Mondays to Thursdays. During this time MPs seek to score party points, establish reputations, humble opponents, or merely indulge their taste for personal publicity. As part of this, Question Time will continue to arouse very varied reactions from participants and observers.

[82] Ibid., p. xiv, para. 43.

4

Questions and Members

Mark Franklin and Philip Norton

Members of Parliament table a substantial number of questions each year. We have looked at the rules that they have to follow. We have looked at their behaviour in Question Time itself. But why do they do it? What purpose do MPs believe is served by tabling parliamentary questions? Where do their questions originate? And what do they do with the answers?

Why MPs table questions has not previously been the subject of systematic study. Chester and Bowring noted that Members may table questions in order to seek information, to press for action in pursuit of a particular grievance or a matter of more general concern, to make a party point, to seek an answer that a minister wants to give (the 'inspired question'), or for personal publicity.[1] Though the order given probably reflects the importance attached to the categories by Chester and his associate, no attempt was made to ask Members themselves why they tabled questions. The analysis was based on a reading of *Hansard* and the Order Paper, supplemented by some secondary sources.

In order to assess the contemporary use of parliamentary questions, we have focused on those who table the questions. Some Members of Parliament have expressed their views in memoirs. The Procedure Committee in its 1991 inquiry into questions sought the comments of those Members who tabled the most questions. These sources we have supplemented by interviews with Members and research assistants and, more systematically, by a survey of a small number of MPs, chosen to be representative of different types of question-askers. The survey provides us with an important insight into Members' perceptions.

---

[1] D. N. Chester and N. Bowring, *Questions in Parliament* (Oxford: Clarendon Press, 1962), 200–27.

The Survey

In 1989 we mailed questionnaires to seventy MPs, of whom thirty-four replied; of those giving their party affiliation, eighteen were Conservative, and fourteen Labour.[2] These were, on the whole, frequent attenders at Question Time (more than twice a week on average, excluding Prime Minister's Questions) and frequent askers of parliamentary questions. It is perhaps significant that none of the MPs chosen as representative of infrequent questioners responded to our survey.

Respondents were asked what functions they thought questions performed, whether these functions ought to be performed by parliamentary questions, and, if so, how well they performed them. They were also asked which of the functions would be their own main reason for asking questions. On the questions they tabled, we asked whether they drafted the questions themselves, and if not, where the questions originated. We also asked what problems they saw with the present state of Question Time and what solutions they would propose to some of these problems. Various follow-up questions were asked about particular functions and problems.

One of the most striking features of the responses was the unanimity of responses, irrespective of party. For example, Conservative and Labour respondents claimed to attend roughly the same number of Question Times each session: an average of ninety-three. (Given the number of sitting days on which questions are asked—an average of just over 134 per session in the 1980s—this constitutes approximately 70 per cent of all Question Times, bearing out the popularity of Question Time among Members generally.) In no case did Labour respondents differ from Conservatives by as much as one point on a five-point scale (very poorly, poorly, so-so, well, very well) or by as much as two-thirds of a point on a three-point scale (often, sometimes, never); and the agreement between respondents of different parties was generally much closer than that. On less than one-fifth of the questions asked did Labour respondents differ from Conservative

---

[2] The response rate, of just under 50%, is not unusually low for a mailed questionnaire.

respondents by as much as half a point on a five-point scale or a third of a point on a three-point scale. Some of these differences will be highlighted in our findings, but it is important to stress that even the largest differences between MPs of different parties are much less than might have been expected. The degree of unanimity recorded in our survey is hardly less than staggering, and mitigates the problems of such a small sample.

Functions

Nine functions were proffered. All or most respondents agreed that PQs should fulfil eight of these functions. Only the function of acting 'as a forum for outside lobbyists' divided Members: almost 40 per cent felt that this was not a function that PQs should fulfil. The other eight functions appeared to be exhaustive as a far as our respondents were concerned. When asked if there were any other functions, most Members failed to identify any, and there was no function identified by more than two of those who did respond.

The eight functions on which there was general agreement are listed in Table 4.1 in the order in which Members felt they were least well performed. Within this list, the functions fall roughly into three groups: first, those to do with influence and account-ability, which MPs think are not performed well; second, concerned with the acquisition of information, on which perform-ance is somewhat better; and third, those which relate less to government activities *per se*, which a majority of respondents believe are performed well by PQs. The function of attacking or defending policy and the workings of government departments occupies a distinctive position in the list. Few respondents felt that PQs performed this function poorly. Less than half felt that they performed it well. However, if the 'so-so' and 'well' responses are combined, it achieves a higher evaluation than any other function.[3]

There was remarkable unanimity between MPs of both parties. The only major disagreement was over the use of PQs for

[3] The percentage of respondents replying 'poorly' was the same for this question (attacking or defending policy and the workings of departments) as for 'publicizing backbench MPs and their concerns'; but the combined percentage replying 'so-so' or 'well' to the latter question was less than 90%, because three respondents did not believe that it was a function that PQs should fulfil.

Table 4.1. *Functions of parliamentary questions (and number of MPs who feel that these functions should* not *be performed)*

Function		Questions perform this function		
		Poorly (%)	So-so (%)	Well (%)
Influencing government policy and actions	(1)	47	38	13
Holding ministers accountable	(0)	35	42	23
Getting hard-to-obtain information	(1)	38	26	32
Attacking or defending workings of government departments	(0)	9	45	45
Getting information on policy, work of government, etc.	(1)	28	22	50
Taking up constituency interests	(0)	13	38	50
Evaluating parliamentary performance	(2)	13	27	54
Publicizing backbench MPs and their concerns	(3)	9	19	63

Note: Numbers in parentheses are for MPs who do *not* think that the function should be performed by PQs.

attacking or defending public policy and the workings of government departments. Where Conservatives, on average, saw this as a function that was performed well, Labour MPs, on average, regarded it as a function that was performed only 'so-so'. This difference may be a consequence of the very nature of constituting the opposition, with opposition MPs feeling frustrated when faced with well-briefed ministers; or it may be a consequence of the political situation at the time. Given that the questionnaire was sent out in 1989, when the Conservative government was encountering economic difficulties and internal divisions on the issue of European union, the more plausible explanation is probably the former.

However, it is the cross-party agreement, rather than the differences, that is remarkable. The other remarkable feature is the extent of dissatisfaction with PQs in fulfilling those functions that are traditionally regarded as core functions of Parliament itself: influencing government policy and actions and holding ministers accountable. The extent of this dissatisfaction should not be exaggerated. The MPs taking part in our survey who felt a particular function was being performed poorly were out-numbered in each instance by those answering 'so-so' and 'well' (or 'very well'). None the less, the figures are sobering: 85 per cent of respondents did not judge the task of influencing government policy and actions to be performed well. Further questions elicited reasons for this dissatisfaction to which we shall return shortly.

Reasons for Asking Questions

MPs have a view, a fairly consensual view, of what functions PQs should fulfil. But why do they actually table questions? And is there any difference between their reasons for tabling oral as opposed to written questions?

Our respondents were themselves heavy users of parliamentary questions. The most frequent reason they gave for putting down PQs for either oral or written answer was in order to hold ministers accountable for their actions and those of their subordinates (see Table 4.2). Only one of our respondents never put down such questions for oral answer, and only three never put down such questions for written answer. The only other reason for tabling PQs that achieved anything like the same level of unanimity was for the purpose of defending or promoting constituency interests. Only three or four of our respondents never asked oral or written questions for this purpose.

Again, the agreement between the two sides of the House was more notable than the disagreement. The major area of disagreement was over the first and third of the reasons listed. Labour Members were more likely to be concerned with influencing government policy and actions, whereas Conservative Members were more likely to be concerned with holding ministers accountable for their actions and those of their subordinates.

Table 4.2 is arranged so as to distinguish between motives that lead primarily to the asking of oral questions (towards the top end of the table) and those that lead primarily to the tabling of written questions (towards the foot of the table), though it should be noted that nearly half the reasons given (those identified by an asterisk in the table) are given virtually as often both types of

Table 4.2. *Reasons for using oral and written parliamentary questions*

Reason		MPs using PQs for each purpose	
		Oral (%)	Written (%)
Holding ministers accountable	*	97	91
Defending or promoting constituency interests	*	91	88
Influencing government policy and actions		86	77
Publicizing government failures, successes, etc.	*	85	87
Because I was asked to		47	82
Auditing departmental performance		61	84
Making ministers aware of points of concern to constituents	*	87	91
Getting the government to make a formal statement		85	94
Discovering information that might be hard to get elsewhere		55	97

Note: Reasons followed by an asterisk are those for which oral and written questions are employed by about equal proportions of respondents.

question. In so far as it is possible to generalize from these figures, it appears that oral questions are employed primarily where the Member considers some publicity is desirable, whereas written questions are employed when it is simply a matter of obtaining information.

Visibility is clearly an important consideration. Eighty-five per cent of respondents mentioned that they found participation in the asking of questions quite helpful or very helpful to their image in their constituency or party. Chester and Bowring, as we have already noted, included 'personal publicity' among the various motivations for tabling questions. Whereas much of what an MP did might not attract publicity, a parliamentary question had 'a much greater chance of being mentioned if not in one of the national dailies, at least in a paper or journal, either circulating in the Member's area or concerned with the subject matter'.[4] However, those who used the procedure frequently were rare. The

[4] Chester and Bowring, 223.

number using PQs has increased, and, we would hypothesize, the
motivation of obtaining publicity is now far greater than in the
1950s and 1960s. The reasons for this have been discussed in the
Introduction. Though the number of marginal seats has decreased,
the level of perceived electoral vulnerability by MPs has increased.[5]
The demands made of MPs by constituents are greater; the
willingness of MPs to respond (indeed, to seek out constituency
problems) is far greater.[6] Parliamentary candidates are increasingly
trained to exploit local media, such as local radio and 'freesheets'.
Parliamentary questions are a relatively cheap way for MPs to
demonstrate that they are doing something in pursuit of their
constituents' interests—or, indeed, a relatively cheap way of
demonstrating that the MPs are simply doing *something*. Written
questions receive replies, but do not require Members to be
physically present at a given time in the chamber; the answers can
be sent to the local newspaper. Indeed, 82 per cent of respondents
said that they sent such answers to the local paper. (As one MP
candidly put it in evidence to the Procedure Committee in 1991,
'PQ answers can act as "hooks" for my press releases.')[7] The value
of tabling oral questions has been increased by the introduction of
television cameras which, in the words of the then Defence
Secretary Tom King, 'has raised the stakes for both MPs and
Ministers'.[8] Members now compete, in effect, for a 'sound bite'.

   Though most respondents find questions useful as a way of
raising their profile in their constituencies, and an even greater
percentage use oral and written questions for the purposes of
defending or promoting constituency interests, there is general
agreement that writing a letter to a minister is more effective in
achieving a desired response. This evaluation is by no means a
recent one. Chester and Bowring called attention to it, and

   [5] See P. Norton and D. M. Wood, *Back from Westminster: The Politics of
Constituency Service* (Lexington, Ky.: Kentucky University Press, forthcoming).
   [6] According to Cain and his associates, 27% of Members adopt a proactive
approach to constituency casework (B. Cain, J. Ferejohn, and M. Fiorina, *The
Personal Vote* (Cambridge, Mass.: Harvard University Press, 1987), 65). That
percentage is likely to be higher following the 1987 general election. See P. Norton
and D. Wood, 'Constituency Service by Members of Parliament: Does it
Contribute to a Personal Vote?' *Parliamentary Affairs*, 43 (2) (Apr. 1990),
196–208.
   [7] *Parliamentary Questions*; HC (1990–91) 178, Appendix 13, p. 53.
   [8] Ibid., Appendix 23, p. 63.

Richard Crossman, as a minister, attested to it.[9] Only 27 per cent of respondents thought that an oral question would be more effective than a letter, and only 8 per cent thought that a written question would be more effective. PQs may be used as a 'second stage' device if letters fail to produce the desired response. However, given the perception of how limited the effectiveness of PQs is compared with that of letter writing, the more importance we may attach to the value of publicity. Letter writing is a private activity; tabling parliamentary questions is a very public one.

One of the more surprising reasons for asking PQs was 'because I was asked to'. Almost half our respondents 'often' or 'sometimes' (overwhelmingly the latter) tabled oral questions because they were asked to; just over two-thirds of respondents (67 per cent) 'sometimes' tabled written questions because they were asked to, and 15 per cent 'often' did so. Only 18 per cent of respondents said they never tabled written questions because they were asked to. The reasons for MPs tabling questions on behalf of others have been discussed in Chapter 1. Lobbying by pressure groups—and constituents—is an increasingly significant feature of parliamentary life. Of those respondents who identified on whose behalf they tabled questions, half mentioned local interest groups and their constituencies, and 15 per cent identified national interest groups. Almost one-third identified colleagues. Given the extent of syndication and planted questions, this figure may be surprising only for the fact that it is not larger.

The recommendations of the Procedure Committee in 1990, which were approved by the House in October of that year, were designed in large measure to reduce the number of oral questions tabled by MPs 'who were asked to' by their colleagues. As Helen Irwin and her colleagues point out (Chapter 2), the requirement that Members hand in their starred questions in person to the Table Office does not appear to have affected significantly the syndication of questions. 'Syndication', in the words of the Principal Clerk of the Table Office, 'is still alive and well.'[10] As one MP told one of the authors in mid-1991, 'Previously my PM's engagements questions were put down for me. Now I receive a reminder each fortnight to table them myself.'[11]

[9] R. Crossman, *The Diaries of a Cabinet Minister*, vol. 1 (London: Hamish Hamilton/Jonathan Cape, 1975), 628–9.
[10] *Parliamentary Questions*, HC (1990–91) 178, q. 4.
[11] Conservative backbencher to Philip Norton, 1991.

Two other findings of our survey are worthy of note. One is the percentage of respondents who claim to use oral questions for defending or promoting constituency interests. This remains as significant a motivation as it was when Chester and Bowring studied the subject. That it does so appears to run counter to the views expressed in 1990 by the Principal Clerk of the Table Office in his evidence to the Procedure Committee. Members, he wrote, 'normally use written rather than oral Questions to ventilate individual constituency matters. . . . The use of oral questions for constituency matters has largely disappeared in recent years as a result of syndication.'[12] The disparity is explained in part by likely differences in defining what constitute 'constituency matters' (for some MPs, questions about levels of unemployment are constituency-related) and also by the fact that our survey did not distinguish between the numbers of questions submitted. Most MPs may occasionally use an oral question to pursue a constituency matter, but more frequently use written questions. Even so, the fact that nine out of ten respondents claimed to use oral questions, however infrequently, for pursuing constituency cases is significant.

The other significant finding is one that we have already touched upon. It is the distinction to be drawn between oral and written questions for the purpose of obtaining information. Chester and Bowring identified obtaining information as one of the principal purposes of tabling parliamentary questions. All bar one of the MPs in our survey considered getting hard-to-obtain information as a function of PQs. In practice, it is a function that is fulfilled more often through written than through oral questions. Just over half our respondents use oral questions for obtaining such information, whereas virtually every one employs written question for this purpose. That this should be so is not particularly surprising. Asking for information as a peg on which to attack or praise the government usually involves information that is already known. (Few Members would run the risk of asking such a question without knowing the likely answer.) Information that is particularly hard to find, especially of a statistical nature, often does not lend itself to a supplementary question.

What our survey confirms is that Members of Parliament ask questions for a variety of reasons. The categories in Table 4.2 are

---

[12] *Parliamentary Questions*, HC (1990–91) 178, Evidence, p. 9.

not mutually exclusive. It is possible that some Members use PQs for reasons they are reluctant to admit. Some may be unwilling to concede that they table oral questions because they are asked to. However, given the number willing to admit that they table written questions for this reason, this would seem unlikely, or at least not likely on a scale that would affect the percentage significantly. Table 4.2 gives, we believe, a reasonable picture of the purposes for which MPs on both sides of the House ask parliamentary questions.

Drafting Questions

Questions are tabled in the name of Members of Parliament. But who actually writes the questions?

According to our survey, most MPs write their own questions. Eighty-two per cent of respondents 'often' write their own oral questions, and 88 per cent 'often' write their own written questions. However, what is particularly interesting is the proportion who often or sometimes have questions written for them by others. Fourteen per cent of respondents often have both oral and written questions prepared for them by research assistants. The view of the Table Office in 1990, with which the Procedure Committee was 'inclined to agree', was that research assistants played a more significant role in the number of written questions tabled.[13] There is some evidence for this from our survey in respect of the proportion who 'sometimes' have written questions prepared by researchers as compared with the number who sometimes have oral questions prepared: 38 per cent as against 21 per cent. However, given that there is no limit on the number of questions that can be tabled for written answer, it is not just the number of MPs who sometimes have questions prepared by researchers that is important; it is the number of questions that those researchers prepare. The example cited in Chapter 1 of the research assistant who handed in at one time 122 written questions, all apparently emanating from the assistant, illustrates well the point. Somewhat more MPs are likely to use research assistants for drafting written questions than for drafting oral

[13] *Oral Questions*, HC (1989–90) 379, p. vii, para. 10.

questions (and, between the parties, Conservative MPs are somewhat more likely than Labour MPs to use assistants for this purpose), and some of those who do use them for drafting written questions utilize them to table a large number.

Beyond that it is difficult to go in generalizing about the relationship between MPs and research assistants. As the Principal Clerk of the Table Office noted in his evidence to the Procedure Committee, there is a high turnover in assistants, and, consequently, some 'are extremely inexperienced and ignorant of the House's rules and procedures'.[14] Others, it has to be recorded, have a good knowledge of Parliament and its procedures, in some cases as good as—if not better than—their Members. Some Members will tell their assistant the gist of what they want to achieve in a particular question and leave it to the assistant to draft it. In other cases, a research assistant may have a standing instruction from a Member to generate as many questions as possible for tabling, the assistant having no guidance other than the Member's known areas of interest. The motivation in the case of oral questions is for the MP to maximize the changes of getting a question called. The more the Member is able to be heard in the House—through a question being called and then through a supplementary—the greater the publicity and the greater the opportunity to make a mark in the House. Our data are insufficient to identify the extent of this practice. It would seem a plausible hypothesis that it is likely to be greater among newer Members, keen to achieve some attention in the House, than among longer-serving, hence established Members. That hypothesis is borne out by interviews with research assistants to a number of Conservative backbenchers. Although the number involved is too small to allow us to draw a firm conclusion, we have discovered no evidence so far that runs counter to our hypothesis.

Another notable finding, though one that is not overly surprising given the increase in parliamentary lobbying (see Chapter 1), is the proportion of MPs who have questions—especially written questions—drafted for them by professional lobbying firms, known by their correct style as political consultancies. Thirty-one per cent of our respondents sometimes had oral questions drafted by such organizations (though none had questions written by them often); 62 per cent sometimes had written questions drafted by

[14] *Parliamentary Questions*, HC (1990–91) 178, Evidence, p. 5, para. 35.

them (and 7 per cent often had such questions drafted by them). In many cases, the MP is seeking to obtain information that outside organizations have had difficulty in obtaining from government departments. In a 'how to' book on lobbying, Charles Miller, the managing director of a leading political consultancy, reproduces a draft letter for any organization wanting to approach an MP to get such information via a PQ.[15] In other cases, a lobbying firm may be seeking to get some comment on the public record, or simply some reference to a matter that a client considers important— which, on occasion, means the client's name. The extent to which MPs are active parties in the process or act 'in the role of a postman for outside bodies'[16] appears to vary considerably. Though there have been various allegations that some MPs have a pecuniary interest in the practice (receiving payment for tabling PQs), the main motivation appears to be a willingness to help— especially if there is a constituency connection—or because of an affinity with the group involved. Lobbyists target potentially sympathetic MPs.

Where a Member expresses an interest in the topic involved and a relationship is established (or where he or she is already known to the consultants), the consultants will often find themselves subsequently assisting with the drafting of parliamentary questions and early day motions, and providing material for inclusion in letters to ministers or speeches on the floor of the House or in committee.[17]

Our survey illustrates the extent of such activity.

The remaining responses to our survey question provide an indication of the extent and source of syndicated and planted questions. Forty per cent of respondents sometimes, and 3 per cent often, had oral questions written for them by 'another member'. (For written questions, the figures were 31 per cent sometimes and 3 per cent often.) In many cases, the 'other member' for Conservative MPs is likely to have been a minister's PPS. Twenty-three per cent of respondents sometimes had oral questions, and 14 per cent sometimes had written questions,

---

[15] C. Miller, *Lobbying*, 2nd edn. (Oxford: Basil Blackwell, 1990), 135.

[16] *Parliamentary Questions*, HC (1990–91) 178, pp. xxiii–xxiv, para. 103. See Ch. 1.

[17] C. Grantham and C. Seymour-Ure, 'Political Consultants', in M. Rush (ed.), *Parliament and Pressure Politics* (Oxford: Clarendon Press, 1990), 69.

written for them by backbench committees. Though backbench committees on both sides of the House are suffering from declining attendance,[18] they remain important as sources of syndicated questions. This was borne out both by our survey data and by independent interviews with backbenchers. The other principal source of questions identified by our respondents was that of party research staff: 3 per cent of respondents often had oral and written questions drafted by them; 40 per cent sometimes had oral and 31 per cent sometimes had written questions drafted by them. These sources emphasize the significance, discussed in Chapter 1, of partisanship in the contemporary House of Commons.

The sources we have identified appear to make up the total. None of our respondents said that they had often had oral questions drafted for them by any other body or bodies, and less than 10 per cent said that they sometimes had written questions drafted for them by other bodies. Two or three MPs sometimes had questions written for them by constituents. Two MPs mentioned whips and front bench teams, thus reinforcing the partisan dimension. No other source was mentioned by more than one Member.

Our findings thus reveal that parliamentary questions emanate from three basic sources: the MP's office (from the MP personally or a research assistant), lobbying organizations and the party (backbench committee, party research staff, minister's PPS). MPs claim to be the principal writers of PQs, a number relying significantly on research assistants, with 'other Members' variously providing them with oral questions and with lobbying bodies variously providing them with written questions. Most Members, though, claim not to use anyone else for drafting oral questions.

Use to which PQs are Put

What do MPs do with the answers to parliamentary questions? For many oral questions, the answer is nothing. Answers to syndicated questions usually achieve their purpose within Question Time itself. They are asked as part of the partisan battle within the

---

[18] See P. Norton, 'The Parliamentary Party', in A. Seldon (ed.), *Conservative Party History* (Oxford: Clarendon Press, forthcoming).

House, the question itself often being drafted on the MP's behalf. Once the Member has used the supplementary to commend or censure the answer given by the minister, the task is complete.

Many of the reasons identified by Members for asking questions, other than for partisan purposes, do not necessarily prompt any further action either. Those that would imply further usage beyond Question Time itself are essentially those requesting information that is difficult to obtain and those tabled on behalf of outside bodies (categories that are not, of course, mutually exclusive). Regardless of the substance of, or overt purpose for tabling, questions, the desire for publicity would also suggest that answers to questions may be utilized for wider purposes.

To get some idea of what MPs do with answers to questions other than those put down for partisan purposes, we focused on written questions. As we have already noted, most respondents— 82 per cent—sent answers to their local papers. (The frequency with which they did so was not specified.) A slightly greater proportion— 85 per cent—said that they variously used written questions as part of a wider campaign. An MP seeking to influence a department on a particular issue will normally use a variety of parliamentary devices, and PQs will constitute part of that activity. Some MPs will focus heavily on written questions, tabling a great many in order to get the department to take notice (and often displaying great procedural ingenuity in ensuring that they are all in order), while others will place the emphasis elsewhere, on letters, EDMs or an adjournment debate. The Procedure Committee in its 1991 Report on Parliamentary Questions distinguished, in effect, between campaigns waged *by* MPs and campaigns waged *through* MPs by particular individuals or bodies, the latter on occasion producing over a period of time a string of badly drafted or disorderly questions; such activity it was keen to discourage.[19]

Not necessarily unrelated to parliamentary campaigns, 62 per cent of respondents also said that they gave the answers to whoever asked them to table the question. Given our earlier figures, this response relates particularly to lobbying organizations. For written questions, as we have seen, just over two-thirds of

---

[19] *Parliamentary Questions*, HC (1990–91) 178, pp. xxiii–xxiv, paras. 101–7. In his evidence to the Committee, the Leader of the House, John MacGregor, also drew attention to the cost of such campaigns.

respondents often or (more likely) sometimes table questions drafted for them by such organizations. A smaller proportion sometimes table questions written for them by other MPs and party research staff. As such, MPs act as conduits, sometimes taking an active interest in the proceedings, at other times—as we have discussed—simply serving as postmen for others.

Most respondents—71 per cent—also said that they variously used answers to written questions in preparing speeches. A member making a partisan speech may seek material that may be used to defend or attack the record of the government or a particular department; a Member speaking to a professional body may seek information to demonstrate knowledge of the subject. Most respondents—74 per cent—also variously table written questions in order to reply to letters. Most letters received by MPs can be, and are, answered through the MP sending the letter to the minister and then writing back enclosing a copy of the minister's reply.[20] Some, though, lend themselves to written questions. Some may be tabled because of a delay or an inadequate response by a minister to a Member's letter. Some of the letters may be from pressure groups, and, as we have seen, may actually request the tabling of a parliamentary question. Most, though, are probably prompted by letters from individual constituents.

A majority of respondents—59 per cent—also reported that they filed the answers to written questions. Our categories are not mutually exclusive, and Members were obviously allowed to give multiple responses. The presumption, therefore, is that this filing took place after some other use had been made of the answers. This presumption is strengthened by the response to the final category. A small proportion of respondents—17 per cent—said that they did 'nothing' with answers to parliamentary questions. This in itself is the most remarkable finding. Two possible explanations suggest themselves. One is that the Member tables questions for the purposes of achieving some publicity, leaving it to the media to pick up on the answers. (It is notable, though possibly coincidental, that the percentage of respondents who do not send PQ answers to the local press is almost identical with the

---

[20] About 250,000 letters a session are now written by MPs to ministers, a significant increase over the past 10 years, and far in excess of the number of written questions tabled in a session. See T. Elms and T. Terry, *Scrutiny of Ministerial Correspondence* (London: Cabinet Office Efficiency Unit, 1990).

proportion who say they do nothing with the answers.) The other is that the MP tables a PQ on behalf of somebody else, and leaves it to that person or organization to scrutinize *Hansard* for the answer, or, alternatively, leaves it to a research assistant to forward the answer. We have some limited evidence that would support the latter explanation.

These responses, again, appear almost exhaustive. Three of the thirty-four MPs in our survey volunteered that they used answers to questions for the purposes of tabling further questions. Two also volunteered that they sent answers to party spokespersons, councillors, local authorities, or candidates, the implication being that this was a fairly regular exercise and that these bodies were not the prompters of the questions. No other usage was reported by two or more MPs.

MPs thus put answers to PQs to a variety of uses. In some cases, their role is fairly passive: just passing the question on to others. In other cases, the answers are important in both the MP's outward-directed—that is, public (speeches) and constituency (letter responding)—activities and his or her more inward-directed role in seeking to influence government departments. In the last category, they are often utilized as part of a wider campaign.

MPs' Assessments

How do MPs themselves assess PQs? Clearly, as we have seen, a significant proportion of MPs in our survey considered that PQs perform 'poorly' a number of the functions they expect them to perform. We explored Members' views of why PQs failed to live up to their expectations. We also explored whether they felt Question Time itself was being abused by some Members and whether it had changed in recent years and, if so, why.

In seeking to identify the causes of dissatisfaction among Members, we asked if there were any rules relating to PQs which prevented them using questions in the way they would like to use them. One of the listed possible responses to the question produced unanimity: every one of our thirty-four respondents said that they were inhibited by the rule restricting questions to matters for which ministers had responsibility. No other reason achieved even majority support. Almost one-third of respondents identified the 'block' that ministers place on questions. Fewer than 20 per cent identified other limitations. In addition to the foregoing responses, 9 per cent of respondents identified other limitations, but none of these was identified by more than two Members.

Though most respondents (56 per cent) favoured some change in the rules governing oral questions and a sizable minority (44 per cent) favoured a change in the rules governing written questions, identifying the need for change proved easier than identifying what that change should be. Ten possible changes were identified, but none was supported by more than three respondents. Indeed, only one (to allow questions on the internal workings of government) was subscribed to by three respondents. Others (such as shortening the fourteen-day advance notice for oral questions, ending blocking answers, and knowing in advance which oral questions were to be grouped by ministers) were identified by two or a single MP. This lack of consensus is also reflected in the letters sent by Members to the Procedure Committee during its inquiry into oral questions and its later inquiry into questions generally, as well as in the survey of MPs reported by Radice, Vallance, and Willis. Of the letters sent to the Procedure Committee during its inquiry into oral questions, a number directed their attention to syndication; otherwise, they were notable for their disparateness in prescription—and occasionally for cancelling one another out. A similar disparateness was apparent in the Radice survey, though here recommendations for change extended beyond the formal rules. They ranged from allowing departmental questions to be tabled to the PM, the PM answering with the help of the relevant minister, to limiting the priority given to the Leader of the Opposition and to Privy Councillors.[21]

Some MPs' criticisms were directed not at the rules and the conventions governing PQs, but rather at fellow Members. Almost one-third of our respondents (principally Conservatives) felt that some Members abused Question Time by making 'poor use' of the occasion. However, more specific criticisms received far less support. Twelve per cent of respondents felt that there was an abuse through easy questions being asked by government sup-

---

[21] L. Radice, E. Vallance, and V. Willis, *Member of Parliament* (London: Macmillan, 1987), 161.

porters. Only 9 per cent actually mentioned planted questions. Other 'abuses' were mentioned by 6 per cent or less of our respondents.

Against the criticisms must be set the positive perceptions that Members generally have of PQs. They feel that PQs fulfil important functions, and are very defensive of their existing rights to utilize them. Questions, declared a member of the shadow Cabinet (Frank Dobson) in 1991, 'are not for the administrative convenience of the Clerks or Ministers—they are a crucial part of the mechanism by which the freely elected members of the legislature attempt to carry out their function of holding the executive to account'.[22] No select committee, he went on to state, should ever contemplate limiting the number of questions for written answer. Respondents in our survey, as we have already recorded, generally found participation in PQs to be helpful or very helpful to their image in their constituencies and their parties (only 15 per cent said it was not helpful, and none said 'not at all helpful'). Just over half our respondents considered oral questions to be helpful in pursuing constituency casework; just over three-quarters (76 per cent) gave a similar response for written questions.

We also found that respondents felt that there had been little change in the attention paid by ministers and civil servants to PQs. Eighty-two per cent said that there had been no change in recent years. The quality of answers, according to Labour backbencher Austin Mitchell, is determined essentially by the particular ministers answering them.

I find that to an extent the way ministers deal with questions bears some relationship to the known characters of the ministers. Some are helpful and see the essential truth that the provision of information informs them and allows effective external audit of their work. Others are just unhelpful, surly clams with devious minds. By their answers shall ye know them.[23]

It is a view borne out by Philip Giddings's study of how departments deal with PQs (Chapter 5) and by a study of the answers that subsequently emerge.

---

[22] *Parliamentary Questions* HC (1990–91) 178, Appendix 10, p. 47.
[23] Ibid., Appendix 21, p. 62.

Conclusion

The picture we get of parliamentary questions on the basis of our survey is, on the whole, a vigorous one. All our respondents employed PQs, most of them in many different ways. Most satisfaction was evinced in regard to their use for self-promotion and for the promotion of constituency interests. Least satisfaction was evinced in regard to the use of PQs for influencing government policy and holding ministers accountable. The major reason for dissatisfaction lies in the rule that restricts questions to those on matters for which the minister is responsible. There was considerable unanimity between respondents of different parties about these assessments, as indeed there is about the reasons for employing PQs.

Though some of our findings may be slightly skewed because of sampling, or in the odd case may not be quite accurate because of respondents' reluctance to admit to (or deny) a particular practice, the other evidence available to us from interviews and from MPs' comments on the public record suggests that the picture we have sketched is a fair one. MPs are conscious of the limitations of PQs, but very protective of their right to use them, viewing them as a central weapon in their parliamentary armoury, and generally being very willing to exploit questions for a variety of purposes. Parliamentary questions constitute essentially a multi-functional, vital mechanism in the relationship between backbench MPs and the executive. That is the view from Westminster.

5

Questions and Departments

Philip Giddings

Ministerial answerability means that parliamentary questions present an organizational challenge to government departments. Questions have to be processed, the relevant information gathered, and draft answers presented to ministers for approval within the timescales required by parliamentary procedures. These timescales may be formidably short, particularly given the number of questions some departments have to deal with. The scale of this organizational task[1] and the way in which it has grown can be seen from a comparison of questions answered in the 1980–81 session with those answered by the six most 'popular' departments (excluding the Prime Minister) in 1988–89, shown in Table 5.1.

Table 5.1. *Answers given by selected departments, 1980–81 and 1988–89*

Depart- ment	Answers (1980–81)		Answers (1988–89)		Index
	Number	%	Number	%	
DHSS	3,475	21.3	7,421	42.4	199
Home	2,277	13.97	3,826	21.86	156
DTI	2,878	17.7	2,587	14.8	84
DoE	2,464	15.1	5,297	30.3	201
DEmp	2,334	14.3	3,347	19.1	134
MoD	1,439	8.8	3,783	21.6	245

Note: Figures in this table—and the succeeding paragraph—were extracted from the POLIS database.

---

[1] See above, Table 2.1. See also *Parliamentary Questions*, HC (1990–91) 178, Appendix 1.

The total number of PQs answered increased from an average of 207 a day in 1980–81 to nearly 304 a day in 1988–89, a figure which conceals the full extent of the growth as, since mid-1984, unreached 'open' questions to the Prime Minister have not been included. Setting aside the Prime Minister, the Department of Health and Social Security (DHSS), the Department of the Environment (DoE), and the Ministry of Agriculture, Fisheries, and Food (MAFF) were answering twice as many questions per day in 1988–89 as they were in 1980–81, the Ministry of Defence (MoD) nearly two and a half times as many. Only the Department of Trade and Industry (DTI) showed a decline; but then the DTI's functions at the end of the decade were notably different from those in 1980–81. And by 1988–89 the DoE was handling over thirty PQs a day, the Home Office and MoD about twenty-two. If the Department of Health (DoH) and the Department of Social Security (DSS) figures are combined for 1988–89, the DHSS equivalent was over forty-two questions a day. At the other end of the scale, in 1988–89 the Department of Energy (DEn) was handling only eight PQs a day, the Northern Ireland Office under nine, and the Welsh Office just over ten. Necessarily such figures reflect the ebb and flow of parliamentary interest as the topicality of issues varies: salmonella and BSE ('mad cow disease') contributed to the growth in MAFF questions, the community charge to those to DoE, and the Education Reform Act to those to the Department of Education and Science (DES).

Organizing Answers

The need to process such numbers of questions within the prescribed timescales has, not surprisingly, produced a similarity of organizational pattern across Whitehall, with minor variations reflecting the different sizes of departments.[2] The essence of this organizational task is the gathering from within the department of the required information and analysis, and the drafting of the results in a form suitable for approval by ministers as a parliamentary

---

[2] The information in this chapter is based on material supplied by the various government departments, largely through interviews with their Parliamentary Clerks, except where other sources are cited. The author is particularly grateful to those Parliamentary Clerks who gave so generously of their time in interviews in the spring and summer of 1990.

answer, all in the timescale set by parliamentary procedures. For this purpose, departments have established a Parliamentary Unit, usually within the Secretary of State's private office, to co-ordinate the process. The Unit will identify (from the Order Paper) and sort the department's questions, allocate them to the appropriate divisions for the production of draft answers, and arrange for the submission of drafts to ministers at the appropriate time. The Unit is headed by the department's Parliamentary Clerk, who is usually a senior or higher executive officer, but in a few of the larger departments may be a Grade 5. Most of the administrative functions relating to questions are usually delegated to junior staff working in the Parliamentary Unit. The Unit is also responsible for dealing with the parliamentary aspects of the department's legislation, adjournments, and most other parliamentary business apart from liaison with the departmentally related select committee, which is often organized separately.

To take the stages of this process in turn: *for questions for written answer*, on receipt of the Order Paper, the department's questions have to be identified. This is usually relatively straightforward, but there are always some questions which would, in the view of departmental officials, be more appropriately answered by a department other than that to which they have been directed. Transfers are accordingly negotiated between departments, usually by their Parliamentary Clerks, but occasionally by divisions directly. Areas of particular difficulty potentially are functions which are dispersed amongst the territorial departments of state, such as schools, agriculture, and hospitals. Parliamentary Clerks will also be concerned at this initial stage to identify questions to other ministers (and in particular the Prime Minister) in which their department might have an interest and for which briefing may be required.

Once the questions have been satisfactorily identified, the Parliamentary Clerk will prepare an allocation of them to ministers (for answer) and to officials (for drafting). Most departments now have a functional delegation of responsibilities by the Secretary of State to junior ministers, and in normal circumstances questions will be allocated accordingly, unless the Secretary of State directs otherwise. The Parliamentary Clerk will also allocate questions to the appropriate part of the department (usually, but not invariably, a division) for the preparation of a

submission to ministers by a specified date—for priority written
questions often within two (now three) working days, unless a
holding answer has to be given, which departments say they seek
to avoid if at all possible.

In some departments, the Parliamentary Unit may provide
briefing for officials in divisions on the MP asking the question,
utilizing reference works like *Dod's Parliamentary Companion*
and also noting the MP's interests as reflected in his other
parliamentary activities. But the primary task of gathering and
analysing the relevant information and drafting an answer is the
responsibility of the division. Depending on the nature of the
question and the degree of judgement required, preparation of the
initial draft may be delegated within the division to a Grade 7, a
senior of higher executive officer, or even an executive officer if
the requirement is for straightforward information. But the draft
will always need to be approved—'signed off'—by the divisional
head, usually a Grade 5 but in some departments a Grade 3,
before being dispatched to the Parliamentary Clerk for submission
to the minister. The Parliamentary Clerk customarily checks the
draft for the appropriate parliamentary terminology and known
ministerial preferences on style and then submits the draft answers
for ministerial approval in the overnight or weekend box.
Ministers are, of course, free to accept, reject, question, or amend
drafts so submitted. However, once a department has got to know
its minister's mind, the proportion of draft answers needing
revision at this stage should be small. Once approved by the
minister, the answer will be transmitted to the House by the
Parliamentary Clerk. In general outline, that is the process for
dealing with questions for written answer, which are the vast
majority.

Briefing Ministers

How to produce a good answer? Draftsmanship of this kind is
reputed to be one of the principal skills of the British higher civil
service. The art of producing succinct, accurate answers which
'give nothing away' is both highly prized and indicative of the
adversarial political culture which has traditionally underlain the
procedure. Brevity and accuracy are certainly deemed important—

though the former marginally less so for written answers. In accordance with the general ethos of the civil service, most departments assume that a civil servant will learn the necessary skills 'on the job'. Nevertheless, as we shall see, not all parts of a department have a significant exposure to parliamentary interest. Accordingly, in most departments the Parliamentary Unit provides initial guidance and assistance when needed, particularly in the subtleties of parliamentary terminology. The Foreign and Common-wealth Office has a briefing session for all new entrants, plus a 'day in Parliament' course for senior officials and a half-day parliamentary course for desk officers. Several departments—for example, the Home Office—provide notes of guidance for officials who have to draft answers. Emphasis is laid on the need for answers to be brief and to the point, as far as possible limited to facts of particular significance. For oral questions it is important for ministers to be able to absorb material easily at a glance when under pressure in the House.

Oral questions require special treatment. The manner in which ministers prepare for Question Time, and in particular equip themselves to deal with supplementaries, varies a good deal. In one sense the timetable is predictable. The department's turn comes at known and regular intervals, and Members are effectively required to give ten sitting days' notice. As we have seen in Chapter 2, under the procedures in operation until November 1990, if a Member found that a proposed oral question came out low in the shuffle, he or she could either unstar or withdraw it, thereby enabling the Member to remain within the quota and table further questions to other ministers. Thus, not all questions initially starred remained so.

Hence, prior to the 1990–91 session, there was a marked disparity between the numbers of oral questions put down and the number reached (a disparity which affected the larger departments to a greater extent). This meant that departments had to make a judgement as to the number of questions on which full briefing should be provided. In practice, it was generally the top twenty-five or thirty on the Order Paper, which left a reasonable margin for late withdrawals and absences.

However, at the end of the 1989–90 session[3] the House agreed

---

[3] *HC Deb.* (1989–90) 178, col. 727.

limitations on the number of oral questions which would be printed on the Order Paper—set now at a maximum of forty for those departments which answer for the full Question Time, thirty for those departments answering until 3.10 or 3.15 p.m., and for the Prime Minister (and the smaller departments which answer for only 5 or 10 minutes) a maximum of ten. A consequence of these changes is that much of the uncertainty as to which questions will be reached has been removed and the departments can prepare their briefings accordingly.

Departments also have to brief their ministers to respond to anticipated supplementaries. The growth in the number of less specific and 'open' original questions has had an inevitable effect upon this process of ministerial preparation. The pattern of preparation varies according to departmental and ministerial preferences, as the following examples of different types of department, some experiencing changes of minister, illustrates.

One form is typified by the *Ministry of Agriculture, Fisheries and Food*. Questions put down for oral answer—until the changes in procedure introduced at the beginning of the 1990–91 session, these normally numbered about 100—are allocated to divisions in the normal way. The Parliamentary Clerk drafts an allocation of these questions to the department's ministers for approval by the minister himself. Draft answers from divisions are submitted to the relevant ministers for approval the weekend before the day for answer. (Prior to the November 1990 changes the top twenty on the list also went to the minister.) Briefing material for dealing with supplementaries is attached for all questions. After the weekend, drafts are returned by ministers with suggested amendments, which will need to be cleared with the relevant divisions. This process should produce a complete set of agreed answers (only the top twenty questions prior to November 1990), which are considered by MAFF ministers collectively the day before the questions are due to be answered. At this collective meeting are the Permanent Secretary, the minister's Parliamentary Private Secretary, the minister's special adviser, and an official from Central Office. As a result of that meeting, which is primarily concerned with presentational and political issues rather than substance, it would not be unusual for about a quarter of the draft answers to require substantial amendment—which would again have to be cleared with the divisions.

A variant of this procedure is operated by what is now the *Department for Education*. After receiving the drafts in the weekend boxes, each minister holds separate briefings, usually involving the Grade 5 and Grade 7 civil servants from the relevant branches and occasionally the Grade 3 too. When Kenneth Baker was Secretary of State, this was followed later by a collective briefing, attended by the Secretary of State, other ministers, the Permanent Secretary, Deputy Secretaries, the Senior HMI, the Chief Information Officer and Press Office, the Secretary of State's special adviser, the Parliamentary Private Secretary, the Principal Private Secretary, and the Parliamentary Clerk. And on question day itself Mr Baker held a 'PQ lunch briefing'. However, these procedures were abandoned after John MacGregor became Secretary of State, illustrating the way in which preparation arrangements are adapted to suit the personal preferences of ministers.

For the *Department of the Environment*, with its extensive responsibilities, Question Time lasts the full 'hour'. Prior to the procedural changes of November 1990, more than 150 questions would appear on the Order Paper, and the department would focus its prime attention on the top thirty. The allocation of that top thirty to ministers was done by the Secretary of State's private office, the remainder being allocated by the Parliamentary Clerk. Draft answers with full briefing used to be required for a ministerial meeting one week before answer day. This meeting comprised all ministers, the Parliamentary Private Secretaries, the private secretaries, and special advisers—essentially a political forum. It could result in requests for additional briefing, commissioned by Private Office direct from the relevant Grade 3 civil servants. However, when Chris Patten became Secretary of State, he discontinued the practice; rather than having a meeting specifically to discuss PQs, that business was absorbed into the regular round of ministerial meetings in the department. This arrangement was continued under Michael Heseltine.

For the *Department of Trade and Industry* the Parliamentary Clerk prepares the ministerial allocation of questions for the Secretary of State's approval on the day they appear on the Order Paper which is Thursday. Questions are then allocated to divisions for return by the following Tuesday. On the subsequent Thursday all draft answers (forty under the procedures operated since

November 1990) and supplementary briefing are reviewed at a meeting comprising all ministers, Parliamentary Private Secretaries, Central Office staff, senior officials, and the Parliamentary Clerk, who is responsible for commissioning any further briefing which may be required. In the days before answer day, ministers will hold their own briefing meetings with officials on individual questions.

In the *Foreign and Commonwealth Office* a 'PQ round-up meeting' is held to prepare for answer day, comprising all ministers, special advisers, and Parliamentary Private Secretaries. By contrast, the *Department of Health* provides oral briefings for its ministers individually at the request of Private Office, usually the day before answers are to be given. This department has also recently introduced a meeting one week before Question Time at which all ministers, Parliamentary Private Secretaries, special advisers, and senior officials discuss outline briefing on the first seventeen questions. This meeting gives a steer to the preparation of full briefing. In the Home Office and the Foreign and Commonwealth Office, on the other hand, ministers receive oral briefing on questions only if they request it, though ministers, Parliamentary Private Secretaries, the whip, and special advisers meet a couple of days before answer day to consider the questions which are likely to be reached.

Departmental practice has also varied as to the form of written briefing provided to ministers for oral answers. Traditionally, departments provided a draft answer to the original question, together with draft answers to anticipated supplementaries and, where appropriate, background briefing. Some departments still follow this practice, relying on the political awareness of officials to identify the key issues likely to be raised to provide succinct, clear notes which ministers can absorb at a glance when under pressure in the House. However, other departments have found that this format did not really meet ministerial needs, particularly in an era of more generalized or open questions.

To cope with this, in 1986 the then Chancellor of the Exchequer Nigel Lawson introduced a 'bull point' format instead of anticipated supplementary questions and answers: bull points, 'elephant traps', and key figures were required, all on one page. John Moore, Mr Lawson's Financial Secretary, introduced this format to the DHSS when he was appointed Secretary of State for Social

Services, with the addition that the department provided notes for supplementaries as well as key points. This system has been continued by his successors in both the DoH and the DSS, and the key points system, or something like it, has been adopted by a growing number of departments, reflecting the greater emphasis on presentation.

The problem of anticipating supplementaries is acute for the *Prime Minister's Office*, given the predominance of the open question. Some MPs—mostly, but not only, government supporters—give No. 10 advance notice of their supplementary. The PM's office may also suggest 'friendly' supplementaries to government supporters. However, it is difficult for officials to predict which MPs will be called by the Speaker to ask supplementaries. Prior to the procedural changes introduced in November 1990, No. 10 would treat the top ten questions (so in practice the top ten questioners) as 'possibles', although in Mrs Thatcher's incumbency it was unusual for more than eight to be reached. Mr Major's answering style is considerably briefer than Mrs Thatcher's, so this may require a revision of the numbers. While known constituency or political interests of MPs are not difficult to identify (though again it is not known which MPs will be called), No. 10 has really to rely on identifying topical subjects from the newspapers, broadcasting media, recently published reports, and so on, as likely sources of supplementaries. Thus the Prime Minister will be provided with briefing on between fifteen and thirty topical subjects, with material obtained from departments where relevant. Again, the Prime Minister's ability to absorb material has to be kept in mind. Mrs Thatcher's practice was to go through the press and media reports early in the morning—not only for PQ purposes—and then to be briefed by her private secretaries over lunch.

The Private Notice Question

Private Notice Questions, as we have seen (Chapter 3), set a particular challenge for departments because of the very short period of time available for preparing an answer.[4] When the Table

---

[4] This account is based on interviews with Parliamentary Clerks.

Office has alerted the department that a PNQ has been put down, the Parliamentary Clerk has to provide background briefing from the department, which is before the Speaker when she decides whether the PNQ will be allowed. The Speaker makes this decision at her midday conference, taking into account the degree of urgency of the question and the availability of other parliamentary opportunities for raising it, as well as the department's background briefing. In the meantime the Parliamentary Clerk will have alerted his minister's private office and the relevant divisions in his department. The Speaker's decision is communicated to the Parliamentary Clerk by about 12.30 p.m. If the question is allowed, the answer is therefore due in three hours, at the end of normal questions. Most departments seek to provide their minister with a written brief within an hour, followed by such oral briefing as is required. This is obviously a very short timescale.

Although some departments hardly ever have a PNQ, others clearly believe they are a growth industry. The opposition's campaigns on food safety led to a substantial number of applications for PNQs to MAFF in the period from November 1988 to February 1990, although only four of these were allowed. Necessarily, departments like Transport and Environment, with their responsibility for government responses to accidents and emergencies, are likely to figure more prominently, as in the first three months of the 1989–90 session, although only two PNQs were allowed. Not surprisingly in view of the unpredictability of world events, the FCO has been a prime target, as in the long session of 1987–88, when nine were allowed, and in the 1989–90 session, when six were allowed.

There have been marked variations in the numbers of PNQs allowed. Table 2.1 reveals the extent of that variation. As Borthwick notes, there is a difference—the full extent of which is not known—between the number of applications made and the number allowed.[5] In the 1980s, it is understood that the proportion allowed averaged about one in eight varying from a high of about one in five in the most 'successful' session to about one in thirteen in the least 'successful'.

It is also the case that departmental responses vary: sometimes

[5] See above, Ch 3, p. 99.

the threat of a PNQ will prompt a department to 'volunteer' a statement or seek a question already on the Order Paper from a government backbencher which can be answered 'at the end of questions'. This enables the government to recover some of the initiative. Ultimately, it is a matter for the Speaker, in the light of the factual briefing from the department (the quality of which inevitably varies), to determine whether a PNQ is allowed.

Ministerial Responses: To Exploit, to Inform or to Block?

It would be a mistake to assume that departments (and their ministers) are merely passive players in the business of parliamentary questions, responding only to what opposition MPs or their own backbenchers choose to ask. Ministers, with the advice of their officials, decide what kind of answers are to be given. They have a choice: they can use the question to obtain good publicity and political credit for the department; they can simply give the information sought or the assurance requested; or, if the subject matter is politically embarrassing, a minimal answer may be given, perhaps amounting to a non-answer—'No, madam'.

Questions can be exploited in a number of ways. Ministers and their departments are very well aware of the publicity value of the parliamentary process and the opportunity it presents for good public relations. But they are also acutely conscious that parliamentary time is a precious commodity, a scarce resource the allocation of which can cause interdepartmental strife. A written answer to a parliamentary question is, therefore, a useful way of making an announcement: it consumes no parliamentary time and provides no immediate opportunity for cross-examination of ministers by MPs, critical or otherwise—in marked contrast to an oral statement at the end of Question Time, which can often produce up to forty-five minutes of questions. In practice, therefore, departments—via the Parliamentary Private Secretary and/or the whips—will arrange for a suitable question to be asked so that the prepared announcement can be made in the form of a written answer.[6] (An example would appear to be the Minister of Agriculture's statement in reply to a question from Conservative

---

[6] This account is based on interviews in government departments.

backbencher Nicholas Bennett on 27 April 1989, proposing a ban on the retail sale of cracked eggs as part of the response to the Agriculture Committee's report on salmonella.[7]) Timing is important here if the department is anxious to obtain media coverage of the announcement. Ministers are responsible primarily to Parliament, and risk criticism from MPs if they make announcements in press conferences in advance of statements in the House of Commons.

Although 'arranged questions' are a well-known feature of the present system, there is some 'tongue in cheek' sensitivity on the subject which makes it difficult to estimate the scale of the practice. Similarly, as we have seen, it is known that not all 'non-arranged' questions originate with the MP who puts them down. Officials in departments are convinced that a proportion of questions originate from MPs' staff, and particularly their research assistants, a view held by many in the House[8] and one for which Mark Franklin and Philip Norton (see Chapter 4) have now provided some empirical support.

It is important not to confuse the practice of 'arranged' written questions with the extensive use of syndicated or inspired oral questions (see Chapter 2).[9] This practice of syndication reflects the view of many Members (but not all) that oral questions are more about political warfare than the obtaining of information—witness the results of the survey detailed in the previous chapter and the questions from David Winnick and Graham Allen in the Procedure Committee's inquiry.[10] Syndication is seen as one more weapon for use in that warfare.

While the 'political warfare' view might not be accepted by all Members, it is widely accepted that ministers find substantial advantages for themselves in oral questions. Leader of the House John MacGregor, with previous experience in the Treasury, the DES, and MAFF, put it like this:

It does enable the ministerial policy position to be put over and to get publicity for some issues which are important to get publicity for. It does actually also have an internal effect sometimes . . oral and written questions sometimes draw to the attention of a Minister an aspect of

---

[7] *HC Deb.* (1988–89) 151, col. 679w.
[8] See above, Ch. 2, and *Parliamentary Questions*, HC (1990–91) 178, p. xix, paras. 76–83.   [9] Ibid., Appendix 3.   [10] Ibid., qs. 35 and 43.

policy, or of the working of his Department with which he was not familiar, and through the briefing that he gets to pursue issues on that particular aspect of policy, and that does sometimes lead to changes.[11]

However, it is also clear that there are many occasions when questions raise matters which are embarrassing to ministers and their departments, and then their response is much less forthcoming. A variety of options is available to ministers in such situations. Perhaps the first is to try to avoid answering the question at all, exploiting the rules of order[12] which require that a question relate to a matter for which a minister is responsible and that it not be fully covered by an answer (or, more significantly in this context, a refusal to answer) given in the same session. As ministers themselves decide how to answer questions, the opportunity exists for them to block questions on topics by an initial answer to the effect that 'it is not the practice to disclose information of this kind'. Questions about the security services are a well-known specific example of this practice. Ministers may also decline to provide information by use of formulas such as that the information is 'not held centrally', can 'only be provided at disproportionate cost' (discussed below), or 'is a matter for some "arms length" body', such as a health authority, a nationalized industry, one of the new regulatory bodies (OFTEL, OFGAS, OFWAT, and so on), or the chief executive of a 'Next Steps' agency.

Once such an answer is given, further questions are blocked, and the Table Office has to decline to accept them. This can be very frustrating to Members, and puts the Table Office in the position of appearing to protect the government by refusing a question.[13] Frustration is intensified by the fact that ministerial practice (and hence the application of blocks) is inconsistent. In his evidence to the Select Committee the Principal Clerk of the Table Office cited four questions in three days from the same MP to the Secretary of State for Wales concerning the Powys Health Authority, two of which received substantive answers on matters of some detail (the replacement of a washing machine on a particular ward and the cost of replacement furniture for a board room) while the other two, on matters of similar detail received the answer 'This is a matter for Powys Health Authority'.[14] The

[11] Ibid., q. 59.
[13] Ibid., Evidence, p. 6.
[12] Ibid., Evidence, pp. 11–15.
[14] Ibid., Appendix 1, Annex A.

Principal Clerk also cited similar inconsistent answers from the Home Office on potential deportees on 24 January.[15] Such examples show that ministers are adept at exploiting the rules to their own advantage. Equally, some Members seek to get round the rules by raising matters which have been subjected to a block as a supplementary to an oral question (often an 'open' one) when the Speaker is in practice unable to enforce the admissibility rules so strictly and ministers are reluctant to refuse an answer.[16]

Nevertheless, generally speaking, ministers prefer to answer if they can—not least because it looks better from a public relations viewpoint, and, as with requests for credit, a refusal may offend. However, answering questions has resource implications of which ministers and officials have to be aware. 'Excessive or disproportionate cost' is, as we have seen, available as a reason for not supplying a substantive answer. For this purpose, the Treasury circulates a guide-line figure as the trigger for considering whether the excessive cost answer should be given.[17] The methodology used in the Treasury estimate was questioned by the Procedure Committee in its recent report, which reasserted that cost considerations, while important, cannot be allowed to predominate.[18] It is, nevertheless, up to ministers to decide whether the 'disproportionate cost' answer should be given. While in many cases ministers are in fact anxious to reply if the answer can be interpreted favourably to their department, Members continue to be frustrated by the number of occasions on which disproportionate cost is cited as the reason for not giving a substantive answer.

In November 1989 Mark Fisher, Labour's shadow Minister for the Arts, frustrated by ministers apparently ducking politically embarrassing written questions by citing 'disproportionate cost' or 'information not held centrally', probed this whole area with a series of questions to departments.[19] He sought information about the number of occasions a Secretary of State had refused to answer a question, the number of times a Secretary of State had declined to give a substantive answer on certain specified grounds (that the information available was not separately recorded, or not recorded

[15] Ibid., Appendix 1, Annex B.
[16] See e.g. ibid., Appendix 12.
[17] Interviews in government departments. At the time of the interviews, it was £250. It has since been increased; see below and *HC Deb.* (1990–91) 201, col. 546w.
[18] *Parliamentary Questions*, HC (1990–91) 178, p. xvii, paras. 67 and 68.
[19] Letter to author.

centrally, or not recorded in government statistics, or could only be provided at disproportionate cost), and the cost of answering a parliamentary question. Such 'round robin' questions occasion consultation between departments as to how best to handle them without causing mutual embarrassment; this usually produces similar rather than uniform answers, as was the case on this occasion.

To the first question about refusals to answer, most departments simply answered 'none'. Three (Education and Science,[20] Energy,[21] and Environment[22]) added as a qualification 'except on grounds of disproportionate cost'. The Department of Health set out five reasons why MPs would normally be 'referred to the responsible health or local authority' for the appropriate information.[23] The Northern Ireland Office reported fifteen refusals, presumably reflecting the security situation there.[24]

To Mr Fisher's probing of the grounds for a non-substantive reply, most departments responded that the information requested was itself either 'not readily available' (MAFF[25]) or could only be produced at disproportionate cost. The DSS added that 'disproportionate cost' had been cited in forty-five instances, which constituted less than 2 per cent of the questions answered in the period concerned.[26] The Department of Employment pointed out that 'to provide the information in the form requested would involve manual scrutiny of some 3,000 replies to parliamentary questions'.[27] However, five departments did provide a substantive answer to this part of the question: Trade and Industry,[28] the Scottish Office,[29] the Attorney-General,[30] the Northern Ireland Office,[31] and Health—the last referring to the first quarter of the session which was considered representative.[32]

On the cost of answering questions, all departments said that information was either not held or could only be ascertained at disproportionate cost—except the Treasury[33] and the Office of Arts and Libraries,[34] which offered figures based on estimates of the average cost (£90 for an oral question, £54 for a written one).

[20] *HC Deb.* (1989–90) 160, cols. 236–7w.
[21] Ibid., cols. 139–40w.
[22] Ibid., col. 132w.
[23] Ibid., cols. 195–6w.
[24] Ibid., col. 158w.
[25] Ibid., cols. 184–5w.
[26] Ibid., col. 168w.
[27] Ibid., cols. 144–5w.
[28] Ibid., col. 114w.
[29] Ibid., col. 174w.
[30] Ibid., col. 117w.
[31] Ibid., col. 158w.
[32] Ibid., cols. 195–6w.
[33] Ibid., col. 489w.
[34] Ibid., col. 172w.

In Chapter 3 Borthwick identifies a central difficulty in producing a 'true' figure for the costs to departments of answering PQs: the fact that questions are but one part of the whole system of parliamentary accountability (as can be seen from the functions of departments' Parliamentary Units). Even if directly related costs, such as a proportion of the running costs of a department's Parliamentary Unit, could be sensibly attributed to questions, the costs in divisions, private offices, and regions would be very difficult to identify with any degree of consistency and reliability. One does have to be careful here, however, since if there is no way of estimating costs accurately, it is hard to justify the assertion that the cost of answering a particular PQ would be excessive or disproportionate. The estimates which are used (as in the Arts Office reply) are therefore based on assumptions about the approximate amount of divisional staff time spent on drafting the typical answer. Nor is it clear how one would estimate the value of any 'benefit', to which the cost of providing an answer would also need to be related.

In practice, however, such difficulties are rather theoretical. If a written PQ arrives which appears likely to involve an excessive amount of work, the department receiving it will prepare an estimate of the time and grades of staff needed to answer it. The cost would then be calculated from this at standard salary rates for the staff involved. The resultant cost would then be compared with the 'tripwire' level (£400 in 1992) for disproportionate costs. If the computed cost exceeds that level, the matter would be brought to the attention of the minister, who has discretion to override the cost consideration if he considers the answer is of particular importance. Thus, in the end, it is the minister who decides the question of disproportionate costs. This can mean that ministers will decide, on political grounds, to incur expenditure considerably in excess of the 'tripwire' level in order to present the government's case.

The Impact upon Departments

Costs are only one feature of the impact of parliamentary questions upon governing departments. Because of the priority given to parliamentary work, particularly given the tight deadlines for producing answers to PQs, the need to draft such answers and prepare ministerial briefs is inevitably a distraction from a department's other work. Although we customarily think in terms of 'a department' as a unit, all are in fact subdivided into branches or divisions or sections. Just as the incidence of questions varies between departments, so within departments there is considerable variation between divisions, with some—particularly policy divisions—exciting much more parliamentary interest than others. Much, of course, turns on current events; the salmonella and BSE food scares, the Lockerbie and Piper Alpha disasters, the NHS Review, and the community charge stimulate MPs' interest. Legislating does so too—witness the 1988 Education Reform Act. MPs have a particular concern for the affairs of their constituencies, so those parts of departments dealing with, for example, the opening and closing of schools, hospitals, railway lines, roads, or other public services can expect to receive particular attention. The result is that the incidence of PQs within departments is disproportionate, and the load upon particular sections at times of high parliamentary concern can be very heavy indeed.

We can illustrate this with an analysis of questions from three rather different departments: Education, Energy, and Health. The *Department of Education and Science* in 1990 was organized into sixteen branches. Of the 204 questions answered by the department in May 1990, the four schools branches were responsible for exactly half, and the four branches dealing with further and higher education and science for nearly a quarter (22.5 per cent). By contrast, one branch (architects and buildings) answered no questions, and three others (HMI support, establishment, and the secretariat) dealt with seven between them. Most DES branches are further subdivided into divisions—forty-two in all. Four divisions answered nearly a quarter (23 per cent) of all the DES questions that month—all on schools. Another quarter were answered by four other divisions (two science, one statistics, and one finance). Thus 98 (48 per cent) of the department's 204 questions in May 1990 were the responsibility of eight of the Department's forty-two divisions.

A similar concentration can be seen with the former *Department of Energy*, which answered 1,711 questions in the 1988–89 session. Of these, 505 (30 per cent) were on electricity, and 374 (22 per cent) on atomic energy. Thus three (electricity has two) of the department's thirteen divisions were responsible for over half its answers. A further three divisions (coal, energy technology, and energy efficiency) takes the proportion up to 80 per cent.

For the *Department of Health*, the 1989–90 session was dominated by four issues: the winter ambulance strike, the NHS Review, the new contract for GPs, and NHS finance. Of the 633 oral answers given by the department in the session, 99 were on the NHS Review, 52 on doctors, 41 on NHS finance, and 32 on the accident and emergency services—25 of them in the December to February period. Thus those four issues accounted for 35 per cent of the department's oral answers. (The DoH analysis is based on forty-two key 'words'.) For the department's questions as a whole, totalling 3,758 in the session, the NHS Review is still the front-runner, with doctors (174), NHS finance (180), and the accident and emergency services (162) also prominent. Equally prominent were questions about disability (185, but only 28 asked orally), children (151), hospitals (165), and NHS management (148), those eight issues accounting for just over a third (34 per cent) of the department's answers.

Those analyses demonstrate—not surprisingly—how the incidence of questions reflects the public visibility of areas of policy and administration. A similar feature is evident with ministerial correspondence. In the last two months of 1988 the Department of Health dealt with just over 2,000 items of ministerial correspondence, 287 a week. The most 'popular' issues raised were nurses' and midwives' pay (269 and 150) and dental and eye charges (94 and 87). In the equivalent period in 1989 the total correspondence load had almost doubled to 3,812 items, 545 per week, and two items dwarfed all others; the NHS Review (555) and the ambulance men's pay dispute (417). Both showed how an issue can 'take off'. In the last week of October 1989 ambulance men's pay was the subject of just eleven letters requiring ministerial answer; by the end of November it had risen to ninety per week, and it continued at that level until the end of January. By early March it had subsided to under thirty a week. Over the same period PQs showed a similar pattern: nine in November, twenty-three in December, sixty-two in January, thirty-two in February. The NHS Review has seen more sustained, and substantial, interest. From four correspondents in the last week of February 1989, volume increased to a peak of 338 a week at the end of April, there being more than 1,100 letters about the review requiring ministerial answer that month. By February 1990 this had dropped to under sixty a week, far from insubstantial. By July the number was down to twenty-nine. In that month there were fifty-one PQs on the subject.

For most MPs, writing to ministers is, as we have seen (Chapter 4), the preferred way of dealing with constituency cases. MPs are thus substantial contributors to the load of ministerial correspondence, which continues to grow apace much as PQs have done. The Department of Energy in 1990 averaged 65 letters a week from MPs, in addition to its weekly average of 52 PQs. The Treasury receives about 800 letters from MPs each month, mostly on constituency cases or lobbying for particular interests. This compares with about 500 PQs and 1,400 letters from members of the public. The Department of Social Security receives over 330 letters per (sitting) week from MPs, compared with just over 80 PQs. For some departments the load of such correspondence is very substantial and rapidly increasing. The Department of the Environment dealt with over 4,150 items of ministerial correspondence in February 1990, compared with its 1985 monthly average of 2,270. The Department of Transport's load increased by one-third between 1984 and 1989, exceeding 18,000 items in the latter year. Such figures do *not* include *all* letters from members of the public, for which many departments do not keep statistics. However, the Foreign and Commonwealth Office did record that it received over 15,000 letters in the two months in 1989 following a television programme about Cambodia. And in that year the FCO dealt with about 3,000 PQs (including both Commons and Lords, oral and written, PNQs and answers provided for Prime Minister's questions) more than 16,000 letters from MPs, and more than 8,500 other 'ministerial letters'.[35]

Two Case Studies

Such figures draw attention to the danger of seeing parliamentary questions in isolation. Just as for MPs they are but one option in an

---

[35] These data, and other information in this section, have been provided by the departments' Parliamentary Clerks.

array of parliamentary and political devices, so for departments they are but one source of external stimulus, albeit one that requires a particular, formal, and rapid public response. MPs concerned about an issue or wishing to make a political point or simply advertise their own activity can put down a parliamentary question; they can also, as noted in the preceding chapter, exploit other procedures like adjournment debates, Ten Minute Rule Bills, Early Day Motions, and so on; or they can write to ministers or approach them personally. Ministers and officials in departments will see parliamentary questions as one of a series of indicators of parliamentary and public concern. Illustrations of this are the salmonella and BSE affairs.

The Salmonella Affair

The salmonella affair took off in parliamentary terms with Mrs Edwina Currie's statement to a television news reporter on 3 December 1988 about the incidence of salmonella in eggs. Prior to that date there had been *relatively* little interest in the subject in the House of Commons—just one oral and six written questions in the thirteen months from the end of October 1987 to the beginning of December 1988.[36] As it happened, MAFF oral questions had been taken in the week preceding Mrs Currie's interview, and in that question session the issue of salmonella was raised only in one supplementary, though two questions on which it might have been raised (one on food poisoning, the other on ministerial meetings with the British Veterinary Association) were not reached.[37] And on 2 December MAFF answered two written questions on food safety, one of which referred to the withdrawal of funding by the AFRC from a research project in Bristol which dealt with salmonella.[38]

However, this low level of interest was transformed by Mrs Currie's statement to the TV news interviewer. On the next sitting day (Monday 5 December) Sir Hal Miller had a Private Notice Question to the Health Secretary allowed,[39] and this was the beginning of a parliamentary storm which drove Mrs Currie from office. In the three months from December 1988 to February 1989,

---

[36] Information provided by POLIS.
[37] *HC Deb.* (1988–89) 142, cols. 866, 319w, and 321w.
[38] Ibid., col. 428w.   [39] *HC Deb.* (1988–89) 143 cols. 19–24.

190 written questions were answered,[40] mostly by MAFF or the Health Department, but some also by the Scottish and Welsh Offices and the Prime Minister. The issue featured strongly at MAFF oral questions on 19 January (a month after Mrs Currie's resignation), when twelve Members referred to it,[41] and another eleven members had put down questions which were not reached.[42] But for the NHS Review White Paper, the issue would probably have surfaced also at Health question time on 24 January or 21 February; but in fact it was not mentioned at all then, and only featured in one supplementary during Health questions on 13 December,[43] a few days before Mrs Currie resigned.

Once the issue had broken in Parliament, the political pressure was unrelenting. Apart from daily written questions probing all aspects of the department's response to the salmonella threat, a senior Conservative backbencher (Robin Maxwell-Hyslop) raised the issue at Prime Minister's questions as early as 6 December (the Tuesday after Mrs Currie's TV 'gaffe'),[44] and the following week an officer of the Tory backbench agriculture committee (Paul Marland) pressed the Prime Minister to dismiss Mrs Currie.[45] The impact upon the egg industry of Mrs Currie's statement (and other publicity about the salmonella threat) led to considerable pressure on MAFF to take action in the form of market support or compensation. Commons business was repeatedly interrupted on Friday 16 December (the day of Mrs Currie's resignation) as MPs pressed for a statement on details of a rumoured package of measures.[46] In the end, the Minister of Agriculture did make an interim statement at 2.30 p.m., and faced forty minutes of questions from twenty-five Members.[47] The Minister's full statement with details of a market support package the following Monday produced a further period of sustained questioning from twenty-two Members.[48] Later that day Sir Hal Miller raised the issue again on the Consolidated Fund Bill,[49] and Sir Peter Emery also raised it in the debate on the Christmas adjournment motion.[50]

[40] Information provided by POLIS.
[41] *HC Deb.* (1988–89) 145, cols. 467–9, 473–5.
[42] But they did receive written answers (ibid., cols. 308–10w).
[43] *HC Deb.* (1988–89) 143, col. 766. [44] Ibid., cols. 168–9.
[45] Ibid., cols. 775–6. [46] Ibid., cols. 1207, 1227–31, 1236–7.
[47] Ibid., cols. 1276–86. [48] *HC Deb.* (1988–89) 144, cols. 21–33.
[49] Ibid., cols. 167–70. [50] Ibid., col. 72.

Thus in December, after Mrs Currie's TV statement, the pressure on MAFF from MPs was intense; and it continued after Mrs Currie's resignation. The pressure was apparent both in questions and the use of other parliamentary opportunities, particularly as Conservative MPs sought to obtain remedial action from MAFF.

In the New Year, questions, particularly written ones, were the principal form of pressure, particularly from the opposition front bench, as they developed a general campaign on food safety in daily questions throughout January, seeking to exploit Conservative vulnerability to the accusation that MAFF was too easy on the farming lobby, with food issues and consumer interests being neglected. Conservative questioners, on the other hand, were seeking to show that the danger of salmonella in eggs had been exaggerated out of all proportion as a result of Mrs Currie's TV 'gaffe' and her subsequent refusal to correct what she had said. The Agriculture Committee's investigation fuelled the issue further, particularly given Mrs Currie's reluctance to give evidence. The opposition kept up the pressure with its choice of motions critical of MAFF as the topic for debate on 24 January (on consumer protection)[51] and again on 21 February (on food and water safety).[52] And on 7 March[53] an Estimates Day was used to debate the Agriculture Committee's Report[54] which had been published at the end of February. However, from March onwards there was a marked decline in questions: no reference was made to salmonella in Agriculture Question Time in April, May, June, or October, and there were just two references in July.[55] Written questions, which had numbered over sixty a month at the height of the affair, fell to twenty-three in March and well below twenty in April to June.

A key element in assessing parliamentary pressure is, of course, its origin. Politically, most potential lies with government backbenchers. Interventions by senior Conservative MPs like Robin Maxwell-Hyslop, Sir Hal Miller, Sir Peter Emery, and Sir Geoffrey Johnson-Smith carried considerable weight. A high

---

[51] *HC Deb.* (1988–89) 145, cols. 880–932.

[52] *HC Deb.* (1988–89) 147, cols. 852–946.

[53] *HC Deb.* (1988–89) 148, cols. 771–841.

[54] First Report from the Agriculture Committee, *Salmonella in Eggs*, HC (1988–89) 108.   [55] *HC Deb.* (1988–89) 157, cols. 1155–6.

proportion of written questions came from the opposition benches: 216 out of 401, 91 from front benchers.[56] Three MPs—Ron Davies and Dr David Clark (opposition front benchers) and Conservative backbencher Teresa Gorman—were together responsible for 142 (35 per cent) of the questions.

In the absence of detailed research into the policy process which cannot be done satisfactorily without access to the papers, it is not possible to be certain about the impact on government decisions of parliamentary pressure generally, never mind questions in particular. It would be hard to deny, however, that such pressure played an important part in forcing Mrs Currie's resignation and the market stabilization package announced by the Minister of Agriculture in his interim statement on 16 December 1988. There followed in 1989 a series of announcements from the minister about measures to control salmonella in eggs and poultry: powers to prevent movement of processed animal protein from contaminated premises were announced in answer to a question from Michael Lord on 1 February;[57] compulsory slaughter of laying flocks in which *Salmonella enteritidis* or *Salmonella typhimurium* had been confirmed was announced on 10 February in answer to a question from Colin Shepherd;[58] testing of poultry flocks was introduced in March and registration of protein processing businesses with daily sampling was announced in April.[59] A ban on the sale of cracked eggs direct to consumers was proposed in a consultation document issued on 27 April, announced in answer to a question from Nicholas Bennett,[60] and a White Paper was published on 27 July announcing further legislation on food safety and consumer protection.[61] New Codes of Practice to control salmonella in animal feeding stuffs and raw materials were introduced in August,[62] replacing guide-lines introduced at the height of the crisis in December 1988. In October 1989 it was announced that compulsory tendering would be extended to hatcheries and that registration of laying flocks (of not less than 100 birds, covering 98 per cent of table egg production in the

---

[56] Based on data from POLIS. [57] *HC Deb.* (1988–89) 146, col. 242w.
[58] Ibid., col. 831w.
[59] MAFF News Release 164/89, 14 Apr. 1989.
[60] *HC Deb.* (1988–89) 151, col. 679w.
[61] *Food Safety—Protecting the Consumer* Cm. 732, July 1989.
[62] MAFF News Release 331/89, 8 Aug. 1989.

United Kingdom), breeding flocks, and hatcheries would apply from April 1990.[63] And in early November the minister, John Gummer, announced in a written answer to Kenneth Hind the setting up of a new 'Food Safety Directorate' to operate within his ministry 'to strengthen the Department's organisation for dealing with food safety issues'.[64]

It cannot, of course, be argued, that these measures were forced on the government by parliamentary pressure alone. But there seems little doubt that sustained parliamentary interest, in the Select Committee and in questions and debates, at the very least increased the salience of the issue for ministers, and accelerated policy responses to the substantive problems presented by the increase in salmonella food poisoning cases. Accountability to Parliament reinforced and intensified the pressure generated by the issue itself. Questions provided a continuing opportunity for MPs, the opposition, and government backbenchers to maintain that pressure.

Political pressure can be inhibiting. One can only speculate as to the reasons for Mrs Currie's reluctance to correct her statement to the TV reporter; but on matters where public confidence in food safety was the key issue, debates and questions in Parliament and the media could be, and were, counter-productive—not least because of the difficulty of interpreting the scientific evidence on the degree of risk involved with eggs. Here the apparent conflict of interest between Health and Agriculture, understandably exploited by the government's critics, added to the difficulties. Disagreement between those interests, particularly as represented by egg producers' organizations and environmental health officers, in interpreting the evidence of linkage to eggs was clearly a reason for the 'extraordinarily sluggish', in the words of the Agriculture Committee,[65] response from government in the summer of 1988 as the extent of the rise of in salmonella food poisoning cases became apparent.

That sluggishness contrasts markedly with the pace of response when the political crisis was at its height in December—as, for example, in the preparation of the market stabilization package, details of which were announced by the Minister of Agriculture on

---

[63] MAFF News Release 386/89, 3 Oct. 1989.
[64] *HC Deb.* (1988–89) 159, cols. 317–18w.
[65] *Salmonella in Eggs*, para. 90.

19 December—and the stream of announcements already noted which followed in 1989. The factors which had inhibited prompt response in mid-1988—differing interpretations of the scientific evidence and political conflict of interest—had not changed significantly. What had changed was the political salience of the issue, particularly in Parliament. In that change, questions had played their part.

BSE ('Mad Cow Disease')

Uncertainty about scientific evidence has been an important factor in the parallel case of BSE (bovine spongiform encephalopathy). While this has not had the added political dimension of a ministerial resignation, there have been marked similarities with the salmonella case, with sustained parliamentary pressure, over a much longer period than with salmonella. Again, a significant feature of questions on BSE has been the prominent part played by opposition front bench spokesmen, who asked over half (258 out of 485) the written questions put down between November 1988 and the end of the 1989–90 parliamentary session.[66] By contrast, Conservative backbenchers were responsible for only sixty questions between them over that same two-year period, and some of those were clearly vehicles for MAFF announcements (for example, William Hague's question on 15 May 1990[67]).

On BSE, as on salmonella, opposition pressure was evident in other parliamentary proceedings. There was a censure motion on food and water safety in February 1989 in which BSE was featured in Neil Kinnock's opening and Dr David Clark's winding-up speeches,[68] an adjournment debate initiated by Ron Davies in May 1989,[69] a debate on EC matters in February 1990[70] (though there was also great pressure in this debate from Conservative backbenchers[71] for 100 per cent compensation for slaughtered stock), and an Opposition Day debate in May 1990.[72] The issue was

[66] Based on data from POLIS.
[67] *HC Deb*. (1989–90) 172, cols. 393–4w.
[68] *HC Deb*. (1988–89) 147, cols. 852–946.
[69] *HC Deb*. (1988–89) 153, cols. 450–8.
[70] *HC Deb*. (1989–90) 166, cols. 782–860.
[71] e.g. *HC Deb*. (1989–90) 166, Paul Marland (col. 804), Robin Maxwell-Hyslop (col. 810), and William Hague (col. 838).
[72] *HC Deb*. (1989–90) 173, cols. 76–120.

raised by opposition spokesmen at MAFF Question Time in December 1988,[73] March 1989,[74] June 1989[75] (when it was also raised in Welsh Office questions[76]), and in each of the first six months of 1990. And it was also raised three times in Prime Minister's questions—by Labour Members on 28 February 1989[77] and 15 February 1990[78] and by a Liberal Democrat[79] on 2 May 1990. Opposition front bench pressure was particularly intense in May 1989, when forty-three questions were put down, and in January and May 1990, when thirty-two questions were put down. In the latter month the Commons Agriculture Committee also began a short inquiry into MAFF's handling of the issue.[80] And in June, after an illegal ban on British beef exports had been introduced in France, Germany, and Italy in response to anxieties about BSE in the UK, the Minister of Agriculture made an emergency statement on the EC Council at which the removal of the ban was negotiated. The statement and the questions to which it gave rise began at 10.53 p.m., and continued for seventy minutes, reflecting the widespread concern among MPs about the issue.[81]

In sum, we have a picture of intense parliamentary pressure on the department, pressure which peaked in debates like the EC one in February 1990 and questions on ministerial statements, as on 7 June 1990, but was also sustained by a steady stream of written questions. The constant stream of questions demonstrated to MAFF the close scrutiny to which their policy on BSE was subject. This confirms the picture given by the salmonella case, although with BSE the pressure was maintained over a much longer period, and without the sensation of a ministerial resignation.

Conclusion

In terms, then, of the impact of parliamentary questions on policy

[73] *HC Deb.* (1988–89) 142, cols. 862–4.
[74] *HC Deb.* (1988–89) 149, cols. 525–6.
[75] *HC Deb.* (1988–89) 155, col. 1100.
[76] *HC Deb.* (1988–89) 154, col. 7.
[77] *HC Deb.* (1988–89) 148, cols. 155–6.
[78] *HC Deb.* (1989–90) 167, col. 392.
[79] *HC Deb.* (1989–90) 173, col. 168.
[80] Fifth Report from the Agriculture Committee, *Bovine Spongiform Encephalopathy*, HC (1989–90) 449.
[81] *HC Deb.* (1989–90) 173, cols. 899–915.

and administration in departments, it is not possible to separate their effect from that of other parliamentary proceedings. That they are an important element in accountability goes without saying. From the ministerial point of view, the key elements in a good reply are brevity and accuracy. In recent years ministers seem to have become more aware of the PR aspects of questions generally, and Question Time in particular. This has been accentuated, as we have seen, by the broadcasting and televising of Parliament. Parliamentary answers provide an opportunity to put across the government's case. Question Time itself has become a much more partisan occasion, a piece of regular political theatre. The changes in the briefing practice of some ministers reflects this.

However, as the statistics show, oral questions are only part of the exercise; the volume of written questions is substantial. Again, accuracy is a prime requirement in the answers, but, as the columns of written answers in *Hansard* show, brevity is not so critical. Further, ministers are aware of the PR opportunities—hence the practice of using written answers as a means of making ministerial announcements, particularly when departments want to release some 'good news'. A high proportion of written PQs nevertheless originate with the opposition front bench as a way of obtaining information, and thus make a significant contribution to the efficient functioning of the opposition. Not only are such questions an important element in the accountability of government to Parliament, they are also an important resource for opposition parties for their own policy making—a crucial means of access to key data, in fact. Whether this is any consolation to the hard-pressed Grade 5 civil servant who has constantly to divert him or herself from other duties to the task of drafting parliamentary answers is a moot point. But under our present constitutional arrangements the civil service has to operate in a context of ministerial accountability to Parliament. Parliamentary questions are just one aspect of that.

6

Questions in the House of Lords

Donald Shell

It is generally agreed that the first recorded parliamentary question was asked in the House of Lords. This, as noted in Chapter 2, was a question put to the Prime Minister, the Earl of Sunderland, by Earl Cowper on 9 February 1721.[1] Gradually thereafter questions became a regularized form of procedure in both Houses. As this happened, the practice of the two Houses diverged. But before drawing attention to the differences between the procedures and practices of the two Houses in relation to questions, it is worth emphasizing that in essence the idea of the parliamentary question is the same in both, as exemplified in that first question in the Lords some 270 years ago. Any Member has the right to put a question, to which a government minister makes a reply. Today in both Houses time for oral questions is provided early in the proceedings of each day. In the Lords, as in the Commons, oral (or starred) questions are submitted in advance to the government, so that replies can be prepared in government departments. The reply to the question is read out by the minister, with opportunity then being given for the asking of oral supplementary questions, to which the government spokesman replies as best he can. In both Houses the time spent on oral questions is generally recognized as the best attended, liveliest, noisiest, and perhaps most unruly part of the day's proceedings. As well as questions for oral answer, Members of both Houses can submit questions for written answer. When they do so, both the question and the answer will be printed in *Hansard* at the end of the day's proceedings.

But while these basic similarities exist, there are also some important contrasts between the two Houses. First, whereas in the Commons the time spent on oral questions each day is strictly limited, in the Lords, rather than strict formal limits being

---

[1] See above, p. 23, and D. N. Chester and N. Bowring, *Questions in Parliament* (Oxford: Clarendon Press, 1962), 12.

imposed on the time spent on questions, the number of questions which may be put down for any one day is limited. Second, questions in the Lords are almost always addressed to the government rather than to a particular minister. This is because not all departments have ministers in the Lords, and even when there is a minister from a particular department, he or she may not be available to answer a particular question. Answers must sometimes be given by ministers in other departments or by 'Lords in Waiting', the title assumed by whips in the Upper House, whose Commons counterparts do not act as departmental spokesmen at all. It follows from this that there is no equivalent in the Lords to the Commons rota for answering questions. Instead, questions are simply put down where there is an available space on the Order Paper, and answered by the most appropriate available government spokesman.

Further differences derive from the absence in the Lords of a presiding officer with powers equivalent to those of the Speaker in the Commons. This has two particular consequences relevant to questions. The first is that whether or not a question is regarded as admissible is a matter for the House as a whole, rather than something on which an officer of the House can give a ruling. Clerks advise about the wording of questions and their admissibility, and although such advice is generally heeded, questions which would be disallowed in the Commons may, and from time to time do, appear on the Order Paper in the Lords. A government spokesman may refuse to answer a certain question, or the House may refuse to allow the question to be put. But if so, this will be on the initiative of a particular peer, not of a presiding officer. The second consequence deriving from the absence of a Speaker is that, as supplementary questions are put, there is no one who has the power simply to move business on or to curtail discussion. In practice, peers look to the Leader of the House, who frequently intervenes to try to keep proceedings orderly and within what are considered reasonable time limits. But in doing so, he has no authority conferred by Standing Orders, a point he needs to remember. Where there are disputes, they may ultimately have to be settled by the House voting on a motion that a particular Lord be no longer heard or a particular question be not put. In practice, each starred question is dealt with at much greater length in the Lords than in the Commons.

Some differences in nomenclature also need to be noted. Both Houses have starred questions, which are answered orally. However, in the Commons some starred questions receive written answers because they are not reached in the time available for oral questions. In the Lords any starred question which appears on the Order Paper and for which the questioner (or a specifically appointed substitute) is present is assured of an oral answer. This has as a corollary that only questions put down for written answer (known as QWAs) receive such an answer in the Lords.

The Lords also has a procedure known as the 'unstarred question'. This is a question on which speeches may be made, in contrast to starred questions, which are supposedly asked for information only, and upon which speeches may certainly not be made. Unstarred questions in the Lords are always the last item of business on the day's Order Paper. The peer who asks the question makes a speech which is followed by other speeches before the minister replies, also with a speech. Because a question is before the House, rather than a motion, the peer who made the first speech asking the question has no right of reply at the end of the debate. But in other respects this procedure is very like a debate on a motion. Topics may be very specific, but in practice they are more usually quite wide-ranging, some of them very much so. The time spent debating unstarred questions varies considerably. Some are dealt with in half an hour or so, the time spent on daily adjournment debates in the Commons. Others may be debated for two hours or even longer. Generally the House debates about fifty unstarred questions a year, or between one and two a week. The procedure allows a debate of indefinite (but sometimes considerable) length to take place at relatively short notice. It is a flexible procedure, the nearest Commons equivalent probably being the strictly time-limited daily adjournment debates. Though the procedure is designated as 'unstarred questions', it will be apparent even from this brief description that it is now a fundamentally different procedure from those associated with all other parliamentary questions.[2]

As in the Commons, it is also possible for Private Notice Questions dealing with matters considered urgent to be put. They

---

[2] On House of Lords procedures and practice, see D. R. Shell, *The House of Lords*, 2nd edn. (Hemel Hempstead: Harvester Wheatsheaf, 1992).

may be tabled at any time up to twelve noon on the day of the sitting at which they are answered, though such questions must be accepted by the Leader of the House.

Questions in the Lords: Increasing Numbers

The vast expansion in the number of questions being tabled in the Commons has already been discussed (see above, Chapter 2). In the Lords there has also been a growth in the number of questions asked, as is shown in Table 6.1, though the numbers still look extremely modest by comparison with those of the Commons. The most striking growth has been in the number of questions for written answer. Until 1970 these averaged less than one per sitting day! By the end of the 1970s the daily average had risen to around seven; but it has not grown very markedly since then. The number of starred questions has also increased, but Private Notice Questions have declined. The fall in the number of PNQs has been brought about partly as a result of successive Leaders of the House being more restrictive in allowing such questions. But a further factor was the decision in 1983 not to make arrangements for a parallel PNQ to be asked in the Lords whenever a PNQ had been accepted in the Commons. Instead, practice in the Lords has been to repeat as ministerial statements answers to Commons PNQs. This has resulted in PNQs becoming rare in the Lords. Such questions may be accepted when the senior minister responsible is a member of the Lords or, of course, if the Upper House is sitting at a time when the Commons is in recess.

Until 1954 up to three starred questions were allowed per day, but only on two days of the week: namely, Tuesdays and Wednesdays. Given that the House very rarely sat more than three days a week, this restriction simply excluded Thursdays, when the House customarily sat at 3.00 p.m. rather than 2.30 p.m. (the later sitting time originally being due to a wish not to overlap with judicial sittings, but in more recent years being convenient for allowing party meetings to take place on Thursday afternoons immediately before the House sits). In 1954 the House agreed to allow each day's business to commence with up to three starred questions. At that time this limit imposed no real constraint. In each session from 1954 to 1958 the average number of starred

Table 6.1. *Number of questions per session, 1961–90*

Session	Number of sittings	Starred questions		QWAs		PNQs
		Number	Average per day	Number	Average per day	
1961–62	115	275	2.4	72	0.6	21
1962–63	127	297	2.3	84	0.7	20
1963–64	110	340	3.1	77	0.7	17
1964–65	124	370	3.0	73	0.6	9
1965–66	50	151	3.0	33	0.7	13
1966–67	191	660	3.5	96	0.5	19
1967–68	139	437	3.0	92	0.7	16
1968–69	109	363	3.3	92	0.8	11
1969–70	83	287	3.5	108	1.3	9
1970–71	153	467	3.1	283	1.8	13
1971–72	141	494	3.5	315	2.2	7
1972–73	128	460	3.6	281	2.2	16
1973–74	45	139	3.1	92	2.0	4
1974	64	192	3.0	171	2.7	3
1974–75	162	560	3.4	350	2.2	6
1975–76	155	553	3.6	517	3.3	1
1976–77	105	385	3.7	380	3.6	8
1977–78	126	439	3.5	544	4.3	5
1978–79	59	217	3.7	432	7.3	7
1979–80	206	765	3.7	1,277	6.2	16
1980–81	143	537	3.8	857	6.0	2
1981–82	147	531	3.6	1,098	7.5	6
1982–83	94	357	3.8	619	6.6	2
1983–84	178	691	3.9	1,350	7.6	1
1984–85	151	573	3.8	1,142	7.6	0
1985–86	165	631	3.8	1,182	7.2	2
1986–87	84	317	3.8	622	7.4	1
1987–88	192	742	3.9	1,405	7.3	3
1988–89	153	572	3.7	1,202	7.9	1
1989–90	147	551	3.7	1,204	8.2	2

Sources: HL 9 (1987–88) and House of Lords Information Office

questions per day was never more than two. Nevertheless in 1959 the limit was raised from three to four per day. Why was this?

Starred questions then as now had to be tabled at a minimum of twenty-four hours notice. Increasing the maximum number that could be dealt with on any single day helped to ensure greater topicality than when questions were perforce spread more evenly. In fact, only on a minority of days were four questions asked; the average number per day remaining below the old limit of three for another four years.

The period since the passage of the Life Peerages Act in 1958 has seen a steady and continuous growth in every aspect of the work of the House. By the mid-1960s the maximum of four starred questions were being asked more often than not. More pertinent than the rule requiring at least twenty-four hours' notice of a question was the standing order—number 41—which forbade the placing of any notice of a question on the Order Paper more than one month ahead. Sometimes almost all the available slots were full, and the argument was being put that the daily quota of starred questions should be increased. Looking at Table 6.1 it can be seen that the average number of starred questions never fell below three after 1964, and since 1975–76 has always been above 3.5. There are various reasons why the average will always fall short of the maximum permissible. One of these is that starred questions are not asked on the first and last days of the session; another is that sittings may be arranged at short notice. Sometimes, too, questions are withdrawn at short notice. If a peer who has a question down does not appear in the chamber when the question is called, that question is not put, unless the peer whose name is against the question on the Order Paper has specifically asked another peer to formally ask the question in his place. For all these reasons a daily average in excess of 3.5 almost certainly masks an Order Paper with no available slots for questions at certain times of the year.

On several occasions the Procedure Committee of the House has considered how this pressure might be alleviated. Increasing the number of questions allowed each day is an obvious possibility and one which the Committee has frequently considered but always rejected. The reason has been the view that such a step would increase too much the time the House spends on questions. Furthermore, it would almost certainly be the more assiduous

156 *Donald Shell*

peers who would quickly fill the extra slots made available, and
there has been a feeling that the House hears quite enough from
these peers already!

Rather than simply allow a general increase in the number of
questions, consideration has been given to proposals that would
allow a 'topical' question to be asked at short notice. A group of
peers set up to advise the Leader of the House in 1971
recommended this, suggesting that the daily maximum be raised to
five, with the fifth slot being filled at no more than three days'
notice. This proposal was not endorsed by the Procedure
Committee, however.[3] A successor group of peers set up to advise
the Leader in 1987 again considered the possibility of an extra slot
for a topical question, but rejected it, partly because of the
difficulty of deciding what was 'topical' (though in the manifest
absence of any objective criteria the 1971 proposal simply to allow
one late question to be tabled seemed appropriate), but also
because the group noted that 'there are usually vacancies for
starred questions'.[4]

The fact that some vacancies usually exist is in part due to
the acceptance of other recommendations made by successive
Procedure Committees. In 1971 the Leader's Advisory Group,
noting the increase in starred questions, recommended that 'Peers
should be encouraged to make increased use of Questions for
Written Answer; many questions at present tabled as Starred
Questions could more properly be tabled as Q.W.A.s.'[5] As can be
seen from Table 6.1, the number of QWAs has increased
substantially, though the main increase did not occur until some
years after this recommendation was made. In the same Report it
was noted that during the previous autumn (1970) all places for
starred questions had been taken a month in advance, partly
because of 'the pre-empting of 25 places by two peers'. However,
the Committee went on to note that 'Some of these 25 questions
were subsequently shared out amongst other members of the
House', and that in Spring 1971 there had been a marked dearth of
starred questions.[6] The Group therefore made no recommendations to restrict the freedom of peers to table questions (beyond

[3] *Tenth Report from the Select Committee on Procedure*, HL (1970–71) 22 n.
[4] *Report by the Group on the Working of the House*, HL 9 (1987–88), paras. 51–2.
[5] *Report by the Group on the Working of the House* (1970–71), para. 43.
[6] Ibid., para. 38.

the already existing rule that no peer could table more than two questions for any one day), though it did 'stress that the abuse of this right, even by a tiny minority, would quickly make a new system necessary'. The fact that the two peers who had pre-empted so many spaces subsequently withdrew some questions, freeing space for other peers, as well as the general tone of the Report just quoted, illustrate the extent to which the House, in ordering its affairs, has preferred to avoid procedural restrictions and instead look to the collective good sense of Members and their capacity for self-discipline.

However, in an increasingly active House, difficulties in finding spaces for questions grew. In 1981 the Procedure Committee recommended as an experiment that no peer be allowed to have more than three starred questions on the Order Paper at any one time.[7] After the experiment had run for a second six-month period the Procedure Committee recommended that this rule be made permanent, and the House accepted this.[8] In 1987 the Leader's Advisory Group noted that some peers asked many more questions than others, and 'a few usually have their full ration of three on the Order Paper at any one time'. The Group accordingly recommended that no peer be allowed more than two starred questions on the Order Paper at any one time, a recommendation subsequently endorsed by the Procedure Committee of the House.[9] So, while the permissible number of questions has not been increased, restrictions designed to ensure that the ration available is more evenly shared among peers have been steadily introduced. But these have not prevented occasions arising when virtually no slots for questions are available. And it remains the case that some peers table many more questions than others.

Increasing the maximum number of questions per day might have won greater favour if the time spent on starred questions had not also risen steadily. In 1959–60, when an average of 2.3 questions were asked each day, the average time spent on starred questions was just over ten minutes, or about four minutes per question. By 1989–90, when the House was usually dealing with

[7] *First Report from the Select Committee on Procedure*, HL (1981–82) 38; see also *HL Deb.* (1981–82) 426, cols. 705–9.
[8] *First Report from the Select Committee on Procedure*, HL (1982–83) 72; see also *HL Deb.* (1982–83) 439, cols. 222–5.
[9] *First Report from the Select Committee on Procedure*, HL (1987–88) 46.

four questions per day, the average time per question had risen to some seven minutes, with question time regularly taking between twenty-five and thirty minutes. Not surprisingly, the House has periodically looked in the direction of imposing limits on the amount of time spent dealing with questions. In 1976 the Procedure Committee recommended that proceedings on starred questions 'normally be concluded within 20 minutes'.[10] This recommendation was frequently reiterated in subsequent years, and was embodied in the Companion to the Standing Orders. But as R. L. Borthwick commented, the '20-minute limit seems a lost cause'; in respect of the 1988–89 session he found that on only one-sixth of the days were starred questions dealt with inside this time limit.[11] Not infrequently, over ten minutes was spent on a single questions, and occasionally questions took forty minutes to complete, twice as long as the recommended maximum. In 1991 the Procedure Committee, recognizing that its previous guidance had been so frequently breached, recommended that the suggested maximum time for questions be increased to thirty minutes.[12] The time spent per question, therefore, is very much greater in the Lords than in the Commons, and this gives Question Time in the Lords a very different character from that which it has in the Lower House.

In the absence of a Speaker, the decision about when to move on to the next question or the next business is one for the House as a whole, as is the decision about who among many peers perhaps attempting to intervene ought to be heard. In practice peers look to the Leader of the House to give guidance in this regard. Typically, if proceedings become protracted, some peers may call 'Next Question', and the Leader is likely to intervene, suggesting perhaps that after one or two more supplementaries the House should move on. The advice of the Leader is normally followed by the House, though for his part assessing the right moment to intervene can be difficult. Lord Whitelaw was criticized by some peers for allowing too lengthy and wide-ranging a discussion to develop during questions, but he defended his approach on the

[10] *First Report from the Select Committee on Procedure*, HL (1975–76) 239; see also *HL Deb.* (1975–76) 372, cols. 1232–7.
[11] R. L. Borthwick, 'Non-Legislative Debate and Questions', in D. Shell and D. Beamish (eds.), *The House of Lords at Work: A Study Based on the 1988–89 Session* (Oxford: Clarendon Press, 1993).
[12] *First Report from the Committee on Procedure*, HL (1990–91) 17, paras. 13–14.

grounds that questions were a very valued part of the proceedings of the House. Nor did he wish to be seen as possibly protecting ministers from hostile questions by moving business along more rapidly. For example, after the Secretary of State for Employment, Lord Young of Graffham, had incurred criticism for being absent from the House, and therefore unavailable to deal with questions about unemployment, Lord Whitelaw allowed discussion of a single question to continue for twenty minutes on 24 October 1985. When Lord Ferrers, the deputy Leader, was in some difficulty coping with a question about police enforcement of speed limits on motorways on 21 June 1990, the Leader, Lord Belstead, declined to intervene, and supplementaries to Lord Ferrers continued for fifteen minutes. The following day Lord Belstead himself answered a question about the jobs taken by ex-ministers which also drew a good many hostile supplementaries; in such circumstances the Leader is even less well-placed to act as the referee and call time, and on this occasion too proceedings on the question lasted fifteen minutes.

While formal time limits have been eschewed, efforts have been repeatedly made to ensure that Standing Order 32 is observed. This states that starred questions are asked 'for information only. . . . No debate may take place on such questions and supplementary questions must be confined to the subject of the original question.' Peers who intervene with supplementaries must therefore phrase these in the form of a question; transgressors generally find the House quick to call them to order, though seasoned parliamentarians do not appear to find this rule a restriction, simply slipping into the interrogatory mode by prefacing the point they wish to make by 'Is the minister aware that . . .?' The Companion to the Standing Orders states that supplementaries should not include statements of opinion, but often opinions are expressed, sometimes by the questioner simply asking 'Is the minister aware that my opinion is . . . ?' In 1985 the Procedure Committee recommended that supplementaries should not raise a number of different points, but in 1987 the Group advising the Leader suggested that a 'workable and sensible restriction' would be to limit supplementaries to two points. A peer asking a lengthy supplementary is sometimes interrupted with cries of 'Two points only'.

Lengthy and verbose supplementaries may be encouraged by

lengthy ministerial replies. It has been customary in the Lords for replies to be longer than in the Commons. One reason for this has been the different character of the Upper House, with its more elaborate and courteous style of speech. Partly, too, it has been because government spokesmen in the Lords have probably on the whole wished to be more helpful to questioners. There has been a tendency in recent sessions, however, to reduce the length of replies. In the 1989–90 session it was much more common than previously to see minimum possible replies such as 'No, My Lords'. But replies of 150 to 200 words are still by no means uncommon, often giving more information than was actually requested in the original question. Where supplementaries go beyond the terms of the original question, it is always open to the government spokesman simply to decline to answer, stating that the supplementary is really a different question. On the whole, ministers in the Lords have taken a fairly relaxed view about supplementaries, though again, in recent sessions, there are signs that some spokesmen are more readily refusing to answer what they view as irrelevant supplementaries.

But, with twelve or more peers taking part in discussion on a single question, and perhaps twice that number attempting to get in, proceedings can still be quite protracted. The peer answering for the government quite often rises ten or more times in dealing with a single question. If spokesmen resort to brief replies which are also sarcastic or deliberately unhelpful, they may find the House that much more reluctant to move on. After some twenty minutes had been spent pretty fruitlessly on a question to do with privatization on 10 November 1983, Lord Alport rebuked the minister dealing with the question, Lord Cockfield, by asking him whether he realized 'that the sarcasm and discourtesy with which he has answered many of the questions put to him this afternoon is not in accordance with the normal traditions of this House?'[13] However, alongside what might be considered abrupt or discourteous replies, there are numerous examples of House of Lords courtesy, with compliments offered where none appear to be deserved, lavish praise, and congratulations to noble lords who happen to have their birthdays or wedding anniversaries or whatever on that particular day!

[13] *HL Deb.* (1983–84) 444, col. 959.

Answering Questions: The Government Front Bench

The government front bench in the Lords generally consists of around twenty members. All governments have at least two Cabinet ministers in the House, the Lord Chancellor and the Leader of the House. Conservative governments have generally had more than two peers in the Cabinet. The Thatcher governments had either three or four until 1988, when the number fell to the minimum of two. There are usually some ten other departmental ministers, with six or seven whips completing the team. This means that not all departments have ministers in the House. Table 6.2 shows that at the commencement of the 1989–90 session, departments without ministers were Education and Science, Energy, Transport, and Wales. Departments in this position will be spoken for either by a minister in another department or by a whip. Sometimes the number of government spokesmen in the Lords has been much lower; in 1974 only fourteen peers were appointed to the Labour government front bench, giving ministerial representation to only seven departments. There were complaints in the House about this, and the number gradually rose to seventeen by 1975. The Thatcher governments always had at least twenty ministers and whips in the House; during 1990, with the appointment of Baroness Blatch as a whip, the number rose to twenty-two.

The relatively small size of the government front bench in the House means that individually its members have a lot of ground to cover. A full departmental minister will be expected to deal with all the business that concerns the department in which he is a minister, though of course his actual ministerial responsibilities will only concern part of it. Thus Lord Arran, who was Under Secretary at Defence (see Table 6.2) held the particular post of Under Secretary of State for the Armed Forces with responsibilities for service personnel and logistic matters and for administrative support of the armed forces. If he were a minister in the Commons, he would expect to answer only questions concerning these particular matters; but in the Lords he dealt with all defence questions, as well as helping a little with Home Office matters. Likewise Lord Ferrers, Minister of State at the Home Office, had direct ministerial responsibility for the police, the Channel Islands and the Isle of Man, charities law and cults, fire service and civil

Table 6.2. *Government Front Bench: allocation of responsibilities, January 1990*

Minister and position	Departments	Number of starred questions answered
Lord MacKay of Clashfern, Lord Chancellor	Legal Affairs	3
Lord Belstead, Lord Privy Seal	Leader of the House Civil Service	5
Lord Fraser of Carmyllie, Lord Advocate	Legal Affairs	0
Earl of Caithness, Paymaster General	Treasury	36
Earl of Ferrers, Minister of State, Home Office	Home Office	21
Lord Brabazon of Tara, Minister of State, FLO	Foreign Office	41
Lord Trefgarne, Minister of State, DTI	DTI	28
	Foreign Affairs	4
	DEmp	3
	Wales	1
	also Transport	1
	DoE	2
Lord Sanderson of Bowden, Minister of State, Scottish Office	Scotland	8
	also Fishing	2
Baroness Trumpington, Minister of State, MAFF	Agriculture	10
	Arts	1
Lord Strathclyde, Under Secretary, DEmp	Employment	20
	DTI	6
	Treasury	2
	also DoE	1
Earl of Arran, Under Secretary, MoD	MoD	16
	Home Office	1
Baroness Hooper, Under Secretary, DoH	DoH	31
	Den	1
Lord Henley, Under Secretary, DSS	DSS	15
	DoH	2
	Treasury[a]	5

Lord Hesketh, Under Secretary, DoE	DoE Arts (Heritage)	47
Lord Skelmersdale, Under Secretary, Northern Ireland Office	Northern Ireland DSS	1
Lord Denham, Captain, Gentlemen at Arms	Chief Whip	0
Viscount Davidson, Captain, Yeomen of the Guard	Deputy Chief Whip Transport Education[a]	 37 8
Viscount Long, Lord in Waiting	Defence Northern Ireland Foreign Affairs	0 0 0

Viscount Ullswater, Lord in Waiting	Energy
	Transport
	Home Office
	DTI
	    also DEmp
	    Treasury
		20
		4
		7
		6
		3
		1

Earl of Strathmore & Kinghorne, Lord in Waiting	Employment
	Agriculture
	Scotland
	Treasury
	    also DoE
	    Transport
		1
		5
		0
		1
		1
		2

Lord Reay, Lord in Waiting	DoE MoD Foreign Affairs	17 5 11
Baroness Blatch, Baroness in Waiting	Education[a] Health[a] DSS[a] also Transport	22 7 2 1

Note: The number of questions answered is the number between the commencement of the session and 23 July, the date of a major ministerial reshuffle.

The departmental responsibilities for ministers and whips have been taken from the General Information booklet issued by the House of Lords. 'Also' denotes that the peer concerned answered questions pertinent to that department even though he or she was not listed as a spokesman for it. Some questions are difficult to allocate to departments, and briefing is sometimes provided by more than one department. But the allocation made here is that which appears correct from a reading of the question concerned in the light of the officially listed departmental responsibilities.

[a] The responsibility was held for only part of this period, consequent on the appointment of Baroness Blatch as an additional whip in January 1990.

defence; in the Lords, however, he also handled prisons, broadcasting, passports, drugs, and all the other rag-bag of responsibilities
handled by the Home Office. It is essential that all departments
have at least two spokesmen in the House so that if one is absent
the other can speak for that department. Where a department has
no minister in the House, the lead spokesman for that department
will probably be a whip. Lords in Waiting are generally given
offices in the department for which they speak most in the House,
and usually in such circumstances they will attend ministerial
meetings in the department.

For a minister or whip who simply answers for a department in
which he or she has no direct ministerial responsibility, an answer
will always be provided by that department, together with some
background material. But having examined this, the only opportunity to seek further briefing or ask questions about it may well
occur just a few minutes before the question concerned is due to
be answered, and may well be with a civil servant whom the
minister has never met before. The results may sometimes leave a
good deal to be desired, though the House tends to be understanding especially where a Lord in Waiting or minister is trying to cope
with a question in an area for which he has no direct responsibility
whatever. Promises to write to peers who put questions which the
spokesman is unable to answer are often made quite freely.
Sometimes the House rushes to the defence of a spokesman, as
happened, for example, when Lord Davidson responded to a
comment by an opposition peer regretting the absence of a
Transport minister in the House by inferring that this was intended
as criticism of his own performance in answering questions on
transport; peers quickly rose to assure him that no such criticism
was intended. However, the House does show its irritation at
times. On 4 December 1990 an opposition spokesman suggested
that a minister answering a question 'did not know what we are
talking about', though the minister concerned averred that he did.
When a Baroness in Waiting was answering a question on the cost
to the NHS of prescriptions, and a supplementary was put which
referred to 'generic' drugs, she confessed that she did not
understand what the term meant. Amidst much muttering and
embarrassment a medically qualified peer rose to explain the term
to her.[14] On another occasion it was reported that a junior minister

[14] *HL Deb.* (1983–84) 447, col. 1140.

was seen to bury his head in his hands while attempting to cope with hostile supplementaries to a question on the state of health services in Birmingham; on this occasion sixteen minutes was spent on a single starred question.[15] According to a newspaper report in 1991, the Chairman of the Association of Conservative Peers, Lord Colnbrook (formerly Mr Humphrey Atkins, a Cabinet minister under Mrs Thatcher in the early 1980s), having observed Lords in Waiting 'getting into deep water when interrogated by acknowledged experts' in the House of Lords, went to see the Prime Minister, and asked him to ensure that better briefing was available for these junior spokesmen; John Major apparently sent a minute to departmental ministers instructing them to this effect.[16]

Table 6.2 shows how questions pertaining to departments without ministers in 1989–90 were handled. Energy questions were all answered by Viscount Ullswater, a Lord in Waiting, who also answered questions on behalf of at least four other departments. Having joined the government in summer 1989, he was promoted to Under Secretary of State at the Department of Employment in summer 1990. Lord Cavendish of Furness, a new whip, began answering for energy, though Lord Ullswater continued to help deal with questions to that department, as well as answering for his new ministerial post. Education questions were initially all dealt with by Viscount Davidson, the deputy Chief Whip; but in January 1990 Baroness Blatch was appointed to a post as a whip, and she took responsibility for education, dealing with all questions to that department. Her experience as leader of Cambridgeshire County Council for four years in the early 1980s gave her a good background for doing this. In July 1990 she too was promoted to ministerial office (at the Department of the Environment), though she continued to handle some education questions, at least until the end of the session.

It is apparent from the table that the burden of answering questions is not by any means shared evenly among ministers and whips. Of the five Lords in Waiting, three dealt with upwards of thirty questions each, while one, Lord Long, though listed as a spokesman for three departments, did not answer a single starred

[15] See *The Independent*, 17 Dec. 1987.
[16] *The Sunday Times*, 19 May 1991.

question. Viscount Long had served as a Lord in Waiting ever since Mrs Thatcher took office in 1979; he and Lord Denham were the only two members of her government to outlast her, remaining in the same posts under John Major as they had been appointed to when Mrs Thatcher first came to office. It is difficult to sack members of the government in the Lords, given the absence of demand among peers for such posts.

More senior ministers tend to concentrate more on questions to their particular department. The Lord Chancellor answered three questions: one asking how often the Director of Public Prosecutions had considered complaints concerning threats to the life of Salman Rushdie and how often proceedings had been authorized, and two concerned with the role of the European Court of Justice. Another question on Salman Rushdie was answered by the Home Office Minister of State, Lord Ferrers, and other questions concerning the relationship between European Community institutions and the United Kingdom were handled by a Foreign Office minister. The Paymaster General, the Earl of Caithness, dealt only with Treasury questions, and the ministers of state at the Home Office and the Foreign Office likewise only answered questions that came within their departmental remit. Lord Sanderson of Bowden, the Scottish Office Minister of State, answered two questions on commercial fishing, as well as all questions concerned with Scotland; and Baroness Trumpington answered one question on the arts (concerned with funding for the Royal Shakespeare Theatre), as well as all agriculture and food questions. On the other hand, Lord Trefgarne, Minister of State at Trade and Industry, answered questions on behalf of six different departments. Lord Trefgarne held eight different posts under Mrs Thatcher between 1979 and his resignation in July 1990. Throughout this period he was a prolific answerer of starred questions; in the 1981–82 session he answered questions orally in the House almost every other day, and he was still a near top performer in 1989–90.

Some ministers answer very few questions, partly because the departments in which they have responsibilities have few questions directed to them. Thus the Lord Advocate, Lord Fraser of Carmyllie, answered no questions during the 1989–90 session; and Lord Skelmersdale, junior minister at the Northern Ireland Office answered only one, that being the sole question specifically concerned with Northern Ireland (it concerned Belfast prison).

The more protracted nature of proceedings on specific questions in the Lords as compared to the Commons can make the process of answering more exacting for government spokesmen. Coping with supplementaries for up to ten or even fifteen minutes, with peers rising from all quarters of the House, some of them with vast experience of the area under consideration, is a very different kind of experience from the quick fire of Commons Question Time. While some ministers exude great authority and command over their subjects (for example, the Lord Chancellor), others are very inexperienced. In particular, in the late 1980s there was some public comment about the apparent difficulties the government was facing in recruiting peers to the front bench in the Upper House. When in August 1989 the 32-year-old 18th Earl of Strathmore and Kinghorne was appointed a Lord in Waiting a few months after entering the House and before he had made his maiden speech, the *Financial Times* commented on the difficulty that the government faced in finding peers prepared to labour in the House for the modest salary involved.[17] When Lord Trefgarne resigned in July 1990, Lord Hesketh was appointed Minister of State at the Department of Trade and Industry; he had first entered the government in autumn 1986, having made his maiden speech in the House a few weeks earlier. Such rapid promotion to a middle-ranking ministerial job would hardly come to even the most able of Commons ministers. It is something of a paradox that in a House supposedly renowned for its expertise and the experience of its members, there should be such difficulty in filling government posts.

The Labour opposition in 1990 had a front bench team of some thirty members, all of them life peers and a third of them former members of the Commons. The opposition front bench spokesmen frequently intervene at Question Time, and certainly in some cases their expertise on the matter concerned is very much greater than that of the minister answering the question. Likewise, many peers on the cross-benches and indeed on the government backbenches are individuals with considerable experience, as their interventions during questions can reveal.

Furthermore, whereas in the Commons a minister will answer questions only on matters for which he has direct ministerial

---

[17] *Financial Times*, 4 Aug. 1989.

responsibility, and then only on certain days at intervals of perhaps three to six weeks (see Chapters 2 and 3), no such pattern prevails in the Lords. A departmental team of ministers in the Commons can spend a good deal of time preparing for their Question Time appearances, ensuring relevant facts are clearly in mind and so on. In the Lords, by contrast, ministers can be called upon to answer questions on virtually any sitting day. For some ministers this imposes quite a heavy burden. The case of Lord Trefgarne has already been referred to. When Lord Young of Graffham, as Secretary of State for Employment, became a particular target for frequent and hostile questions from Labour peers, he contrasted his position as a minister in the Lords unfavourably with that of a Commons' minister precisely because he had to answer questions so relatively frequently.[18]

Questioners and their Questions

Peers, like MPs, differ in how much use they make of the device of the parliamentary question. Table 6.3 gives figures for two recent sessions (and one session further back) for the number of peers asking questions and the number of questions asked, by party affiliation. In 1984–85 only 15 per cent of the peers who attended the House during the session asked any starred questions, and this represented only 25 per cent of the peers who took some part in debates on the Floor of the House. The figures for 1988–89 were very similar. Of the 150 peers who asked starred questions in the latter session, 59 asked one question only, and only 12 asked ten questions or more. These twelve asked 41 per cent of all the starred questions asked.[19] This is a very similar proportion to that asked by the twelve most frequent questioners in 1971.[20]

A high proportion of those who ask most questions are former MPs. Nine of the thirteen peers who asked most starred questions in 1984–85 had been members of the Lower House, and seven of the twelve most frequent questioners in 1988–89 were also former MPs. Generally the questions of the most active questioners ranged widely in terms of subject matter. Such peers appear to be

---

[18] *HL Deb.* (1985–86) 472, col. 87.
[19] See Borthwick, 'Non-Legislative Debate'.
[20] *HL Deb.* (1972) 327, col. 1127.

Table 6.3. *Questions asked, by party affiliation*

Party	1988–89		1984–85		1955–56	
	Starred questions					
	No. of peers asking	No. of questions asked	No. of peers asking	No. of questions asked	No. of peers asking	No. of questions asked
Conservative	62	229	57	203	21	41
Labour	39	200	30	231	14	29
Liberal SDP	24	89	23	107	5	35
Cross-bench	25	54	17	35	8	25
TOTAL	150	572	127	576	48	129
	Questions for written answer					
Conservative	100	481	77	331		
Labour	41	294	51	430		
Liberal SDP	25	291	25	239		
Cross-bench	25	155	25	132		
TOTAL	191	1221	177	1132		

Sources: For 1988–89, R. Borthwick, 'Non-Legislative Debate and Questions', in Shell and Beamish (eds.), *The House of Lords at Work* (Oxford: Clarendon Press, 1993). For 1984–85, D. Shell, *The House of Lords*, 2nd edn. (Hemel Hempstead; Harvester-Wheatsheaf, 1992). For 1955–56, P. A. Bromhead, *The House of Lords and Contemporary Politics* (London: Routledge & Kegan Paul, 1958).

concerned to ask questions which expose the weaknesses of the opposite party or act as helpful pointers to the achievements of their party in office. A few examples can be used to illustrate this.

Ever since his arrival in the House of Lords in 1978, Lord Hatch of Lusby has been a prolific asker of starred questions. He was for many years Commonwealth correspondent for the *New Statesman*, but never sat in the Commons. In both the 1983–84 and 1984–85 sessions he asked more questions than any other peer (forty and thirty-seven respectively). In 1988–89 and 1989–90 he was still one of the top twelve questioners. In the earlier sessions his questions tended to concentrate on foreign affairs and defence matters, though they also dealt with many other topics. In 1989–90 almost half his questions were answered by an Energy spokesman, but the other half continued to cover a miscellany of topics. Another

Labour backbench peer who asked many questions was Lord
Molloy, a former MP who had also been active in the trade union
movement. In 1989–90 his thirty questions received answers from
spokesmen on behalf of eleven different government departments.
Neither of these were front bench spokesmen, but some front
benchers in the Lords do table a good many questions (unlike
front benchers in the Commons). Thus Lord Dean of Beswick
asked some two dozen questions in the 1989–90 session, concen-
trating on housing, for which he was the party spokesman.

These Labour peers had their Conservative counterparts. Lord
Boyd-Carpenter, formerly an MP and a Chief Secretary to the
Treasury and until 1990 Chairman of the Association of Conservative Peers (the Lords equivalent to the 1922 Committee) was one
such. Not only did he ask many questions over a wide range of
topics, but he intervened frequently with supplementaries which
were invariably elegant and eloquent and often also sharply
partisan. Lord Campbell of Croy, a former Secretary of State for
Scotland while an MP, asked more questions than any other peer
in the 1988–89 session, and again he covered many subjects. Two
hereditary peers who had never sat in the Commons but were also
frequent questioners on the Conservative side in the late 1980s
were Lord Gainford and Baroness Strange, the latter's questions
frequently having an almost adulatory character. Clearly some
government backbench peers are eager to ensure a steady flow of
what might be called friendly questions, though it has to be said
that, given the extended nature of supplementary questioning,
what begins as a friendly question can easily end up as something
distinctly less so. Matters of current political controversy regularly
surface in questions. During 1990 the climbing inflation rate
encouraged a number of Labour peers to table questions asking
for specific comparisons with earlier rates or explanations of the
present rate in the light of past statements by ministers. The peers
who did this included Lord Donoughue, the former head of the
Prime Minister's policy unit under Jim Callaghan, and Lord
Dormand, who as a Labour MP had been Chairman of the
Parliamentary Labour Party before becoming a peer in 1987.

Some peers specialize very noticeably. Baroness Burton of
Coventry, who was a Labour MP in the 1950s before taking a life
peerage in 1962, has for almost three decades regularly asked
questions with regard to consumer interests. In 1990 her particular

concern was to galvanize the government into taking more seriously than it appeared to be doing the need to make provision for extra airport capacity, a subject about which she asked questions on six occasions between April and June. Lord St John of Fawsley, formerly the Conservative Cabinet minister Norman St John-Stevas, asked three questions on the proposed export of the statue known as 'The Three Graces', and also a couple about religious broadcasting. Lord Merrivale, a hereditary Conservative backbench peer, clearly had a particular concern about the Algeciras to Gibraltar ferry service, while Baroness Sharples, another Conservative backbencher, asked about the Blandford fly, and was openly lost for words when in answer to a question on 1 May 1990 the government announced that it was spending up to £70,000 to try to rid the River Stour of this particular unwelcome form of wild life. Questions from a number of peers in 1990 were directed at impressing concern on the government about a proposed 'over the horizon' radar installation on the St Davids peninsula.

Some peers ask very occasional questions. In 1988–89 Borthwick found that over a third of those who asked starred questions asked only one. The position was very similar in the early 1980s. The Bishop of Worcester asked about homelessness in London on 21 February 1989. Lord Callaghan of Cardiff, former Prime Minister, asked about Soviet and East European Studies in the UK on 26 July, and the resulting exchanges lasted fifteen minutes. Lord Halsbury asked about the Tower of London on 26 April 1990; most unusually he prefaced his question by making a personal statement in which he declared his interest as President of the Association of Friends of the Chapels Royal and referred to his late wife's work. The burden of his question concerned changed administrative arrangements in regard to the Tower and their introduction without proper consultation; but he was also concerned at the possible removal of some of the treasures from the Jewel house for display elsewhere. Baroness Birk, the Labour opposition spokesperson, had clearly checked out the facts involved in this case. The Duke of Norfolk added historical detail. Lord Hesketh, replying for the government, was able to say that he had dined at the Tower the previous evening, so perhaps he too was trying to find out what had been going on. In any event, this was another question which occupied the House for a full fifteen minutes.

Questions for Written Answer

Reference has already been made to Table 6.1, which shows the very considerable increase that has taken place in questions for written answer. From encouraging peers to use this procedure so as to alleviate pressure on starred questions in the early 1970s, the Select Committee on Procedure was considering whether to introduce any restriction on the number of QWAs any individual peer might have on the Order Paper at one time by the late 1970s. This has never been done; nor does it seem to be necessary. Table 6.3 reveals that rather more peers table QWAs than ask starred questions, but the numbers doing so are still modest; fewer than 200 members of the House made any use of QWAs in 1988–89.[21]

Again, however, we find that a small number of peers ask a high proportion of the total of QWAs. In 1984–85 seventeen peers asked over half of all QWAs, and in 1988–89 the position was only slightly different.[22] Those who make considerable use of the QWA procedure are not infrequently peers who ask very few if any starred questions. For example, Lord Kennet asked 173 QWAs in 1988–89 but only five starred questions, while four of the top eleven askers of QWAs tabled no starred questions at all. This should probably be taken to indicate nothing more than a personal preference. If the main concern of a peer is to obtain a piece of information, then the QWA remains a sensible, efficient way of going about it, at least from the peer's point of view. In addition, some peers who find it inconvenient to attend the House or whose reliable attendance cannot be guaranteed because of age or infirmity may prefer to ask a QWA.

Lord Kennet was a Labour minister in the 1960s, but then joined the SDP, becoming their spokesman on defence and foreign affairs; in 1989, however, he moved away to the cross-benches. His questions concentrated on defence and foreign affairs. Another peer who very frequently tabled QWAs in the early 1980s was Lord Avebury, formerly the Liberal MP Eric Lubbock, who used his position in the Lords to ask numerous questions about immigrants and prisoners. In the late 1980s Lord Hylton, a hereditary cross-bench peer, appeared to have become the resident spokesman for such folk in the Upper House. Other

[21] Borthwick, 'Non-Legislative Debate'.
[22] Shell, *House of Lords*, 206, Borthwick, 'Non-Legislative Debate'.

peers who often asked QWAs were Lord O'Hagan, the MEP for Devon, whose questions invariably had a European slant, Lord Jenkins of Putney on nuclear-related matters, and Lord Mason of Barnsley (formerly the Labour Cabinet minister Roy Mason) on salmon fishing.

About one third of those who ask QWAs in a session ask but a single question.[23] The device of the QWA permits any peer with a particular concern to table a question to the government. In some cases the purpose lying behind the question is clear enough. A peer may be gathering information in advance of some debate or other proceeding in the House. Perhaps he or she is concerned to update information or simply to know when the government expects some document to become available. A QWA may even be used to remind the government of some commitment it has given, or at least remind the government that the peer asking the question is still looking for an answer.

Some of these questions are 'inspired' (see above, p. 63). A calculation made in 1985 suggested that this might well be true of about one-third of Lords' QWAs, that being the proportion that had almost identical parallel questions for written answer in the Commons. The relatively modest use of this device in the Lords is no doubt in part related to its very heavy use in the Commons. Peers can easily access the Commons *Hansard*, using the POLIS index system freely available within the Palace of Westminster. Written answers in the Commons are a mine of information. Furthermore, peers do not have constituency concerns, though some peers certainly take up particular cases, as Lord Avebury frequently did in respect of prisoners. Peers sometimes ask about particular local interests—for example, planning decisions—but their concern is generally expressed as a general point about procedures and practices. Examination of *Hansard* suggests that the written parliamentary question is a useful device for all parliamentarians.

Conclusion

Although some peers have from time to time expressed concern that the character of proceedings in the Lords with respect to

---

[23] Shell, *House of Lords*, and Borthwick, 'Non-Legislative Debate'.

starred questions has been more and more approximating that of the Commons, this hardly seems a justified anxiety. Certainly Lords questions are dealt with today in a very different manner from that which prevailed twenty or thirty years ago. There is a much greater eagerness to participate in questions now than there was then. It is very unusual for three or four peers not to join in with supplementaries on a question, and as we have noted, sometimes the number doing so is considerably more. There is in general a sharper cut and thrust of a party-political kind than used to be the case. In 1958 Peter Bromhead wrote that 'opposition peers rarely ask questions with the intention of embarrassing or annoying the Government'.[24] This could certainly not be said today! At the same time the proceedings have not become so dominated by party-political point scoring as they have in the Commons. In particular, the longer time given to each question allows for more probing supplementaries. Government spokesmen who answer questions know that if the House is not satisfied, it will probably linger on a question. They are therefore less inclined to try answers that dodge the point of the question or present information different from that which was requested. At least some former MPs who have become peers contrast proceedings on questions between the two Houses in a way that is favourable to the Lords; for example, Lord Jenkins of Putney, a former MP, commented: 'On the whole I find the question procedures here [that is, in the Lords] rather preferable.'[25]

At the same time, because of the absence of any real semblance of power and hence the lack of a genuine or developed sense of ministerial responsibility to the House, questions in the Lords often have the appearance of being mere shadow-boxing. The hard political action is clearly taking place elsewhere. How much notice is taken of proceedings in the House is very difficult to say. It seems hard to believe that the Prime Minister 'always reads *Hansard*', as Baroness Trumpington suggested in the House when answering a supplementary question in April 1990.[26] But proceedings on a question may be shown on television to many thousands of viewers the following day. The possibility of influencing the

[24] P. A. Bromhead, *The House of Lords and Contemporary Politics* (London: Routledge and Kegan Paul, 1958), 225.
[25] *HL Deb.* (1981–82) 431, col. 707.
[26] *HL Deb.* (1989–90) 518, col. 107.

course of events through a well-made point during questions is always present, even if the reality is most of the time much more mundane.

In C. P. Snow's final novel in the *Strangers and Brothers* sequence, *Last Things*, the hero, Lewis Eliot, is created a peer (as indeed was C. P. Snow himself). An episode in this novel, published in 1970, has Lord Eliot involved in a question in the House of Lords. Though on the surface everything is quite normal, there is no doubt from the way the scene is written up that for the participants the proceedings are regarded as being of considerable importance.[27] Questions in the Lords can draw contributions from the very well informed and from individuals whose reputation virtually ensures that what they say is at least listened to by those who hold power. At the same time, they can appear as a boring and rather meaningless exercise, of interest to almost no one but the participants themselves. But, allowing for all the differences in style, much the same could probably be said about the Commons.

[27] C. P. Snow, *Last Things* (London: Macmillan, 1970).

7

Questions outside Parliament

*Philip Norton**

Question Time, as we have seen, is a popular spectator event. It is popular with MPs themselves, and is popular with the media. The entry of the television cameras, discussed by Borthwick in Chapter 3, has added a new dimension. What happens in the chamber is now seen by millions, as opposed to the hundred or so spectators in the Strangers Gallery. Tabling questions, as we have seen (Chapter 2), is also very popular with Members of Parliament. Indeed, PQs could be described as a significant growth industry in recent decades.

Yet what use is actually made of the answers to the questions? Televised coverage of Question Time focuses as much, indeed more, on how questions are answered—and supplementaries asked—as on the substance of the answers. There is little interest beyond the adversarial clash of competing parties. What happens, then, to the printed word, to the answers to oral and written questions published in *Hansard*? Are they left to gather dust, of interest only to the occasional researcher or vain MP? Or have they a wider audience?

Some questions, as we have seen (Chapter 4), are tabled for partisan purposes. This applies especially to oral questions. Once asked in the chamber, their purpose is fulfilled. Some questions are tabled by MPs seeking information for speeches or projects. Some are tabled by MPs wanting to raise their profile in the House. The act of tabling questions is thus more important than the substance of the answers they receive. Yet the data in Chapter 4, identifying the reasons why Members table questions, suggest that a large number of questions have a utility that extends beyond the Palace of Westminster.

Answers to PQs have at least two consequences that extend

* For reading and commenting on a draft of this chapter, I am especially grateful to Simon Denegri, Cliff Grantham, Nick de Luca, and Paul Willis.

beyond Westminster. One is functional: they provide information of use to outside bodies. As we shall see, the uses to which that information can be put are several. The other is to enhance the legitimacy of Parliament.

Making use of Answers

The bodies outside Westminster that make greatest use of answers to parliamentary questions can be subsumed under two heads: interest groups and the mass media.

That interest groups make use of answers—and do so on a much more significant scale than ever before—can be deduced from three important pieces of data. The first is the increase, noted in the Introduction, in the number of interest groups. Such groups have burgeoned in number since 1960. They have made more demands of the political system, and have increasingly lobbied Parliament, seeing this as a route of supplementary influence—sometimes as an alternative route—to that of government departments. A consequence of the increased activity of pressure groups in the political arena, we would hypothesize, would be to make use of PQs as means of raising issues and to monitor answers in order to gauge departmental thinking and intentions, as well as obtain useful information.

The second set of data is drawn from surveys of interest groups and Members. A survey of more than 250 interest groups in 1986 found that the overwhelming majority (189, almost 75 per cent of the total) had regular or frequent contact with one or more MPs. Of the groups maintaining such contact, more than 80 per cent had asked an MP to table a question. This percentage exceeded that for all other types of demands made of Members (Table 7.1).[1] It is a finding reinforced by our own survey of MPs. As we detailed in Chapter 4, only 18 per cent of respondents said that they never tabled questions when they were asked to. Almost two-thirds had

---

[1] The percentage asking peers to put down questions was smaller (48.6%), hardly surprising given the limited opportunity to table PQs in the House of Lords. However, it remained a large proportion compared with the other requests to peers. Only asking a peer to arrange a meeting at the Lords atracted an affirmative response from a larger percentage of groups (53.7%). M. Rush (ed.), *Parliament and Pressure Politics* (Oxford: Clarendon Press, 1990), 290, q. 11(e).

178   *Philip Norton*

Table 7.1. *Interest group requests to MPs*

Request	Answering 'yes'	
	Number	%
Have you ever asked an MP to:		
Put down a parliamentary question	157	83.1
Table a motion	97	51.3
Introduce or sponsor a Private Member's Bill	70	37.0
Table an amendment to a Bill	117	61.9
Arrange a meeting for you or your organization at the House of Commons	148	78.3
Arrange a dinner or reception or similar function at the Commons	78	41.3
Arrange a meeting with a minister	94	49.7

Note: Survey conducted in 1986 of 253 organized groups. Table based on 189 respondents who said they maintained regular or frequent contact with one or more MPs.
Source: M. Rush (ed.), *Parliament and Pressure Politics* (Oxford: Clarendon Press, 1990), 281.

questions drafted for them on occasion by political consultants. Some Members also rely heavily on research assistants, a number of whom have links with outside groups. Some researchers and secretaries in Westminster are actually financed by such groups. The 1986 survey of interest groups found that, of the 189 having regular contact with MPs, twenty provided secretarial or some form of assistance to one or more Members.[2]

The third and possibly most relevant set of data in this context cover the growth in the number of political consultants in the UK. Though popularly known as lobbyists, the term 'political consultants' is perhaps most appropriate when considering the uses made of answers to PQs. Lobbying implies a proactive stance, making representations to government—and Parliament—in order to influence public policy. This is clearly part of the activity of consultants, and using PQs as part of this activity is obviously important. (Groups—well-organized consumer and labour groups

[2] Ibid. 281, q. 1(e).

in particular—will often demonstrate their concern over proposed legislation by asking Members to table questions.[3]) However, their activity is reactive as well as proactive. Indeed, a large proportion of the time of political consultants is given over to monitoring parliamentary developments. Some companies, such as Randalls and PMS (Parliamentary Monitoring Service), exist principally or exclusively for the purpose of monitoring. The most central and time-consuming aspect of this work is the monitoring of answers to parliamentary questions.

Recent years have witnessed a significant growth in the number of political consultancy firms in the UK. They were virtually unknown, albeit not non-existent, in the 1960s and early 1970s. But since 1979, they have expanded in number, and flourished.[4] (The 1992 edition of *Dod's Parliamentary Companion* lists forty-one such firms.) They are supplemented by a large number of free-lance consultants and also by consultants employed by firms and other organized interests on an in-house basis. A 1985 survey of 180 sizeable companies found that more than 40 per cent utilized the services of political consultants.[5] The 1986 survey of interest groups found that 20 per cent employed the services of a public relations consultant or firm. However, reflecting the extent of in-house work, almost 40 per cent said they employed someone to monitor or keep in touch with what was happening in Parliament.[6] The emphasis on monitoring is significant.

When bidding for clients, political consultants will emphasize their monitoring services. Checking *Hansard* on a daily basis is a task assigned to researchers, the workhorses starting their career in the lobbying field. (Senior executives advise clients, and generally undertake the tasks associated with lobbying.) Any material covering the client's area of interest is photocopied and forwarded, either in raw form or as part of a more analytic

---

[3] P. Norton, 'Public Legislation', ibid. 184.

[4] See esp. C. Grantham, 'Parliament and Political Consultants', *Parliamentary Affairs*, 42 4 (Oct. 1989), 503–18. See also C. Grantham and C. Seymour-Ure, 'Political Consultants', in Rush (ed.), *Parliament and Pressure Politics*, 45–84, and *Parliamentary Lobbying: Third Report from the Select Committee on Members' Interests*, HC (1990–91) 586 (London: HMSO, 1991), paras. 18, 19.

[5] *Financial Times*, 23 Dec. 1985.

[6] Rush (ed.) *Parliament and Pressure Politics*, 293, q. 14, 15. The person employed to monitor Parliament was usually a full-time employee, but not one whose time was devoted exclusively to Parliament.

package. Given that each government department normally answers several—sometimes many—written questions each week, it is not surprising that answers constitute the bulk of this package.

Consultants thus act as conduits between parliamentary activity and clients. Clients include firms and professional bodies, as well as a number of interest groups. Those clients will use the answers in a number of ways. One is straightforwardly as information-providers, using factual answers to add to their store of knowledge about their sector and the effects of public policy. Another is as a form of political intelligence, using answers to gauge government intentions and, as we shall see, to identify friends and enemies. Some clients—particularly interest groups—will also act as conduits themselves, publishing a selection of answers in their trade or professional journals. This serves both to convey information to a wider audience and to help justify the existence of the group providing the service. Others do little with the answers, recognizing that they need to do something to keep up with their competitors—hence hiring consultants—but not quite sure what to do with the material they are given.

Other firms and interest groups use their own employees to undertake a similar exercise. Few such organizations will have in-house specialists on anything approaching the scale of the larger political consultancies. Even some of the large national utilities, for example, will have no more than two or three employees working full-time on governmental and parliamentary relations. Where only a single employee is involved, monitoring PQs constitutes a major proportion of the workload. Where there are two or three employees, one is normally assigned responsibility for monitoring.

Both consultants and in-house researchers make use of PQs as a valuable means of identifying the particular interests of MPs and, indeed, their stance on those issues. 'The question', as one leading consultant observed, 'may be less important than the motivation of the questioner.'[7] MPs who table 'friendly' questions will not only be noted, but also, in many cases, approached with offers of information and advice and, implicitly or explicitly, encouragement to help the cause. This is especially important for promotional groups—animal welfare organizations, for example—who need to

---

[7] C. Miller, *Lobbying*, 2nd edn., (Oxford: Basil Blackwell, 1990), 143–4.

raise the public profile of their campaigns through parliamentary devices such as Private Members' legislation. PQs offer a valuable resource for identifying possible sponsors and supporters. 'Hostile' Members will be identified for the purpose of avoidance or else for approach in order to counter their claims or misgivings. From the point of view of utility companies, to take a particular example, this category will include Members who have power-generating plants in their constituencies and who table questions concerning the safety and environmental records of those plants. For the utility company responsible for the plant, the PQ is often the first indication they have of an MP's concern. The moment the PQ is picked up in the previous day's *Hansard*, a letter is immediately sent to the Member.[8] For bodies wanting to utilize Parliament for lobbying purposes, an analysis of PQs thus constitutes an important initial step. It is central to the exercise of mapping the political terrain.

The evidence would thus seem sufficient to bear out our hypothesis. As more and more pressure groups have come into existence and sought to influence public policy, the greater the use they have made of in-house or bought-in-expertise in order to monitor as well as lobby. Such groups, as we have seen, are significant prompters of parliamentary questions. They are also significant consumers.

Indeed, it would probably be fair to say that organized interests—ranging from City firms to small pressure groups—constitute far more avid consumers of answers to PQs than the mass media—or at least the print media. For the press, poring over answers to PQs is not an overly rewarding exercise. It is none the less an exercise that is engaged in. There is always the chance of finding a significant answer slipped in under the guise of a routine answer to a written question. Those occasions are relatively rare, and PQs do not figure significantly in newspapers' daily output. For serious national dailies, answers to PQs will be utilized to fill a few column inches. The occasion of Question Time—the atmo-sphere, the cut and thrust—is likely to occupy more space as part of a parliamentary sketch-writer's column. Answers will only be utilized in the tabloid press if they prove controversial or convey

---

[8] Former parliamentary officer of a national utility to Philip Norton, interview, 1992.

information that is colourful or unusual. Answers to PQs are too dated to be utilized on any regular basis by the Sunday papers.

All this despite the fact that Question Time comes at prime time in the parliamentary day and attracts a good audience in the Press Gallery, and that departments go out of their way to ensure that the Gallery receives copies of answers to questions. Question Time falls at a good time for the purpose of meeting copy deadlines. Relative to opportunity, the coverage given to PQs is thus limited. But this is not all that surprising. There is little value in covering a routine answer. The coverage is of the party clash and the exceptional. The increase in the number of PQs tabled has not been matched by an increase in newsworthiness. The more questions that are tabled, the harder MPs—and departments—have to work in order to get a particular answer noticed.

The position is different with the broadcast media. Question Time has traditionally received a significant proportion of the time in 'Today in Parliament', the daily radio programme devoted to parliamentary proceedings. Coverage by television programmes for most of the period under review was limited, a fact explicable by the absence of pictures from the chamber. All that changed with the entry of the cameras in November 1989. The initial fear of many opponents of TV coverage was that too much attention would be given to PM's Question Time and not enough to the rest of Question Time and to the other activities—especially the committee work—of the House. In the event, those fears have not been borne out. A review of the first fifteen weeks of parliamentary broadcasting found that PM's Question Time occupied a signifi-cant, but not overwhelming, proportion of the time given by the national programmes—ranging from 10 per cent on the daily BBC 'Westminster' programme to 38 per cent on ITV's 'News at Ten'.[9] The committee work of the House received more coverage than many parliamentarians expected—especially on the dedicated weekly programmes[10]—as did, far more significantly in terms of time, the rest of Question Time. Though daily news programmes,

---

[9] *Review of the Experiment in Televising the Proceedings of the House: First Report from the Select Committee on the Televising of Proceedings of the House*, HC (1989–90) 265-I (London: HMSO, 1990), Annex 4, Table 4, p. 41.

[10] The review of the experiment (ibid.) found that committee coverage occupied more than one-third of the time of the BBC2 'Westminster' programme. There is also now a BBC2 weekly programme, 'Scrutiny', devoted to covering the work of parliamentary committees.

with the exception of 'News at Ten', tended to give somewhat more time to PM's Question Time than the rest of Question Time, the position was generally reversed on the dedicated programmes. The BBC programmes 'Westminster' and the 'Westminster Week' were especially noteworthy for the proportion of air time they gave to Question Time other than the PM's, the average being 36 per cent in each case. When added to PM's Question Time, the time given over to questions by the two programmes was 61 per cent and 50 per cent respectively.[11]

Question Time has thus enjoyed significant coverage, especially on the dedicated programmes. These programmes have a much smaller audience than the news broadcasts in the evenings, but far higher than many broadcasters anticipated. Evening news coverage can reach between eleven and fifteen million people. The dedicated daily programmes, according to the data from the first few months of broadcasts, can draw anything from 100,000 to 250,000 viewers, and the weekly round-ups about 300,000 to 350,000. Live coverage of PM's Question Time can draw a seven-figure audience.[12]

Though the introduction of cameras into the Commons has also had, as Borthwick has noted (Chapter 3), some negative effects— including, it might be added, largely squeezing out coverage of proceedings in the House of Lords—it has served to open up Question Time in the House, at least in visual terms, to a far larger audience than was ever previously possible.

These observations apply to national coverage. A different position emerges in terms of regional coverage. Regional television programmes have tended to give greater emphasis to speeches made by local MPs in debates.[13] Indeed, once one moves below national level, PQs appear to assume more prominence in the print than the broadcast media. The explanation for this may well rest in the nature and scope of the different media. Sub-national television is organized on a regional basis. Local radio stations operate at a sub-regional level, but each covering an area that usually encompasses several parliamentary constituencies. For each television and local radio station, there is likely to be at least

---

[11] Ibid., Annex 4, p. 13, and Table 4, p. 41.
[12] Ibid., p. xxix. See also A. Hetherington, K. Weaver, and M. Ryle, *Cameras in the Commons* (London: Hansard Society, 1990).
[13] *Televising the Proceedings of the House*, Annex 4, pp. 13, 33–5.

one MP within its transmission area who—if not each day, certainly each week—has made a speech in the chamber or otherwise attracted attention. By contrast, many local papers— especially in rural areas—have a readership confined to one particular constituency. Some large rural constituencies may encompass a number of local papers. For them, whatever the local MP does at Westminster constitutes political news. Given that a backbencher may table a number of PQs each week but only make—to take the parliamentary average—four speeches a session, PQs constitute the most regular source of Westminster news for the local paper. MPs themselves are well aware of this. As we saw in Chapter 4, 82 per cent of the Members we questioned said they sent copies of their PQ answers to the local press.

Furthermore, for local papers, there is often the problem of finding news to fill the space available. Material sent by the MP is essentially cheap copy, not requiring the despatch of a journalist or—usually—significant editorial work. For TV and local radio, there is competition for air time, with news occupying a small proportion of the total transmission time. Beyond the confines of the local constituency, a routine PQ is not newsworthy.

This relationship of MPs to the local press is nothing new. Chester and Bowring commented on it.[14] What has changed, as we have seen (Chapter 2), has been the number of PQs that Members table. In the 1950s and 1960s, a PQ was more significant because of its relative rarity. It was thus possible, to take a particular example, for an MP, a businessman who was not always notably active in Westminster or his constituency, to give the impression of parliamentary activity by regularly tabling written questions and sending the answers to the local newspaper. The answers would be duly published, thus conveying the intended impression. Today, PQs are more numerous and, not least now as a result of radio and TV coverage, somewhat better understood. Consequently, though they might get quantitatively more coverage than before, individually they have less impact. Indeed, to take an ironic example, the present-day successor to the MP just mentioned ran into criticism in the local press in 1990 for being silent in the chamber. The fact that he tabled written questions was not enough to protect him from such criticism.

[14] D. N. Chester and N. Bowring, *Questions in Parliament* (Oxford: Clarendon Press, 1962), 176–7.

Parliamentary questions none the less remain important sources

Parliamentary questions none the less remain important sources of copy for local newspapers. Added to this, we now have the much wider coverage of Question Time itself by the broadcast media. The attention given to PQs by organized interests has also increased in extent and significance. As a result, the audience for PQs—oral and written—is now far more significant than at any time before in the history of parliamentary questions. It is a development that has important implications for the political system.

Enhancing Legitimacy

The implications are not uniformly positive. As we saw in Chapter 3, TV coverage of Question Time has some negative consequences, to some extent undermining the legitimacy of the 'territorial' Question Times through the greater involvement—for publicity purposes—of MPs from other parts of the UK. Critics of televising proceedings would also see the coverage of Question Time—especially PM's Question Time—as encouraging, and being part of, a form of popular entertainment, rather than recording the serious questioning of ministers.

The involvement of lobbyists in instigating PQs has also aroused fears of both unequal access to, and manipulation of, the parliamentary process. The use made of answers to PQs by lobbying firms may also enhance the perceived legitimacy of such bodies, giving the impression to potential clients of some form of superior knowledge of parliamentary proceedings. The monitoring service offered by a firm may mask a relatively fickle grasp of the intricacies of both Whitehall and Westminster. Thus there exists a problem of accountability derived not so much from the lobbyist–MP relationship (democratic accountability) as from the client–lobbyist relationship (consumer accountability).[15]

It is difficult to deny that there are some negative implications. Some MPs may play to the cameras, raising bogus points of order.[16] The competence of political consultancies—and individual

[15] P. Norton and C. Grantham, 'The Hyphen in British Politics? Parliament and Professional Lobbying', *British Politics Group Newsletter* (USA), 45 (Summer 1986), 4–8. See also Grantham, 'Parliament and Political Consultants'.
[16] See the Speaker's observations in *Televising the Proceedings of the House*, para. 142.

consultants—varies considerably. In the 1986 survey of interest groups, more than 20 per cent of respondents said that they were aware of abuses in the lobbying process.[17] (As Grantham and Seymour-Ure record, there are occasional rumours of a 'going rate' for putting down a PQ, said to be about £150 in 1985.[18]) There is no professional body to police the industry. In 1991, in addressing this problem, the Select Committee on Members' Interests took the step of recommending the establishment of a Register of Political Lobbyists,[19] something it had previously recommended against.

These problems are essentially at the margins, however. What has been notable about the televising of proceedings has been the extent to which MPs' behaviour in the chamber has shown no significant change.[20] The Select Committee on Members' Interests, in its 1991 report on political lobbying, noted that no organization had come forward to claim that it had been 'conned' by a lobbying company, and it was unable to find any evidence of serious misdeeds.[21] This is not to claim that there is not a problem. Perceptions are sometimes more potent than the reality of what actually takes place. So long as there is perceived to be a problem associated with the activities of lobbyists, then that constitutes a problem.

Nevertheless, these problems pale alongside the advantages that accrue from the use made of PQs by the mass media as well as by consultants and outside interests. As the Members' Interests Committee recorded in its 1991 report, the free flow of information is an essential part of the democratic process.[22] Parliamentary questions are important in contributing to that flow. As we have seen, there are significant restrictions. When answers are given, they often provide no substantive information or else give data that are already in the public domain. However, those PQs that elicit information not already available from other sources make an important contribution to a more open system. Furthermore, Question Time itself has a symbolic significance, providing a

[17] Rush (ed.), *Parliament and Pressure Politics*, 296, q. 20.
[18] Grantham and Seymour-Ure, 'Political Consultants', 77.
[19] *Parliamentary Lobbying*, pp. xx–xxv.
[20] P. Riddell, *The Times*, 23 Dec. 1991. *Televising the Proceedings of the House*, paras. 143, 144.   [21] *Parliamentary Lobbying*, para. 17, p. ix.
[22] Ibid., para. 13, p. viii.

public manifestation of ministers being questioned by the people's elected representatives. The spectacle of the head of government making twice-weekly appearances to be questioned in the House of Commons is held up as one of the more positive elements of openness in the British system—often contrasted with the position in presidential systems, not least in the United States.

The departmental select committees have contributed significantly to greater openness.[23] So have the developments we have outlined, enhancing the legitimacy of the House among both the general public and attentive publics. The televising of proceedings has contributed to greater openness, through coverage not only of committee proceedings but also—more significantly in terms of the amount of air time—of Question Time. With that openness has come greater awareness. Surveys of both MPs and members of the public in 1990 revealed remarkably similar perceptions of the effects of televised proceedings. Seventy-four per cent of MPs questioned felt that 'the public probably now knows more about how Parliament works'; more than 80 per cent of the public questioned (in two waves, in October–November 1989 and March 1990) felt that the effect of televising would be to increase understanding of how Parliament works, with more than 70 per cent believing that it would make people feel more involved in what is going on in Parliament.[24] The same survey also found a greater number of respondents giving correct answers in 1990 than in late 1989 to twelve questions about politicians and Parliament, though the increase was not statistically significant.

Too much should not be read into these findings. The survey of members of the public found little change in levels of cynicism towards politicians and the relationship between politicians and the public. The same survey also showed little change in perceptions of MPs' intelligence and working habits, though this was hardly something about which MPs were likely to complain, given that most respondents thought that MPs were intelligent and worked hard.[25] A MORI poll in April 1991 showed that 59 per

[23] P. Norton, 'The Changing Face of Parliament: Lobbying and its Consequences', in P. Norton (ed.), *New Directions in British Politics?* (Aldershot: Edward Elgar, 1991). 73–5.
[24] *Televising the Proceedings of the House*, p. xxxvi, para. 139, and Appendix 16, p. 84. See also Hetherington, Weaver, and Ryle, *Cameras in the Commons*, 7–8.
[25] *Televising the Proceedings of the House*, Appendix 16, pp. 84–5.

cent of respondents thought that Parliament worked well; not dissimilar results had been obtained in earlier decades.[26] Televised proceedings have not changed significantly, if at all, these particular perceptions; in other words, while not necessarily generating a more positive perception, they have not contributed either to a more negative one.

Overall, the effect, on the initial evidence available, is that the entry of the cameras has either been neutral (regarding levels of cynicism) or positive (generating greater knowledge/awareness of parliamentary proceedings). There appear to have been no significant negative effects at a systemic level.

More pervasively, television fulfils the function of latent legitimation of the political system.

> By operating within that system and accepting its norms, newspapers and television help maintain its popular legitimacy. When a political crisis arises, journalists and TV reporters descend on ministers and MPs for comment, hence accepting and reinforcing the legitimacy of those questioned to comment on the matter at hand. There is regular coverage of parliamentary proceedings.[27]

The willingness of TV companies to utilize the access to proceedings given them by the House reinforces the perceived legitimacy of the institution. Question Time constitutes a central feature of what the broadcasters choose to cover.

The greater dissemination of the answers to PQs to attentive publics—in other words, organized interests—has also contributed to a greater awareness of parliamentary proceedings and, to some degree, to a better knowledge of Parliament's relevance in the political system. Many companies and pressure groups have a history of little or no knowledge of the parliamentary process. The work of political consultants—or the self-taught approach of many groups—has resulted in a greater awareness of what Parliament has to offer. Obtaining answers to PQs has added not only to their substantive knowledge of their own sector but, combined with other parliamentary material and observation, to their knowledge of Parliament. The more such groups become consumers of answers to PQs, and instigate their tabling, the greater the

[26] *The Times*, 25 Apr. 1991. See also P. Norton, *Parliament in Perspective* (Hull: Hull University Press, 1987), 9.
[27] P. Norton, *The British Polity*, 2nd edn. (New York: Longman, 1991), 371.

attachment to the existing system. The 1986 survey of interest groups found that the overwhelming majority (over 92 per cent) rated their contact with MPs as 'useful' or 'very useful'.[28] We would hypothesize that, as groups become even more vigorous in seeking to have some input in to the parliamentary system—not least through PQs—as well as being more avid consumers of its outputs, then the level of satisfaction and attachment to the system that produces that satisfaction are likely to increase.

There remains the problem of access. The televising of proceedings has increased awareness of Question Time. More and more groups are seeking, through a self-taught approach or with professional assistance, to achieve some access to the parliamentary process. Available evidence would suggest that the principal bar to access is ignorance of how to go about it rather than than an unwillingness on the part of parliamentarians to listen and be persuaded. As knowledge increases, access is likely to follow. Parliamentary Questions, consequently, are likely to reach an even wider audience.

Appendix. Group Publications and Parliamentary Questions

The publications of pressure groups and other organised interests often use material drawn from answers to PQs. This extract constitutes one page—out of five—dealing with Parliament, principally PQs, in the August 1988 issue of *Atom*, the monthly journal of the United Kingdom Atomic Energy Authority.

Uranium
23 May
Mr Spicer informed Dr Thomas that the UKAEA has imported no uranium from Namibia since May 1979. Uranium for the UK civil nuclear programme has not been imported from South Africa since 1973 or from Namibia since 1984. BNFL receives uranium ore concentrate from over-seas customers for processing and re-export. The origin of such uranium is a matter for its customers who remain the owners of the material.

All uranium imported into the UK for these purposes is subject to

---

[28] Rush (ed.), *Parliament and Pressure Politics*, 282, q. 1(g).

Euratom safeguards and to the terms of the UK/Euratom/IAEA
safeguards agreement. (WA 7–8).

Uranium discharges
7 June
Mr Alton asked for information on levels of uranium discharged into
Rivacre Brook and from there into the River Mersey by BNFL from 1983
to 1988, and whether the secretary of state for the environment would
impose an absolute level on discharges of uranium by BNFL at
Capenhurst. Replying, Mr Moynihan gave the following figures for the
annual uranium alpha activity discharged into Rivacre Brook by BNFL for
its Capenhurst works from 1983 to 1986. Data for 1987 and 1988 are not
yet available.

Year	Annual discharge in mega becquerels
1983	500
1984	800
1985	900
1986	2000

Mr Moynihan stressed that these levels demonstrated that the discharge
represented an insignificant radiological hazard to members of the public.

The certificate of authorisation for the disposal of low level liquid
radioactive waste from BNFL Capenhurst works into Rivacre Brook
which sets concentration limits on uranium discharges is currently subject
to review by the authorising departments. It is the intention to include
limits on total quantities discharged. The review will be completed before
the end of the year. (WA 483).

Plutonium (Japan)
13 June
Mr Spicer told Mr Flynn that the Department of Energy has not made an
independent assessment of the quantity of plutonium required by Japan
for its fast breeder reactor and MOX fuel programmes to ensure that the
conditions for the export of fissile material to a non-nuclear weapons state
are adhered to. The return of plutonium from the reprocessing of spent
fuel at Thorp to its country of origin or to any other destination will not
take place for several years and will be made only on receipt of assurances
covering peaceful use, application of safeguards, physical protection and

controls on re-transfer in line with the statement made by the then foreign secretary, James Callaghan, on 31 March 1976. (WA 35).

Thorp
20 May
Dr Thomas asked what proportion of the current contracts signed for Thorp at Sellafield with non-UK companies is allocated for the expenditure to be incurred by (a) UK Nirex Ltd, (b) its successor body if reorganised under privatisation and (c) BNFL for the disposal of (i) low level wastes and (ii) intermediate level wastes to be retained in the UK after reprocessing.

Replying, Mr Spicer said, 'Since 1976 BNFL's contracts for the reprocessing of overseas spent fuel have contained options for the return of wastes. Contracts signed before 1976 do not contain such options and therefore cover the costs of long term storage and disposal of low and intermediate level wastes. I understand from BNFL that the costs of such storage and disposal are established to be less than 5 per cent of the total costs associated with current contracts signed for Thorp without return of waste options.' (WA 594–5).

9 June
In reply to Mr Foulkes, Mr Spicer said that Thorp is expected to begin commercial reprocessing in late 1992. The lifetime of the plant will be governed by a combination of economic, commercial and operational factors. Experience of other reprocessing plants suggests that Thorp can be expected to operate well into the second decade of the 21st century.

Mr Foulkes also asked for information on countries currently sending spent fuel to Sellafield for reprocessing and what countries are expecting to use and are currently in negotiation for the use of Thorp. Replying, Mr Spicer indicated that BNFL currently receives spent magnox fuel from Italy and Japan. Utilities in the Federal Republic of Germany, Italy, Japan, Netherlands, Spain, Sweden and Switzerland have entered into contracts for reprocessing in Thorp. On-going negotiations with potential customers are commercially confidential. (WA 633).

Radioactive waste
20 May
In reply to Dr Thomas, Mr Moynihan said that 25 UK delegates attended the IAEA/CEC symposium on low and intermediate level waste held in Stockholm from 16 to 20 May. The organisations represented were: HM Inspector of Pollution, HM Industrial Pollution Inspectorate, UKAEA, CEGB, SSEB, BNFL, NRPB, Taywood Engineering Ltd, Associated Nuclear Services and the Open University.

Dr Thomas also asked what physical checks were made on consignments of radioactive wastes on arrival at Drigg to ensure that the packaged waste contains only what HM Pollution Inspectorate authorisations allow. Mr Moynihan indicated that BNFL is responsible for quality assurance monitoring at the Drigg site. Inspectors of pollution also carry out quality checking. Material can be removed to an independent laboratory for analysis by inspectors.

Asked by Dr Thomas to provide details on the total radioactivity content in becquerels of nuclear wastes currently deposited at Drigg, Mr Moynihan indicated that 470 becquerels were disposed of at Drigg up to 1 January 1986. An authorisation controlling the disposal of solid radioactive waste to the Drigg site was issued on 1 February 1988 and will be reviewed by 1992.

Dr Thomas also made enquiries about the total plutonium content of material currently deposited at Drigg and the development of methods to extract plutonium. Mr Moynihan indicated that he had been advised by BNFL that there were about 500g of plutonium dispersed throughout $700\,000m^3$ of low level radioactive waste currently deposited at Drigg. The radioactive content of this is estimated to be approximately 25 terabecquerels. Much research has been carried out into methods to remove plutonium from wastes prior to disposal. However, none has proved to be worthwhile.

In reply to a further question from Dr Thomas concerning the proportion of radioactive wastes arising from contracts made with foreign companies or governments, Mr Moynihan stated that approximately 4 per cent by volume of the radioactive waste disposed of by burial into the ground at the Drigg disposal site up to the end of 1987 arose from BNFL contracts with foreign customers. This percentage is not expected to change significantly in the period to 2010.

Dr Thomas also asked for a statement on policy towards the import by the UK of foreign nuclear wastes in low and intermediate categories for (a) treatment, incineration and compaction and (b) disposal once Nirex has finalised its search for a suitable deep disposal site. Responding, Mr Moynihan stressed that no low and intermediate waste arising from anywhere in the world is imported into the United Kingdom. Any proposal to do so would be considered on its merits, with a view to ensuring that neither the public nor the environment should be placed at any risk. (WA 602–4).

26 May
Asked by Mr Chapman to make a statement on the disposal of the radioactive wastes prepared for sea disposal in 1983, Mr Parkinson indicated that the government had decided not to resume sea dumping of

drummed radioactive wastes. Instead, these will be prepared for eventual disposal in the deep facility for low and intermediate level wastes which Nirex has been asked to develop.

The government nevertheless remains in no doubt that sea disposal makes good sense for some categories of waste, and intends to keep open this option for large items arising from decommissioning operations. (WA 233).

8

Questions and the
Role of Parliament

Philip Norton

It is more than 270 years since Earl Cowper rose to put his question to the administration of Lord Sunderland. Since then, as this volume testifies, parliamentary questions have become a central feature of parliamentary life in the United Kingdom. It is difficult to imagine a week in the life of the House of Commons without thinking of Question Time. It is difficult to imagine *Hansard* without its pages of answers to written questions. So quickly has the practice become entrenched that it is now difficult to imagine what it was like just over thirty years ago when there was no fixed Prime Minister's Question Time. The introduction of television cameras has served not only to illuminate but also to entrench Question Time. As we have seen, it is highly televisual, especially Prime Minister's Question Time.

PQs and Question Time are parliamentary fixtures. Yet, as the foregoing chapters have shown, both have been subject to significant changes. Indeed, reference to the television cameras reflects one of the most recent changes. Other changes are likely, in part as a consequence of wider systemic and political develop-ments, in part as a more planned consequence of recommendations emanating from the Select Committee on Procedure. As we enter a new era, following the general election of 1992, it is a good time to take stock and to contemplate the future.

The most appropriate way to do this is to examine the pros and cons, drawing on the findings of the preceding chapters. As we have seen, there are many problems associated with PQs in general and Question Time in particular. On the other hand, both have considerable benefits—to Members of Parliament, to Parlia-ment, and to the wider political system. Those benefits are such that any consideration of change must be in order to strengthen, not destroy.

The Limitations

The limitations of Question Time in the 1990s may be succinctly stated. It offers an opportunity to ask relatively few questions. As we have seen (Chapter 2), demand far exceeds the supply of time available. Those that are asked are increasingly asked for partisan purposes. This has been a notable trend since Chester and Bowring wrote *Questions in Parliament*. It has not been an even trend. The incidence of partisan questions became marked especially in 1991 and the months of 1992 immediately preceding the dissolution of Parliament: a result of the confluence of the presence of television cameras and the proximity of a general election.

Of those questions that are partisan in nature, a large proportion—in the case of some departments, a majority—are the product of syndication (discussed in Chapter 2), Members tabling questions at the prompting of party colleagues. On the government side, this has tended to be at the prompting of the whips and the minister's Parliamentary Private Secretary. Hence, a significant number are tabled essentially on behalf of those who are to answer them. The reforms introduced in 1990 have not put an end to the practice. Many who are invited to table questions are now also offered supplementary questions to follow them up. Instead of being a spontaneous response from the questioner, many supplementaries are part of a well-rehearsed, sometimes not so well-rehearsed, script.

The most apparent incidence of partisan questions comes, as we have seen (Chapter 3), during Prime Minister's Question Time. Much of this takes the form of gladiatorial combat between the PM and the Leader of the Opposition. The latter often takes more than one bite of the cherry, thereby reducing the opportunity for backbench participation.

The 1980s witnessed a further change. Instead of questioning the Prime Minister about government policy, there was an increasing tendency among government backbenchers to question the PM about the opposition's policies. As the PM had no responsibility for opposition policies, the backbenchers had to front-load the questions with something ostensibly geared to the PM or public policy. Some questioners fell foul of the Speaker;

some got their lines wrong;[1] some fluffed their lines altogether.[2] The tendency to use the occasion to attack the opposition increased in the months leading up to the 1992 general election.

The result has been a partisan and largely predictable occasion. As Edward Heath noted in his evidence to the Procedure Committee in 1991, the Prime Minister turns up with an album of answers, and flicks over the page to whichever question it is. 'We get that Tuesday and Thursday after Tuesday and Thursday—talking perfectly bluntly—and that was not the purpose of Prime Minister's Questions.'[3]

And for those supplementaries that come from the other side of the House (or from recalcitrant backbenchers on one's own side), the extensive briefing that ministers receive ensures that difficult questions can be deflected with ease, the minister often giving away nothing that is not already in the public domain. Philip Giddings (Chapter 5) had described how the process operates within departments. By the time a ministerial team takes its place on the Treasury bench, each member of that team is already armed with a full set of briefing notes. Those notes, combined with the limitations of time, ensure that a minister is rarely caught off guard.

The greater partisanship has the effect of squeezing out the genuine non-partisan questions. Members keen to pursue particular constituency problems or issues outside the partisan arena have to compete with the increasing mass of party-inspired questions.

Away from the Floor of the House, it is the non-partisan question as much as the partisan question that is now a problem in contributing to the volume of written PQs. As we have seen (Chapters 4 and 7), pressure groups are significant prompters—as well as consumers—of PQs. Getting a PQ tabled may be a valuable way of raising an issue. It may also be used by political

---

[1] Like the Conservative Member, who asked Margaret Thatcher if she had seen a report that morning in the *Morning Star* and received the icy response: 'No, but I have seen a report in the *Daily Star*'.

[2] As in Nov. 1991 when the Conservative Member for Welwyn and Hatfield, David Evans, stumbled over a supplementary, and then reached in his pocket to pull out a prepared question. The occasion was subsequently pounced on by Roy Hattersley. See R. Hattersley, 'The Beggaring of PM's Question Time', *The Guardian*, 28 Jan. 1992.

[3] *Report of the Select Committee on Sittings of the House, Session 1991–91*, Vol. 2: *Minutes of Evidence with Appendices*, HC 20–II (London: HMSO, 1992), 30, q. 97.

consultancies for the purpose of impressing clients and even getting the name of their clients mentioned in *Hansard*. This might not matter too much were it not for the fact that the more questions that are tabled, the less impact each one has. Hence an important issue can virtually drown in a sea of minor questions. Furthermore, answering questions places a significant burden on ministers and, especially in terms of time and resources, their departments. The limitation introduced in 1990 on the number of starred questions that appear on the Order Paper has reduced the burden in respect of oral questions. The position as far as written questions are concerned remains the same.

In short, then, the past thirty years have seen a growth of partisanship in the House of Commons, a major increase in the number of questions tabled (both for oral and for written answer), and an increased burden on those responsible for answering them. These changes, in the eyes of critics, have had the effect of producing more heat and less light.

The House of Lords, as Donald Shell has outlined (Chapter 6), has witnessed pressures not totally dissimilar to those of the Commons, but the procedures and practices of the Upper House have ensured that it has avoided the excesses of the elected chamber. The problems associated with questions in Parliament are principally those of the House of Commons, not the House of Lords.

Strengths

Despite these various and significant limitations, Question Time, and PQs generally, offer a number of benefits—benefits, as we have mentioned, to Members, Parliament, and the political system.

For Members, PQs are an invaluable device for getting noticed. Each backbencher can expect on average to speak in four major debates each session. Question Time offers an opportunity to contribute more frequently. As Borthwick has shown (Chapter 3), some Members are more fortunate than others in the number of times their questions are among the top twenty in the daily shuffle. PQs also provide an opportunity to keep one's name in the local press (Chapter 7). The introduction of television cameras has added to the attraction.

PQs also benefit Members, and Parliament itself, in a number of other ways. As we have seen (Chapter 4), they serve a number of purposes. They serve to bring particular issues to the attention of ministers. The extensive briefing that ministers receive is, in this context, a benefit rather than a limitation. Questions can serve to elicit information for a variety of purposes: for the benefit of Members (in preparing speeches), their constituents, their party, and for particular groups. Obtaining information not previously on the public record also serves a wider systemic purpose. Prior to the creation of the departmental select committees, PQs constituted probably the most important tool for facilitating some degree of openness in government.

Question Time also serves to keep ministers on their toes, literally as well as metaphorically. It is a testing occasion. The folders full of briefing notes are, as one former Cabinet minister recalled, 'a much-needed boost to morale. In practice it is virtually impossible to find the right page among the reams of paper while listening to and trying to comprehend the precise point of supplementaries.'[4] There is always the possibility of a minister being caught off guard. The occasions are rare, but, as Borthwick has illustrated, they do happen. The process is—politically at least—a healthy one,[5] requiring ministers to keep on top of their subjects and be able to defend their positions in a public and critical forum.

PQs are also a means of putting pressure on ministers to achieve a particular outcome. A starred question that comes high in the ballot helps to ensure that a minister is briefed about the subject. However, written questions are especially valuable as a means of harrying government. Since there is no limit on the number that can be tabled, a Member may table several—albeit in different forms—in order to put pressure on a particular department or several departments. This tactic can be employed in defence of a particular constituency interest or in order to achieve some change in public policy. The changes may not be at the level of high policy, but they are important to individuals and to particular groups in society, be it, to take two particular examples, workers

---

[4] J. Biffen, *Inside the House of Commons* (London: Grafton Books, 1989), 43.
[5] The process is not always physically a healthy one. See the comments of D. Davis, *The BBC Viewer's Guide to Parliament* (London: BBC, 1989).

in a factory saved from closure or safety groups keen to ensure some change in regulations governing the sale of electrical appliances.

Though the partisanship apparent at Question Time, especially Prime Minister's Time, is increasingly seen as detrimental to Parliament, there is nevertheless a beneficial dimension to the clash of parties that it represents. Not only are individual ministers having to run the gauntlet of critical interrogation, so too is the government as a whole. A poor performance at Question Time can undermine the morale of the governing party, and have an important ripple effect in terms of the government's standing in the opinion polls.

The clash of views that takes place also serves an important safety-valve function. As one MP noted, the public may complain that the noise and the interruptions make the House seem ridiculous and childish. 'Yet Parliament represents deep divisions of opinion and those divisions need to be expressed and argued about. When passions are aroused, even the most modest of men are unlikely to remain entirely silent.'[6] Question Time serves to release—and to some extent channel—the tensions and passions aroused by disagreement between the parties.

Question Time, as we have seen (Chapter 7), also serves a wider support role. It acts as a means through which outside groups and constituents can obtain information and, by persuading a Member to table a question, feel that some purpose is served by Parliament. The regular and public nature of Question Time serves a valuable symbolic purpose as well. The fact that an ordinary backbencher—in any part of the House—can ask a question of the Prime Minister and other ministers, and expect an answer, stands as an exemplar of parliamentary democracy.

PQs and Question Time thus serve valuable purposes. The importance of PQs is clearly recognized by MPs themselves (Chapter 4). As we have seen, Members' criticisms are not directed at the existence of PQs, but rather at the limitations that exist in answering them. Question Time is a fixture in the parliamentary day—'there could', as John Biffen observed, 'be worse ways of warming up'[7]—and its future is not in serious doubt.

---

[6] R. Needham, *Honourable Member* (Cambridge: Patrick Stephens, 1983), 109.
[7] Biffen, *Inside the House of Commons*, 44.

What is in question, given the costs of the exercise, is the shape it will take.

Where to From Here?

There are four main debates about the shape that PQs, and Question Time in particular, should take in future. The first may be described as the 'breadth versus depth' argument alluded to by Borthwick in Chapter 3. The second is that of information seeking versus partisanship, variously touched upon throughout the volume. The third, also already identified as increasingly important since the time of Chester and Bowring, is that of a backbench versus a front bench occasion. The final one, which again has become prominent since the 1960s, is that of public interest versus pressure groups.

Breadth versus Depth

Should the Speaker seek to take as many questions as possible during Question Time, thus ensuring that a good many Members have an opportunity to be called? Or should she allow supplementaries to run on where questions cover an important topic and the answering Minister appears to be on the defensive, thus ensuring more detailed questioning but reducing the number of starred questions actually answered during Question Time?

As Helen Irwin and her colleagues have noted (Chapter 2), the practice of the Speaker has varied with the occupant of the office. There is a natural tendency to plump for breadth (getting through as many questions as possible), not least given the pressure from attention-seeking Members. Selwyn Lloyd, by contrast, was more attracted to depth (allowing particular questions to be pursued). During his two Parliaments as Speaker, Bernard Weatherill sought to achieve a balance between the two.

In a memorandum to the Procedure Committee in 1990, Speaker Weatherill expressed a desire to get through as many questions as possible: 'It seems to me no more than fair that as large a number of Members as possible are rewarded for taking the trouble to table an oral question.'[8] At the same time, he

---

[8] *Oral Questions*, HC (1989–90) 379, Appendix 21, p. xxxiii.

recognized that there were some subjects of topical interest 'on which the House generally will expect me to allow an extended line of questioning to develop'.[9] His solution was not to reduce the number of supplementary questions asked but rather to reduce the long-windedness of both supplementaries (not least where several questions were contained in one supplementary) and ministers' answers. The Procedure Committee added its endorsement to what it called 'the doctrine of brevity'—it noted that Speaker Hylton-Foster was known to interrupt and call the next question if he felt a minister was taking too long to reply—and the need to achieve a balance between breadth and depth.[10]

Achieving such a balance is likely to prove increasingly difficult. The demand to ask questions will continue to exceed the supply of time available. Attention-seeking Members will want to have their moment of glory. Partisanship will increase the pressure for self-serving, frequently long-winded, questions (often prefaced with 'Will the minister not agree with me that') rather than short inquisitorial questions. The most effective are usually the shortest—notably Tam Dalyell's supplementaries consisting of the one word 'Why?'—but they are very much the exception.

There is thus the danger of the self-interest of Members—and of parties—overwhelming what is in the interests of Parliament. 'The primary purpose of Question Time is to submit the executive to parliamentary scrutiny and not to ensure that as many Members as possible are recognised by the Chair. These two goals—scrutiny and allowing as many Members as possible to be called—are not mutually exclusive but neither are they synonymous.'[11] Ensuring a balance is the responsibility of the Speaker. In time, the powers of the Chair may prove insufficient to maintain that balance. A change both in the attitudes of Members and the practices of the House may be necessary.

Information Seeking versus Partisanship

Obtaining hard-to-get information was identified by Chester and Bowring as one purpose of PQs. As we found from our survey of

---

[9] Ibid., pp. viii–ix, and Appendix 21, p. xxxiii.
[10] Ibid., pp. ix–xi.
[11] Ibid., Appendix 18, p. xxxi.

Members (Chapter 4), it remains important, written questions in particular being employed for this purpose.

Here we use the term 'information seeking' to encompass more than straightforward factual data. It overlaps with other functions identified as important by MPs. It encompasses the probing question designed to elicit a response helpful to a particular cause being pursued by the Member *qua* Member—in other words, not as a party MP. It even extends to probing critical questions asked by individual opposition Members for the purposes of catching the government out. In short, it encompasses questions that have three distinguishing characteristics: first, that they require a substantive answer; second, that they are not pre-arranged; and, third, that they are not syndicated.

This distinguishes them, by definition, from syndicated questions and from the increasing number of supplementary questions that are lobbed at ministers in order that a pre-arranged answer can be given or requiring an affirmative response to a particular statement. Partisan statements dressed up as questions are, as we have seen, a particular feature of Prime Minister's questions, and have facilitated the perception of a slanging match between the two sides of the House. For many Members, as well as television–viewers, the perception is one of trivialization: 'more "playtime" than Question Time' as one MP put it.[12]

Again, there is need for balance. Question Time, along with debates, is an occasion for the clash between contending beliefs. Some partisanship is unavoidable and, as we have claimed already, politically healthy. However, it is not healthy if it predominates to the extent of squeezing out the information-seeking question. If there is to be an imbalance between the two, then it is one that in our view should favour the latter (information seeking) rather than the former (partisanship). The information-seeking question is at the heart of the principal functions of PQs as identified by Members themselves (Chapter 4). The fact that it is being squeezed out by partisan 'questions' lies at the root, we suspect, of a large proportion of Members in our survey (one in three) complaining of a poor use of Question Time.

Some attempts have been made to restore the balance. The 1990

---

[12] Quoted in L. Radice, E. Vallance, and V. Willis, *Member of Parliament* (London: Macmillan, 1987), 161.

reforms aimed at curbing syndication constitute the most significant (even if they have not, as we have seen, had quite the effect hoped for). The Procedure Committee, in its 1991 report on PQs, also endorsed a recommendation of the Principal Clerk of the Table Office that 'open' questions to departments should, as far as possible, indicate a particular subject matter.[13] A further change that may limit partisanship is a restriction on front bench involvement, discussed below. However, at the end of the day, procedural reforms are not likely to curb the partisan instincts of Members. If there is to be a reduction in what the Principal Clerk of the Table Office referred to in 1991 as 'party verbal fisticuffs',[14] the restraint may have to come from outside. Popular distaste for excessive partisanship may provide the ultimate check.

Backbench versus Front Bench

Allied to the information seeking versus partisan debate is that of the relationship between front and backbenches. Since the time of Chester and Bowring, opposition front bench involvement has become a pronounced feature of Question Time. What was 'not a major Front Bench activity' in 1960[15] soon became one. As the opening chapters of this volume have revealed, front bench participation is now routine. It is pronounced at PM's questions, and frequent during departmental questions. It is the focus of television coverage of the chamber.

The clash between ministers and their shadows on the opposition front bench is now part of the political battle, and ensures that ministers are denied an easy ride in answering questions. Ministers know that what they say may be—indeed, is likely to be— challenged by their opposite numbers. As such, it could be argued that supplementaries from shadow ministers contribute to the critical scrutiny of government by the House.

There is, however, clearly a negative side. This has two dimensions. One, already discussed, is the nature of the clash between the two front benches. The partisanship, especially at PM's questions, has reached a level that undermines the occasion

---

[13] *Parliamentary Questions*, HC (1990–91) 178, pp. xiii–xi, paras. 40–3.
[14] Ibid., Evidence, p. 9.
[15] D. N. Chester and N. Bowring, *Questions in Parliament* (Oxford: Clarendon Press, 1962), 274.

in the eyes of television-viewers and, indeed, Members themselves. The second, more significant for this particular discussion,
is that it occupies time that would otherwise be given over to
backbenchers. Question Time is essentially an opportunity for
backbenchers to question ministers. Along with the half-hour
adjournment debate at the end of the day, it is the only regular
opportunity that backbenchers have to probe government outside
the context of party control. Greater party involvement, notably
through syndication, undermines the backbench nature of the
occasion; so too does the greater role played by the opposition
front bench. Question Time is increasingly becoming an extension
of the party clash that takes place during debates.

It would be naïve to expect opposition front benchers to take a
self-denying ordinance, and it would remove an important critical
capacity if those front benchers were barred from participating
during Question Time. The need, again, is for some measure of
balance, allowing front benchers to participate, but not to an
extent that squeezes out backbench participation. As Bernard
Weatherill noted in his evidence to the Procedure Committee in
1990, the opposition front bench has a number of other opportunities to raise issues, including Opposition Days.[16] Backbenchers
are not so fortunate, having to work within a business agenda set
largely by business managers. Given that, he recognized a case for
reducing—but not eliminating—front bench interventions during
Question Time.

Achieving that end is more difficult than establishing the case
for it. Mr Weatherill raised the possibility of not every member of
the front bench team being called at every Question Time and of
the most senior member being called only once rather than, as had
become the practice, twice. If there was cross-party agreement on
such a restriction, he would do his best to enforce it.[17] The
Procedure Committee, noting that the matter was one of 'the
utmost delicacy', declined to make a recommendation, saying that
'Some Members would no doubt take the view that this is a
problem better dealt with as a matter of internal party management
or discipline.'[18] Why party discipline should be considered
relevant in this context was not explained. However, what is clear

---

[16] *Oral Questions*, Appendix 21, p. xxxiii.
[17] Ibid., Appendix 21, pp. xxxiii–xxxiv.   [18] Ibid., p. x.

is that if there is to be an opportunity for more backbench interventions, it will have to be as a result either of internal party pressure on the opposition side of the House or else of the Speaker taking the initiative and implementing the proposals advanced by Speaker Weatherill in his 1990 memorandum.

Public Interest versus Pressure Groups

The growth in the number of pressure groups in the UK since 1960 was established in the Introduction. The effect of those groups on Parliament has been significant. MPs are now heavily lobbied by them (Chapter 1), and such groups are particularly active both in trying to get MPs to table questions (Chapter 4) and in utilizing answers as a valuable form of political intelligence (Chapter 7). The main focus of this activity, as we have seen, is written questions.

Groups ask MPs to table questions to obtain information that is useful to them. Constituents and other individuals—academic researchers, for example—may make similar requests. As the Procedure Committee recorded in its inquiry into PQs in 1991, there is nothing inherently wrong in this. 'But for this to remain within the bounds of legitimacy, Members must genuinely be an active party to the process. This implies some degree of interest both in the form of the question and the likely content of the answer.'[19] For Members to act as unthinking conduits relegates them from being critical agents of enquiry to little more than post-boxes. The advantage to groups is that these particular post-boxes can provide a first-class delivery service. The disadvantage to Parliament is that it undermines the effectiveness of PQs. The more that are asked, the less impact each one has. And if MPs are not acting at least as critical gate-keepers to group requests to ask questions, the greater the number that go down on the Order Paper. The consequence is more time spent by civil servants—with a considerable opportunity cost involved—in answering questions which are not designed to assist MPs in fulfilling their parliamentary duties.

There is also a further disadvantage to Parliament. The greater the involvement of pressure groups in tabling PQs, the greater the danger of such groups being seen as enjoying disproportionate—

---

[19] *Parliamentary Questions* HC (1990–91) 178, pp. xxiii–xxiv, para. 103.

and hence unfair—access to the political system. Even if these
fears are not well founded, the fact that they exist serves to
undermine the legitimacy of the parliamentary process in the eyes
of the public.

The problem, however, is easier to state than to tackle. Pressure
groups have a legitimate interest in persuading MPs to pursue a
particular issue and in briefing Members on what to ask. MPs with
a keen interest in animal welfare, for example, will be briefed by
animal welfare groups on what issues are important and which of
them might usefully be addressed through the medium of PQs.
The MPs in question are active participants in the process, and will
use the answers in deciding how best to pursue the cause of animal
welfare. The answers may form the basis for seeking a change in
public policy, through a Private Member's Bill or through writing
to the minister. As such, PQs form part of what the Principal Clerk
of the Table Office termed 'legitimate' campaigns. 'Illegitimate'
campaigns involve multiple questions designed to badger a
minister, but with no intention of eliciting information or
encouraging action[20]—a primary source of such campaigns being
pressure groups and research assistants, the latter often acting at
the behest of (and sometimes employed by) the former. Policing
the line between the legitimate and illegitimate campaigns is the
difficult part of the exercise.

Both the Principal Clerk of the Table Office and the Procedure
Committee have recognized the difficulty—indeed, the near
impossibility—of creating rules that would allow the distinction to
be enforced.[21] However, the Committee did recommend that a
ruling of Selwyn Lloyd in 1971, authorizing the Table Office to
disallow questions recognizably emanating from an individual who
over a period of time had sought via various Members to table a
large number of PQs (many of the questions being disorderly or
repeating attempts previously disallowed), should be used as a
precedent for authorizing similar disallowals in future.[22] 'In
deciding whether his intervention was justified, Mr Speaker might
have regard to the extent to which a Member was allowing himself
to be used as the agent of outside individuals or lobbies.'[23]

---

[20] Ibid., Evidence, p. 8.
[21] Ibid., p. xxiv, para. 105.   [22] Ibid., p. xxiv, para. 106.
[23] Ibid., p. xxiv, para. 107.

Such intervention may have some effect at the margins. It is not likely to have any major impact on the volume of PQs tabled. It will normally be impossible to determine the genesis of most PQs. Members themselves may not be certain; for example, a research assistant may have been influenced by some external source not known to the Member. Though, as we have seen (Chapter 4), Members are willing to admit the extent to which they table questions because they are asked to, they are unlikely to be willing to admit to being no more than post-boxes.

The ultimate control would be to restrict the number of written questions that a Member may table. The problem with this is that it would remove the advantages that flow from the present arrangements. The 'legitimate' campaign would suffer as much as the 'illegitimate' one. Though a restriction of this sort may be popular with the civil servants who have to answer PQs, it is not likely to commend itself to Members. If Members are to act as active participants in the process, the solution lies much more with them than it does with the Speaker.

Conclusion

Parliamentary questions are a much criticized, but indispensable, part of the parliamentary process. In terms of their form, the rules governing them, and the use made of them by Members of Parliament, they have changed enormously since they achieved their prominence as the *hors d'oeuvres* of the parliamentary day. Oral and written questions have not been immune from wider pressures in the political system. Those pressures have moulded them, and precipitated the various changes in the rules governing them. In this volume, we have identified the wider pressures, the rule changes, and their consequent effects over the course of the past thirty years. We have sought to establish both the context and the dynamic of PQs generally and of Question Time in particular. The changes that have given rise to increased demands on, and changes in, parliamentary questions are neither static nor constant in form. They have given rise to various conjoined debates about the shape that PQs and Question Time should take in future years. How—and if—those debates are resolved will determine the nature of parliamentary questions in the twenty-first century.

INDEX